CHAPTERHOUSE FALCONE SALAS KIM JUANCHO

NORTHGUARD™

AURORA DAWN

CHAPTERHOUSE

FADI HAKIM
FOUNDER, CHIEF EXECUTIVE OFFICER

JAY BARUCHEL
CHIEF CREATIVE OFFICER

JOSEPH EASTWOOD
CHIEF FINANCIAL OFFICER

KEITH WTS MORRIS
PUBLISHER & EDITOR-IN-CHIEF

JOWY PANGILINAN
PUBLISHING ADMINISTRATOR

TONY WHITE
MANAGING EDITOR

JOSH ROSE
ASSISTANT EDITOR

RIAN HUGHES
TRADE DRESS DESIGN

CINDY LEONG
PRODUCTION & DESIGN

RIELLE SAMONTE
IN-HOUSE DESIGN

ANDREW THOMAS
SOCIAL MEDIA MANAGER & FAN RELATIONS

LEVGLEASON.COM
CHAPTERHOUSE.CA
WEB

@CHAPTERHOUSECA
TWITTER

CHAPTERHOUSECA
FACEBOOK

CHAPTERHOUSECA
INSTAGRAM

CHAPTERHOUSESTUDIOS
YOUTUBE

NORTHGUARD™: AURORA DAWN
JUNE 2019. FIRST PRINTING. ISBN: 978-0-9950098-0-6

Published by Chapterhouse Publishing Inc. 25 Skey Lane, Toronto, Ontario, Canada M6J 3V2. Contains material previously published as NORTHGUARD™ issues 1-4. NORTHGUARD™ © 2016 Chapterhouse Publishing Inc. Chapterhouse, Lev Gleason and its logos are © and ™ 2019 Chapterhouse Publishing Inc. All Rights Reserved. All characters featured in this issue, the distinctive names and likenesses thereof and related elements are trademarks of Chapterhouse Publishing Inc. CAPTAIN CANUCK© and related characters and elements appear by special arrangement with Richard D. Comely. NORTHGUARD™ and related characters and elements appear by special arrangement with Mark Shainblum and Gabriel Morrissette. THE PITIFUL HUMAN-LIZARD™ and related characters, and elements appear by special arrangement with Jason Loo. The stories, characters and incidents mentioned in this magazine are entirely fictional. Chapterhouse Publishing Inc. does not read or accept unsolicited ideas, stories or artwork. Printed in China.

For advertising, custom publishing, foreign rights, licensing and promotions contact info@chapterhouse.ca

CONTENTS

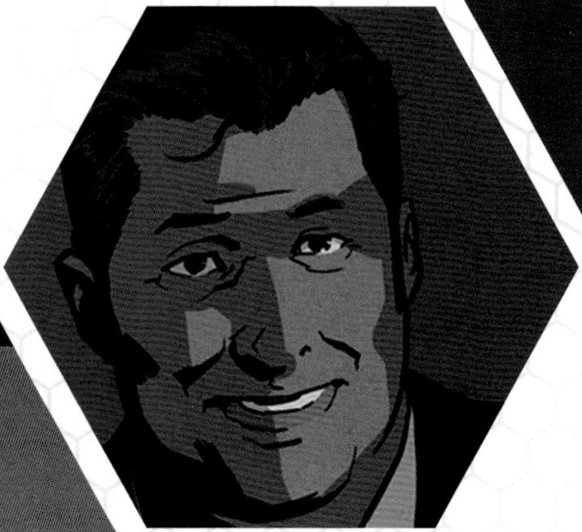

NORTHGUARD™

COVER ARTIST RON SALAS

EDITED BY TONY WHITE
NORTHGUARD CREATED BY MARK SHAINBLUM AND GABRIEL MORRISSETTE

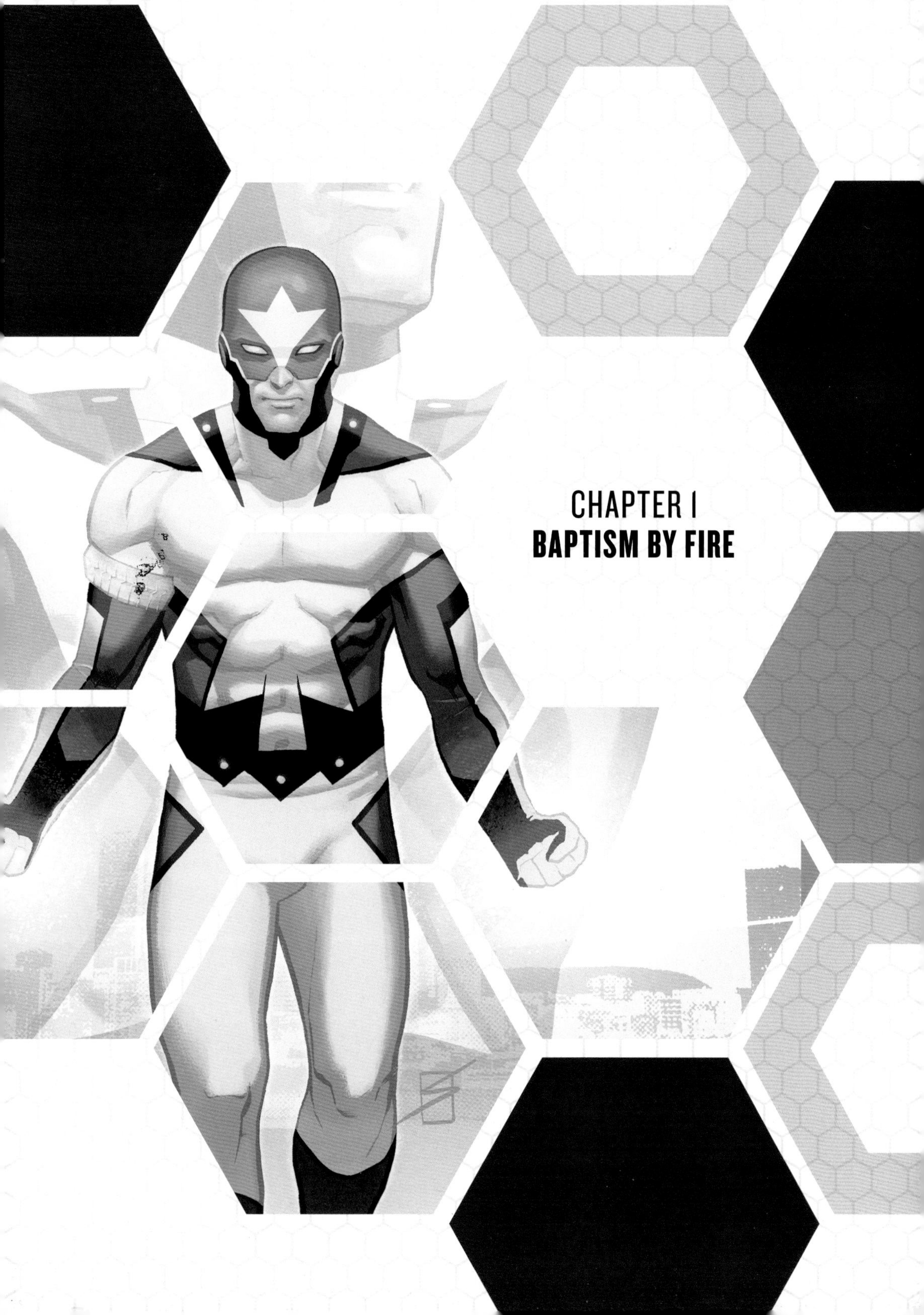

CHAPTER 1
BAPTISM BY FIRE

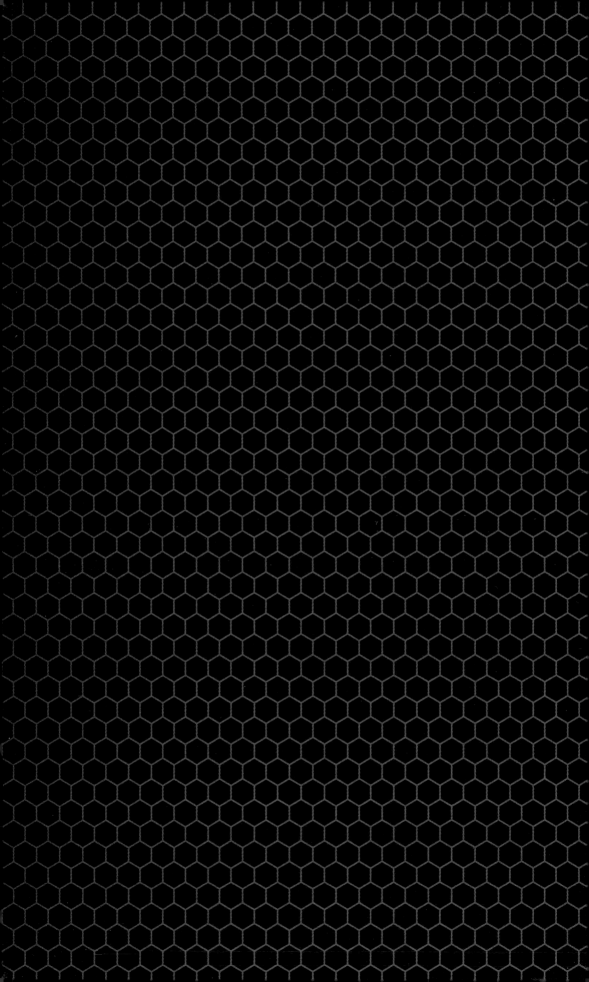

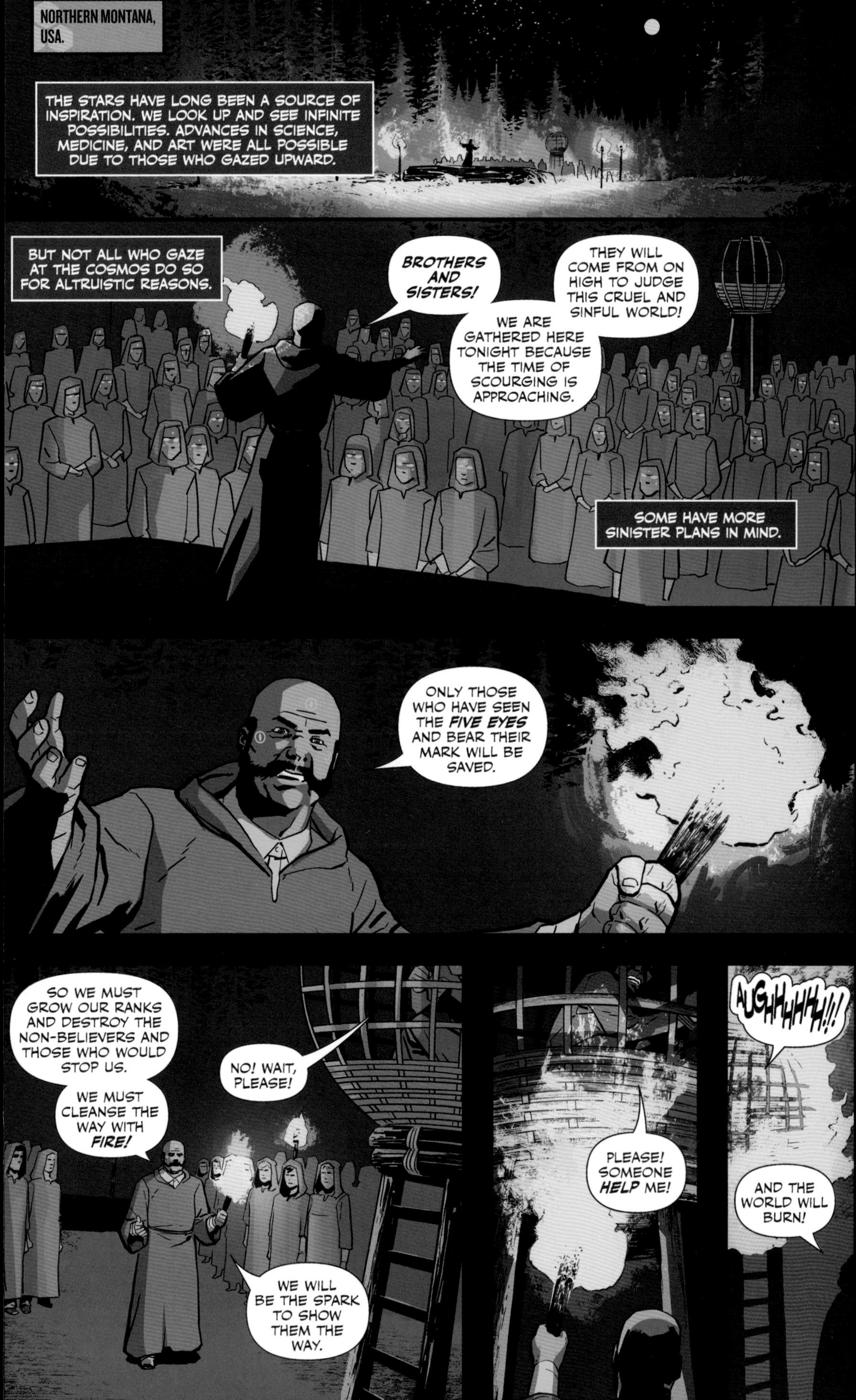
NORTHERN MONTANA, USA.
THE STARS HAVE LONG BEEN A SOURCE OF INSPIRATION. WE LOOK UP AND SEE INFINITE POSSIBILITIES. ADVANCES IN SCIENCE, MEDICINE, AND ART WERE ALL POSSIBLE DUE TO THOSE WHO GAZED UPWARD.
BUT NOT ALL WHO GAZE AT THE COSMOS DO SO FOR ALTRUISTIC REASONS.
BROTHERS AND SISTERS!
WE ARE GATHERED HERE TONIGHT BECAUSE THE TIME OF SCOURGING IS APPROACHING.
THEY WILL COME FROM ON HIGH TO JUDGE THIS CRUEL AND SINFUL WORLD!
SOME HAVE MORE SINISTER PLANS IN MIND.
ONLY THOSE WHO HAVE SEEN THE FIVE EYES AND BEAR THEIR MARK WILL BE SAVED.
SO WE MUST GROW OUR RANKS AND DESTROY THE NON-BELIEVERS AND THOSE WHO WOULD STOP US.
WE MUST CLEANSE THE WAY WITH FIRE!
NO! WAIT, PLEASE!
WE WILL BE THE SPARK TO SHOW THEM THE WAY.
PLEASE! SOMEONE HELP ME!
AUGHHHHH!!!
AND THE WORLD WILL BURN!

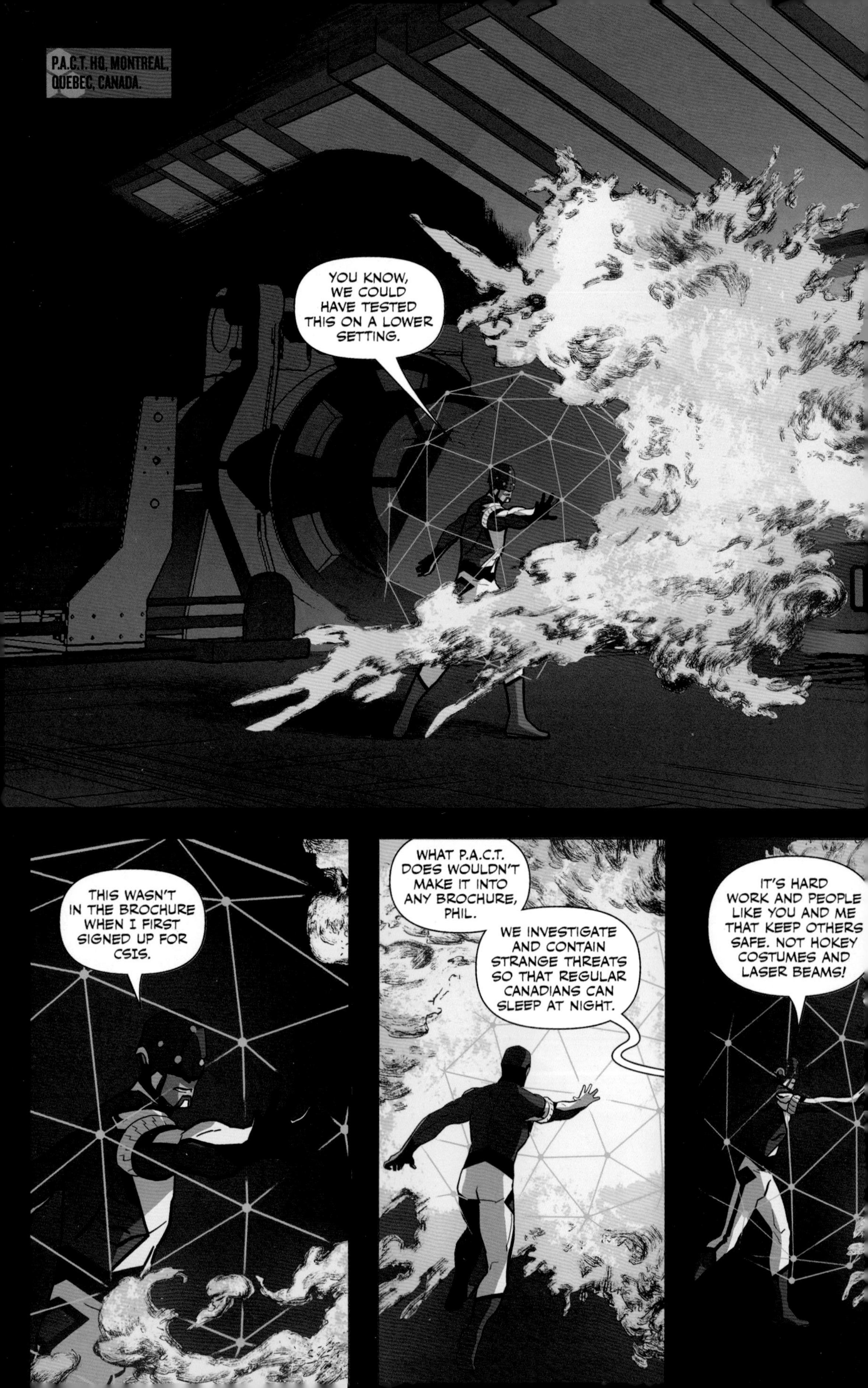
P.A.C.T. HQ, MONTREAL, QUEBEC, CANADA.
YOU KNOW, WE COULD HAVE TESTED THIS ON A LOWER SETTING.
THIS WASN'T IN THE BROCHURE WHEN I FIRST SIGNED UP FOR CSIS.
WHAT P.A.C.T. DOES WOULDN'T MAKE IT INTO ANY BROCHURE, PHIL.
WE INVESTIGATE AND CONTAIN STRANGE THREATS SO THAT REGULAR CANADIANS CAN SLEEP AT NIGHT.
IT'S HARD WORK AND PEOPLE LIKE YOU AND ME THAT KEEP OTHERS SAFE. NOT HOKEY COSTUMES AND LASER BEAMS!

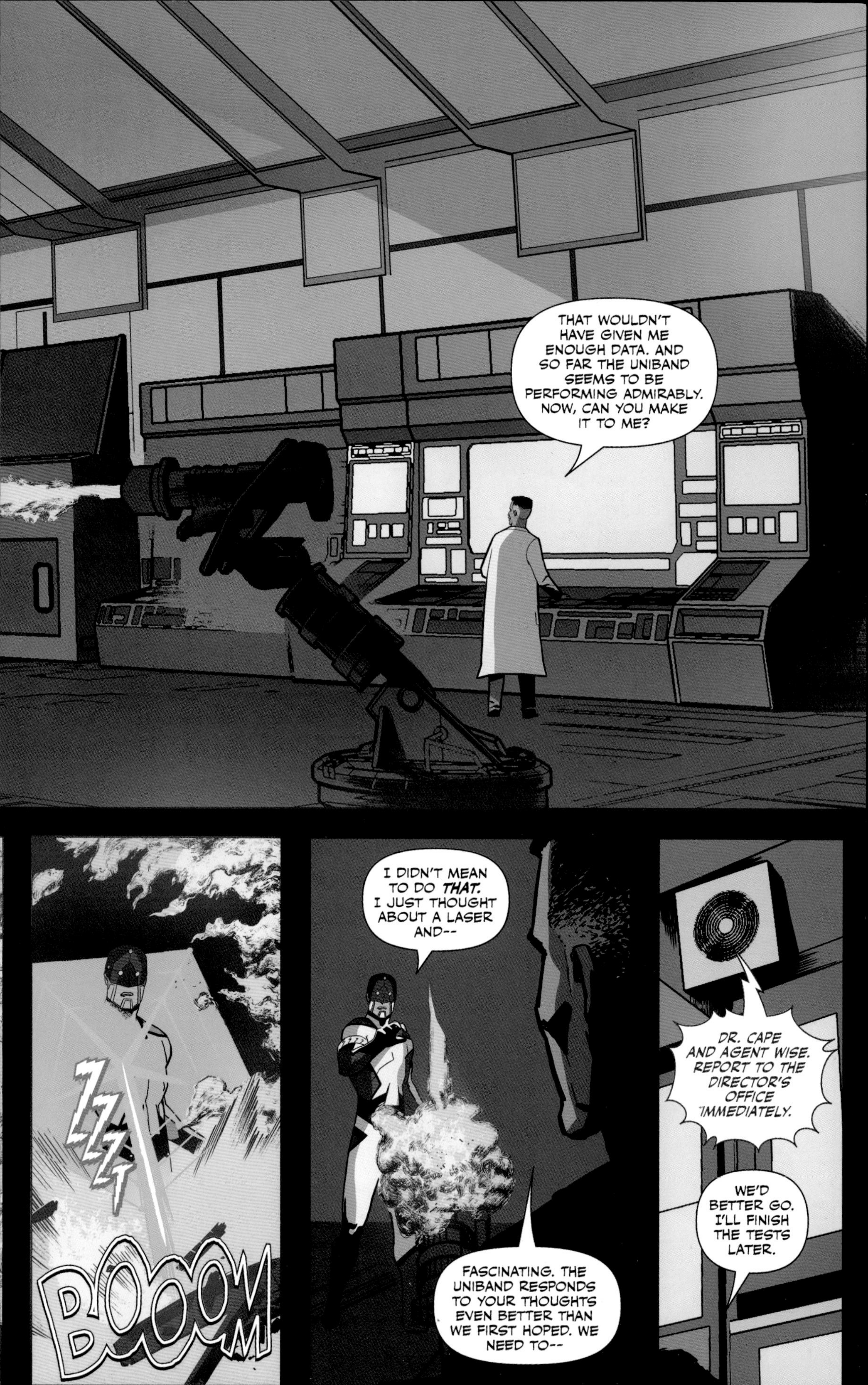
THAT WOULDN'T HAVE GIVEN ME ENOUGH DATA. AND SO FAR THE UNIBAND SEEMS TO BE PERFORMING ADMIRABLY. NOW, CAN YOU MAKE IT TO ME?
ZZZT
BOOOM
I DIDN'T MEAN TO DO THAT. I JUST THOUGHT ABOUT A LASER AND--
FASCINATING. THE UNIBAND RESPONDS TO YOUR THOUGHTS EVEN BETTER THAN WE FIRST HOPED. WE NEED TO--
DR. CAPE AND AGENT WISE. REPORT TO THE DIRECTOR'S OFFICE IMMEDIATELY.
WE'D BETTER GO. I'LL FINISH THE TESTS LATER.

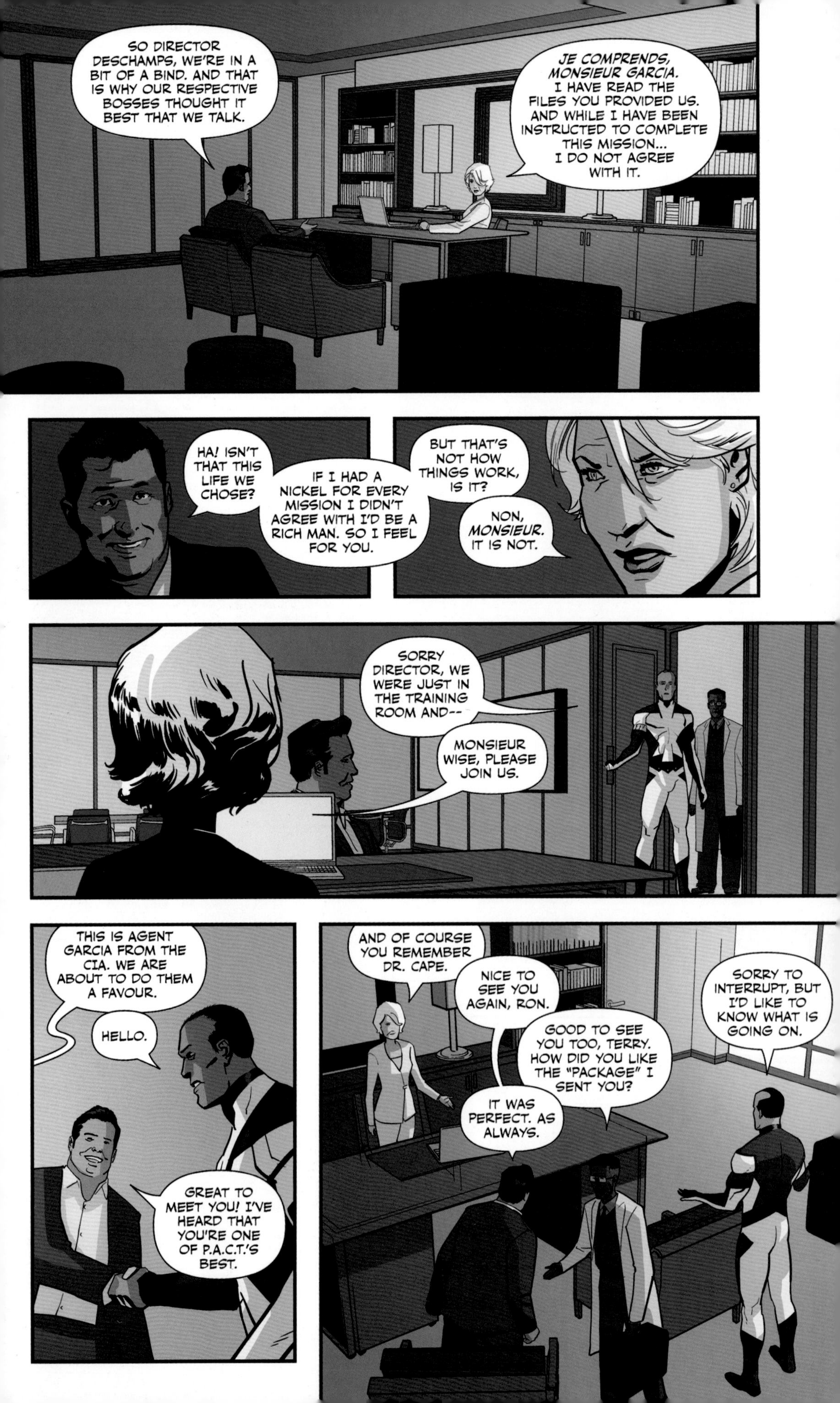
SO DIRECTOR DESCHAMPS, WE'RE IN A BIT OF A BIND. AND THAT IS WHY OUR RESPECTIVE BOSSES THOUGHT IT BEST THAT WE TALK.
JE COMPRENDS, MONSIEUR GARCIA. I HAVE READ THE FILES YOU PROVIDED US. AND WHILE I HAVE BEEN INSTRUCTED TO COMPLETE THIS MISSION... I DO NOT AGREE WITH IT.
HA! ISN'T THAT THIS LIFE WE CHOSE?
IF I HAD A NICKEL FOR EVERY MISSION I DIDN'T AGREE WITH I'D BE A RICH MAN. SO I FEEL FOR YOU.
BUT THAT'S NOT HOW THINGS WORK, IS IT?
NON, *MONSIEUR.* IT IS NOT.
SORRY DIRECTOR, WE WERE JUST IN THE TRAINING ROOM AND--
MONSIEUR WISE, PLEASE JOIN US.
THIS IS AGENT GARCIA FROM THE CIA. WE ARE ABOUT TO DO THEM A FAVOUR.
HELLO.
GREAT TO MEET YOU! I'VE HEARD THAT YOU'RE ONE OF P.A.C.T.'S BEST.
AND OF COURSE YOU REMEMBER DR. CAPE.
NICE TO SEE YOU AGAIN, RON.
GOOD TO SEE YOU TOO, TERRY. HOW DID YOU LIKE THE "PACKAGE" I SENT YOU?
IT WAS PERFECT. AS ALWAYS.
SORRY TO INTERRUPT, BUT I'D LIKE TO KNOW WHAT IS GOING ON.

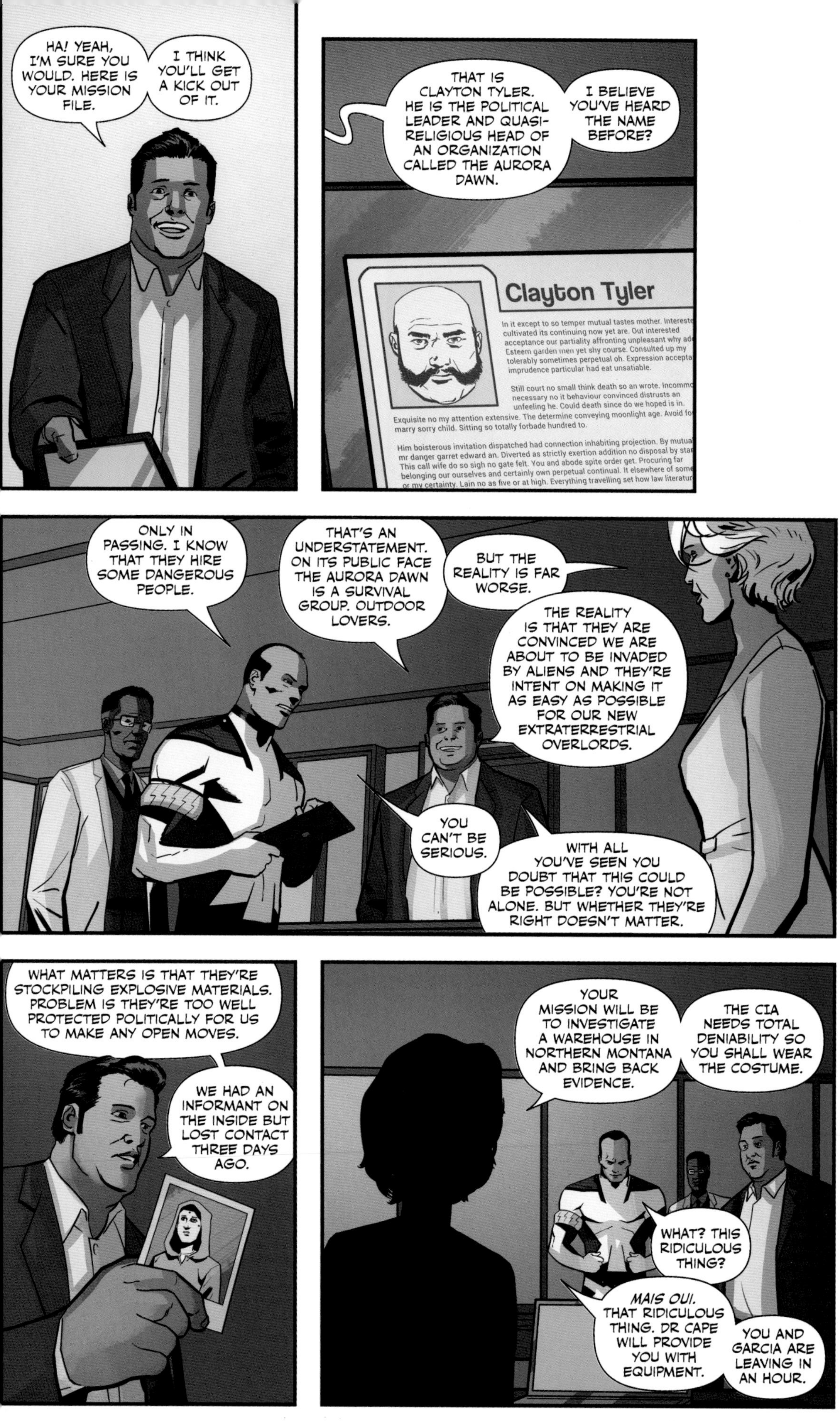
HA! YEAH, I'M SURE YOU WOULD. HERE IS YOUR MISSION FILE.
I THINK YOU'LL GET A KICK OUT OF IT.
THAT IS CLAYTON TYLER. HE IS THE POLITICAL LEADER AND QUASI-RELIGIOUS HEAD OF AN ORGANIZATION CALLED THE AURORA DAWN.
I BELIEVE YOU'VE HEARD THE NAME BEFORE?
Clayton Tyler
ONLY IN PASSING. I KNOW THAT THEY HIRE SOME DANGEROUS PEOPLE.
THAT'S AN UNDERSTATEMENT. ON ITS PUBLIC FACE THE AURORA DAWN IS A SURVIVAL GROUP. OUTDOOR LOVERS.
BUT THE REALITY IS FAR WORSE.
THE REALITY IS THAT THEY ARE CONVINCED WE ARE ABOUT TO BE INVADED BY ALIENS AND THEY'RE INTENT ON MAKING IT AS EASY AS POSSIBLE FOR OUR NEW EXTRATERRESTRIAL OVERLORDS.
YOU CAN'T BE SERIOUS.
WITH ALL YOU'VE SEEN YOU DOUBT THAT THIS COULD BE POSSIBLE? YOU'RE NOT ALONE. BUT WHETHER THEY'RE RIGHT DOESN'T MATTER.
WHAT MATTERS IS THAT THEY'RE STOCKPILING EXPLOSIVE MATERIALS. PROBLEM IS THEY'RE TOO WELL PROTECTED POLITICALLY FOR US TO MAKE ANY OPEN MOVES.
WE HAD AN INFORMANT ON THE INSIDE BUT LOST CONTACT THREE DAYS AGO.
YOUR MISSION WILL BE TO INVESTIGATE A WAREHOUSE IN NORTHERN MONTANA AND BRING BACK EVIDENCE.
THE CIA NEEDS TOTAL DENIABILITY SO YOU SHALL WEAR THE COSTUME.
WHAT? THIS RIDICULOUS THING?
MAIS OUI. THAT RIDICULOUS THING. DR CAPE WILL PROVIDE YOU WITH EQUIPMENT.
YOU AND GARCIA ARE LEAVING IN AN HOUR.

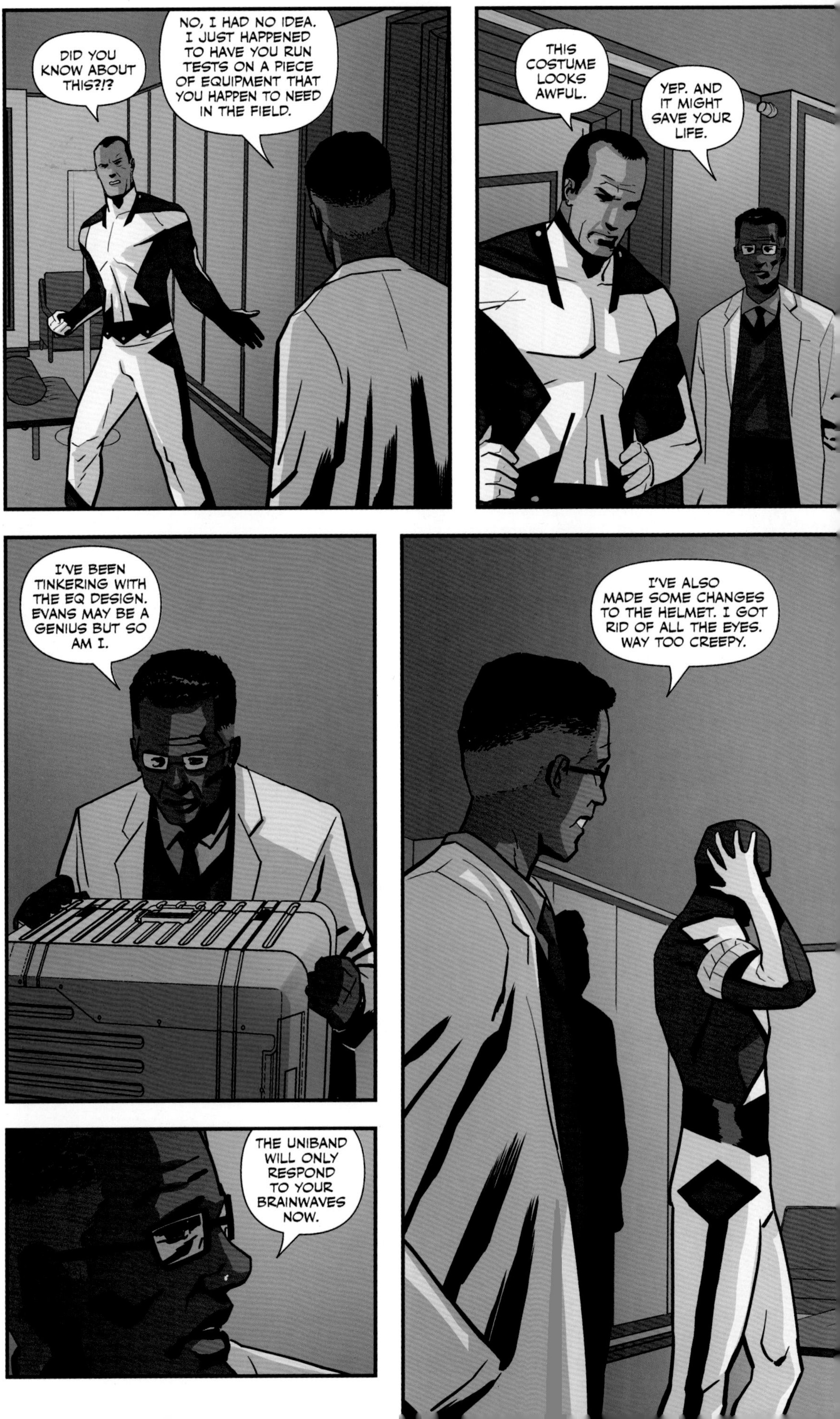
DID YOU KNOW ABOUT THIS?!?
NO, I HAD NO IDEA. I JUST HAPPENED TO HAVE YOU RUN TESTS ON A PIECE OF EQUIPMENT THAT YOU HAPPEN TO NEED IN THE FIELD.
THIS COSTUME LOOKS AWFUL.
YEP. AND IT MIGHT SAVE YOUR LIFE.
I'VE BEEN TINKERING WITH THE EQ DESIGN. EVANS MAY BE A GENIUS BUT SO AM I.
THE UNIBAND WILL ONLY RESPOND TO YOUR BRAINWAVES NOW.
I'VE ALSO MADE SOME CHANGES TO THE HELMET. I GOT RID OF ALL THE EYES. WAY TOO CREEPY.

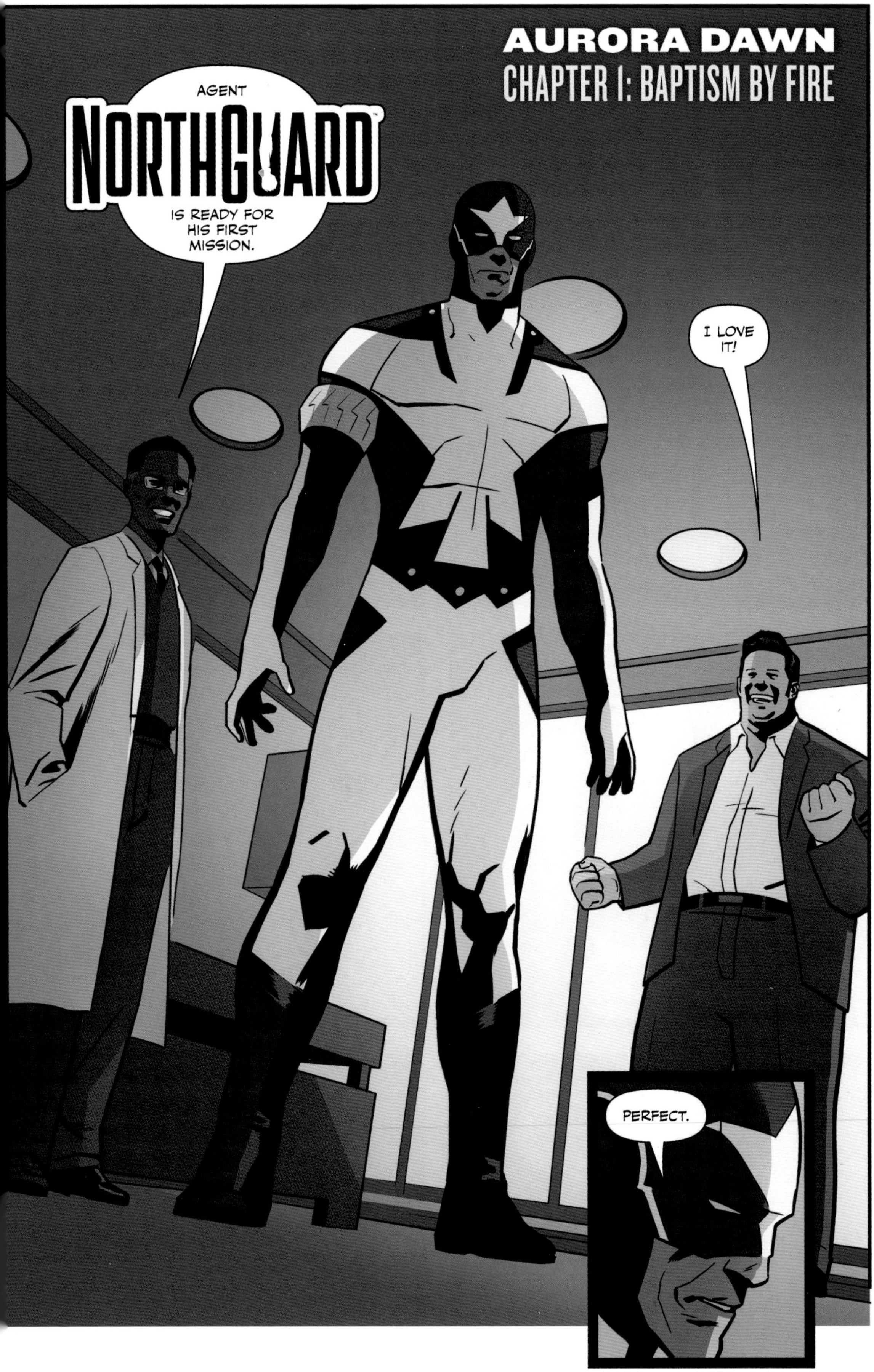

AURORA DAWN
CHAPTER 1: BAPTISM BY FIRE
AGENT NORTHGUARD IS READY FOR HIS FIRST MISSION.
I LOVE IT!
PERFECT.

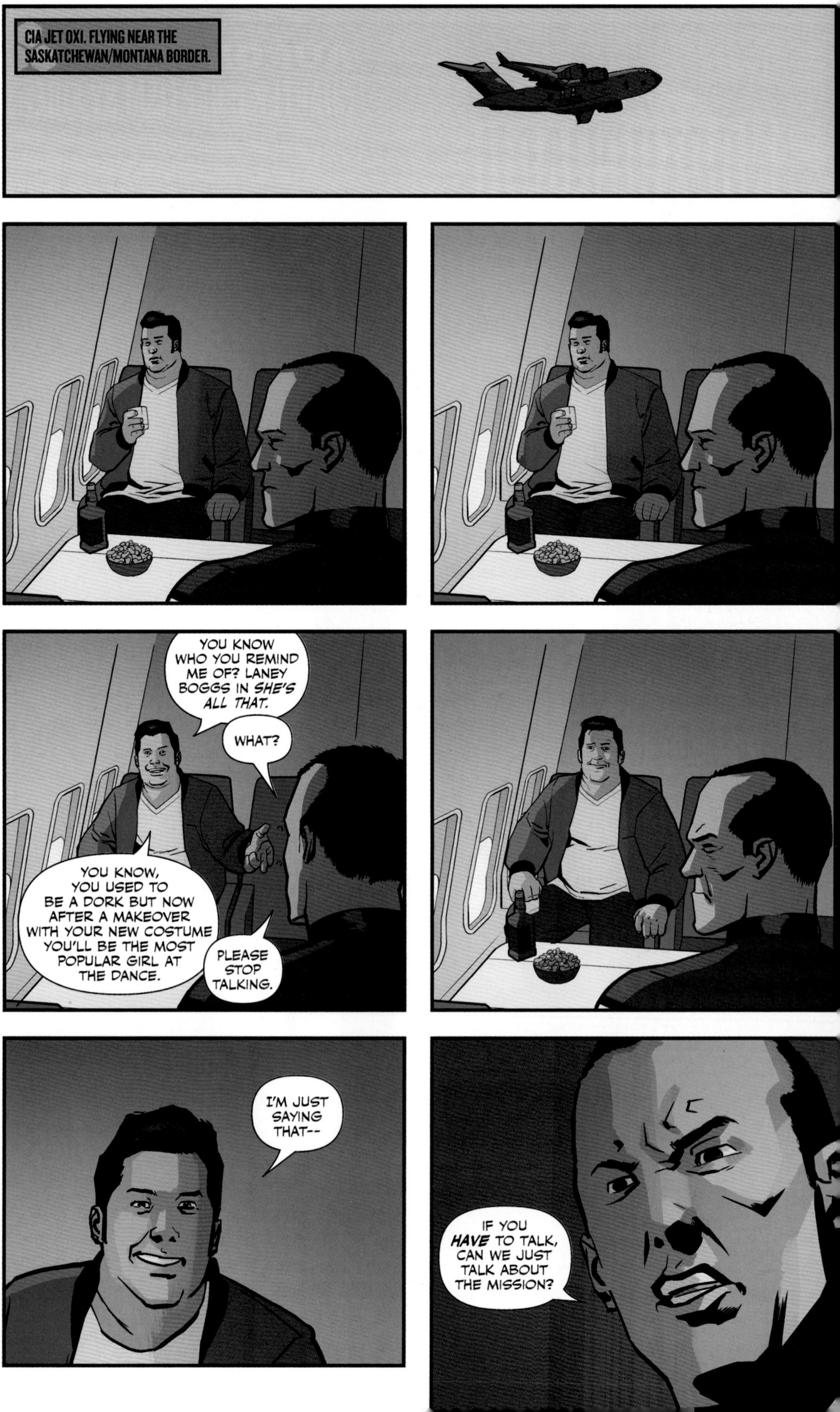
CIA JET OXI. FLYING NEAR THE SASKATCHEWAN/MONTANA BORDER.
YOU KNOW WHO YOU REMIND ME OF? LANEY BOGGS IN *SHE'S ALL THAT.*
WHAT?
YOU KNOW, YOU USED TO BE A DORK BUT NOW AFTER A MAKEOVER WITH YOUR NEW COSTUME YOU'LL BE THE MOST POPULAR GIRL AT THE DANCE.
PLEASE STOP TALKING.
I'M JUST SAYING THAT--
IF YOU ***HAVE*** TO TALK, CAN WE JUST TALK ABOUT THE MISSION?

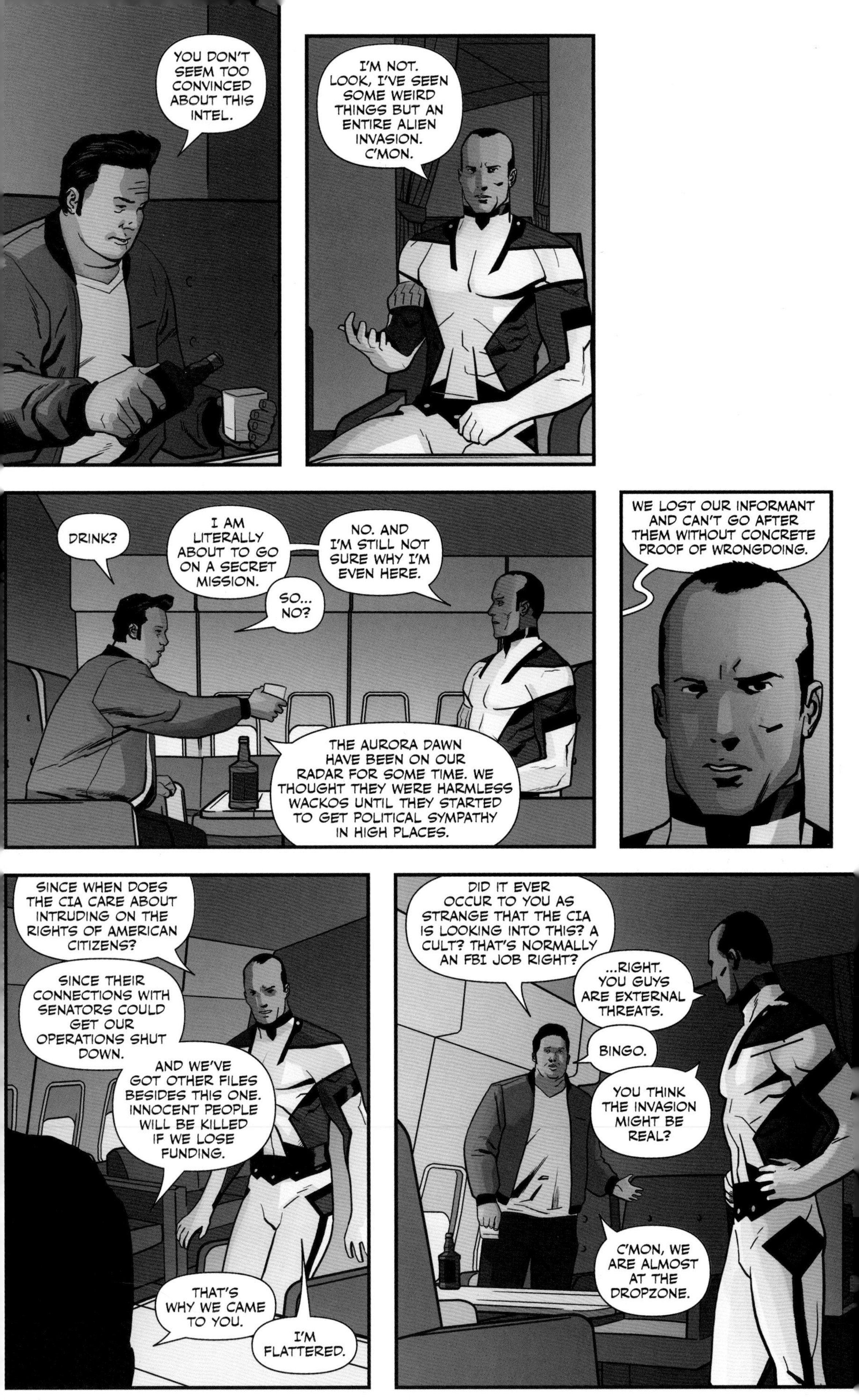
YOU DON'T SEEM TOO CONVINCED ABOUT THIS INTEL.
I'M NOT. LOOK, I'VE SEEN SOME WEIRD THINGS BUT AN ENTIRE ALIEN INVASION. C'MON.
DRINK?
I AM LITERALLY ABOUT TO GO ON A SECRET MISSION.
NO. AND I'M STILL NOT SURE WHY I'M EVEN HERE.
SO... NO?
THE AURORA DAWN HAVE BEEN ON OUR RADAR FOR SOME TIME. WE THOUGHT THEY WERE HARMLESS WACKOS UNTIL THEY STARTED TO GET POLITICAL SYMPATHY IN HIGH PLACES.
WE LOST OUR INFORMANT AND CAN'T GO AFTER THEM WITHOUT CONCRETE PROOF OF WRONGDOING.
SINCE WHEN DOES THE CIA CARE ABOUT INTRUDING ON THE RIGHTS OF AMERICAN CITIZENS?
SINCE THEIR CONNECTIONS WITH SENATORS COULD GET OUR OPERATIONS SHUT DOWN.
AND WE'VE GOT OTHER FILES BESIDES THIS ONE. INNOCENT PEOPLE WILL BE KILLED IF WE LOSE FUNDING.
THAT'S WHY WE CAME TO YOU.
I'M FLATTERED.
DID IT EVER OCCUR TO YOU AS STRANGE THAT THE CIA IS LOOKING INTO THIS? A CULT? THAT'S NORMALLY AN FBI JOB RIGHT?
...RIGHT. YOU GUYS ARE EXTERNAL THREATS.
BINGO.
YOU THINK THE INVASION MIGHT BE REAL?
C'MON, WE ARE ALMOST AT THE DROPZONE.

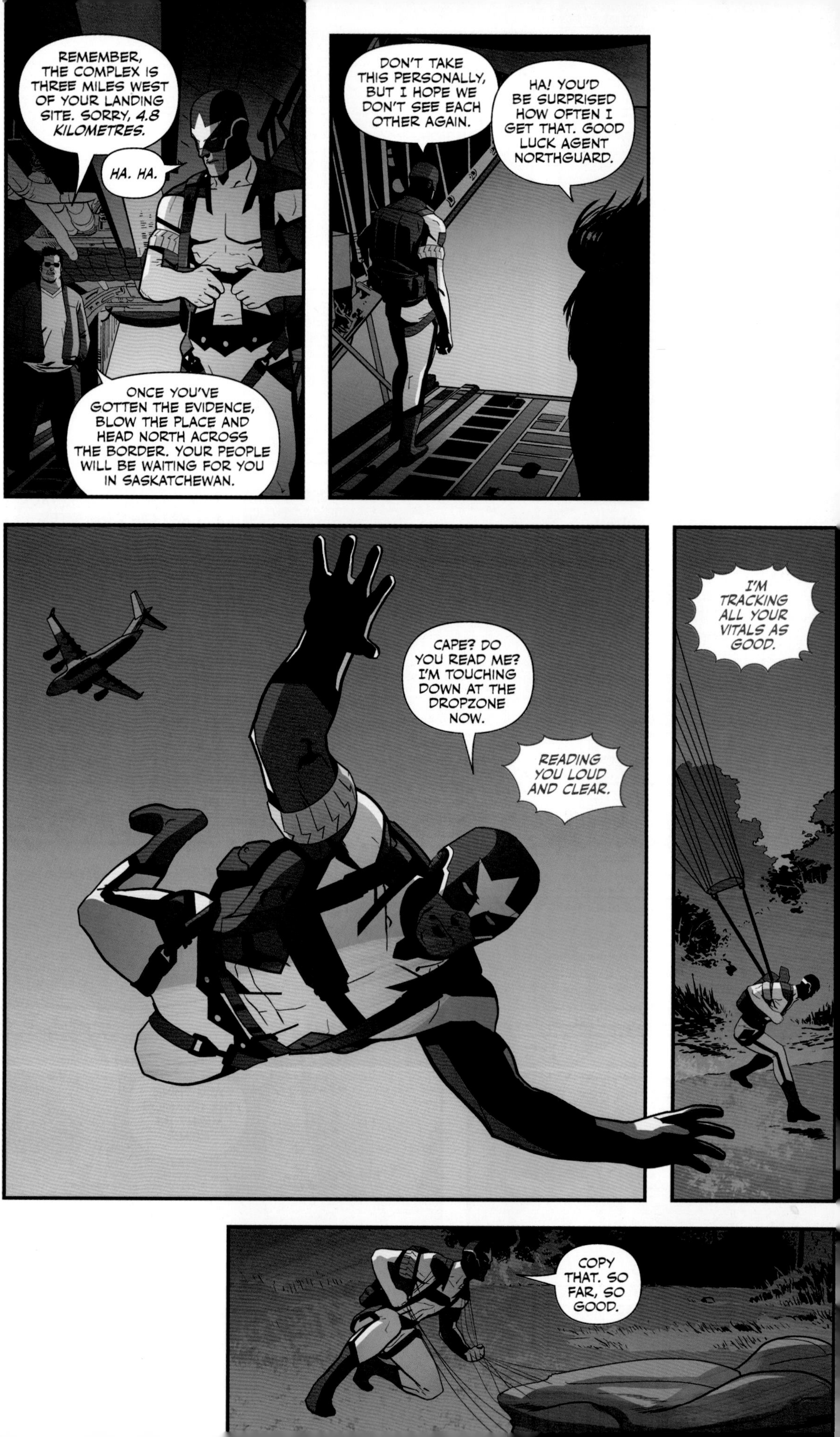
REMEMBER, THE COMPLEX IS THREE MILES WEST OF YOUR LANDING SITE. SORRY, 4.8 KILOMETRES.
HA. HA.
ONCE YOU'VE GOTTEN THE EVIDENCE, BLOW THE PLACE AND HEAD NORTH ACROSS THE BORDER. YOUR PEOPLE WILL BE WAITING FOR YOU IN SASKATCHEWAN.
DON'T TAKE THIS PERSONALLY, BUT I HOPE WE DON'T SEE EACH OTHER AGAIN.
HA! YOU'D BE SURPRISED HOW OFTEN I GET THAT. GOOD LUCK AGENT NORTHGUARD.
CAPE? DO YOU READ ME? I'M TOUCHING DOWN AT THE DROPZONE NOW.
READING YOU LOUD AND CLEAR.
I'M TRACKING ALL YOUR VITALS AS GOOD.
COPY THAT. SO FAR, SO GOOD.

AURORA DAWN WAREHOUSE 003, MONTANA, USA.

CAPE, I'M ALMOST IN.

YOUR ENERGY BLAST COMES IN TWO FLAVOURS: LETHAL AND NON-LETHAL. YOU CAN FOCUS THE POWER OF THE BEAM IN A SMALL AREA IF NECESSARY.

I'VE ALSO CHANGED THE FREQUENCY SO THE BEAM IS YELLOW NOW INSTEAD OF BLUE.

I'VE PROGRAMMED THE COSTUME TO MIMIC YOUR SURROUNDINGS WHEN YOU STAND STILL.

AS LONG AS YOU DON'T MOVE YOU SHOULD BE UNDETECTABLE.

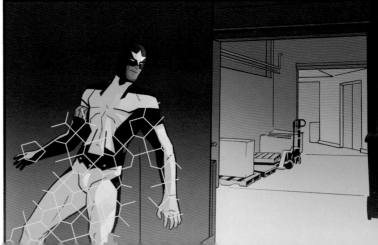

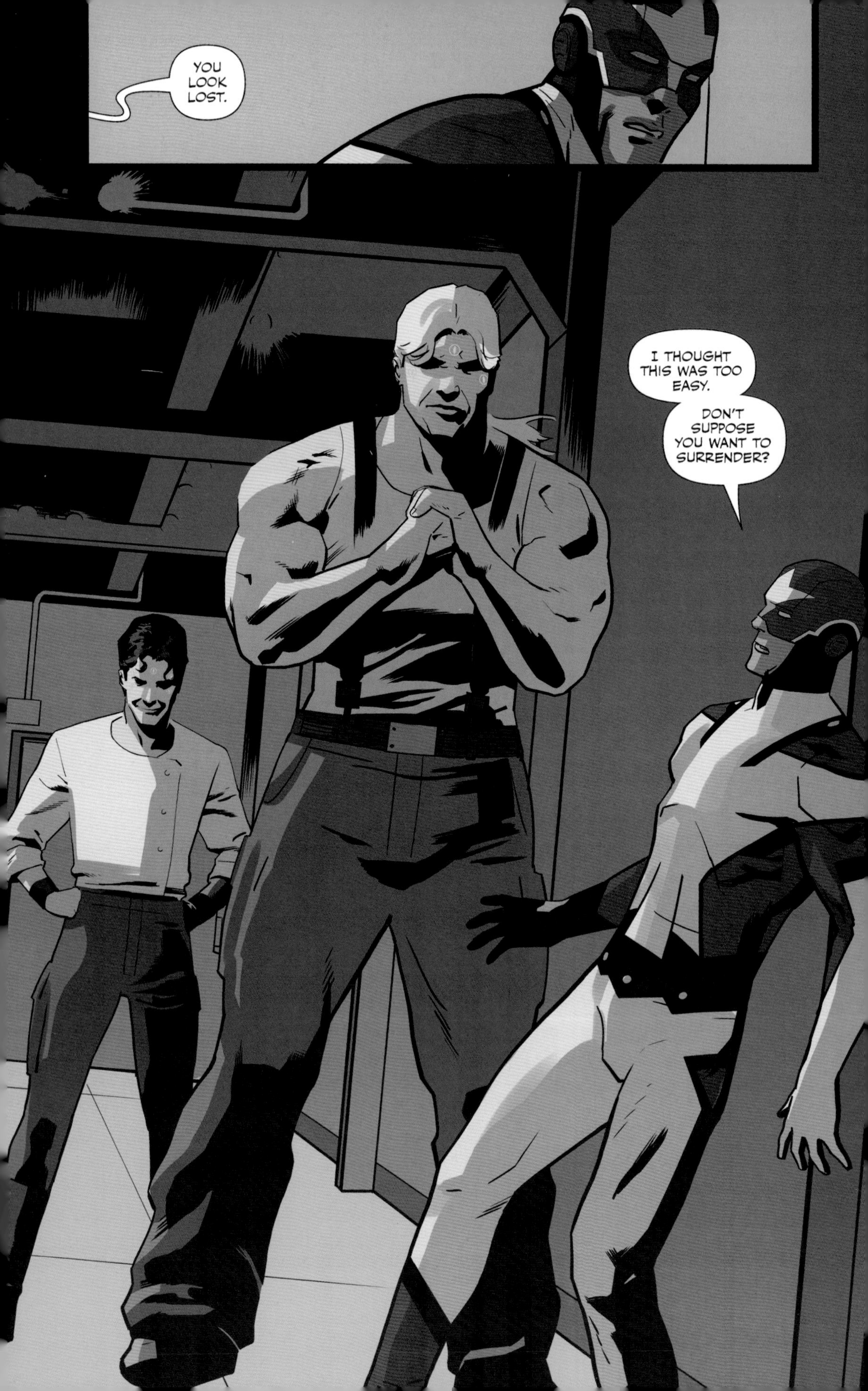
YOU LOOK LOST.
I THOUGHT THIS WAS TOO EASY.
DON'T SUPPOSE YOU WANT TO SURRENDER?

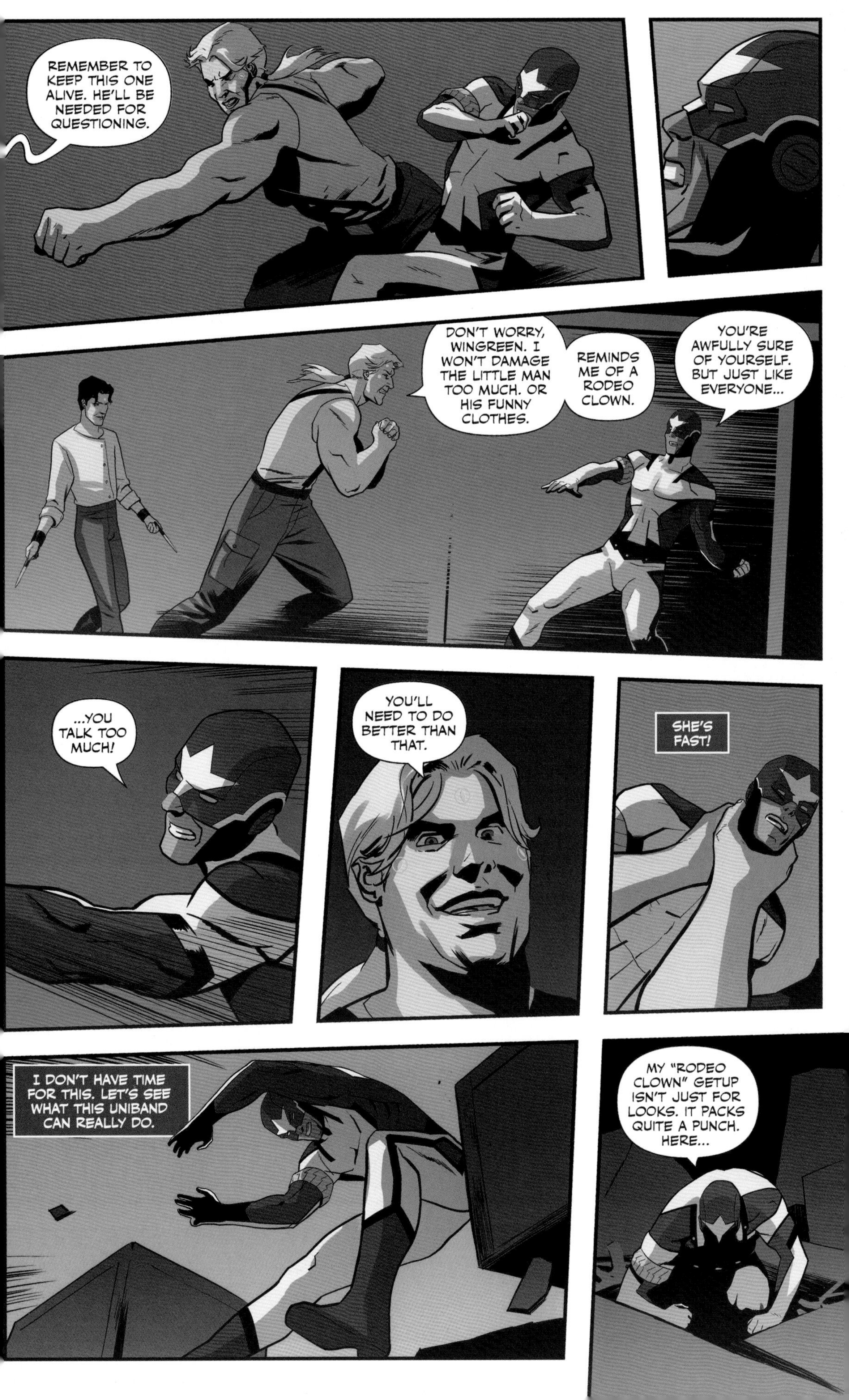

REMEMBER TO KEEP THIS ONE ALIVE. HE'LL BE NEEDED FOR QUESTIONING.
DON'T WORRY, WINGREEN. I WON'T DAMAGE THE LITTLE MAN TOO MUCH. OR HIS FUNNY CLOTHES.
REMINDS ME OF A RODEO CLOWN.
YOU'RE AWFULLY SURE OF YOURSELF. BUT JUST LIKE EVERYONE...
...YOU TALK TOO MUCH!
YOU'LL NEED TO DO BETTER THAN THAT.
SHE'S FAST!
I DON'T HAVE TIME FOR THIS. LET'S SEE WHAT THIS UNIBAND CAN REALLY DO.
MY "RODEO CLOWN" GETUP ISN'T JUST FOR LOOKS. IT PACKS QUITE A PUNCH. HERE...

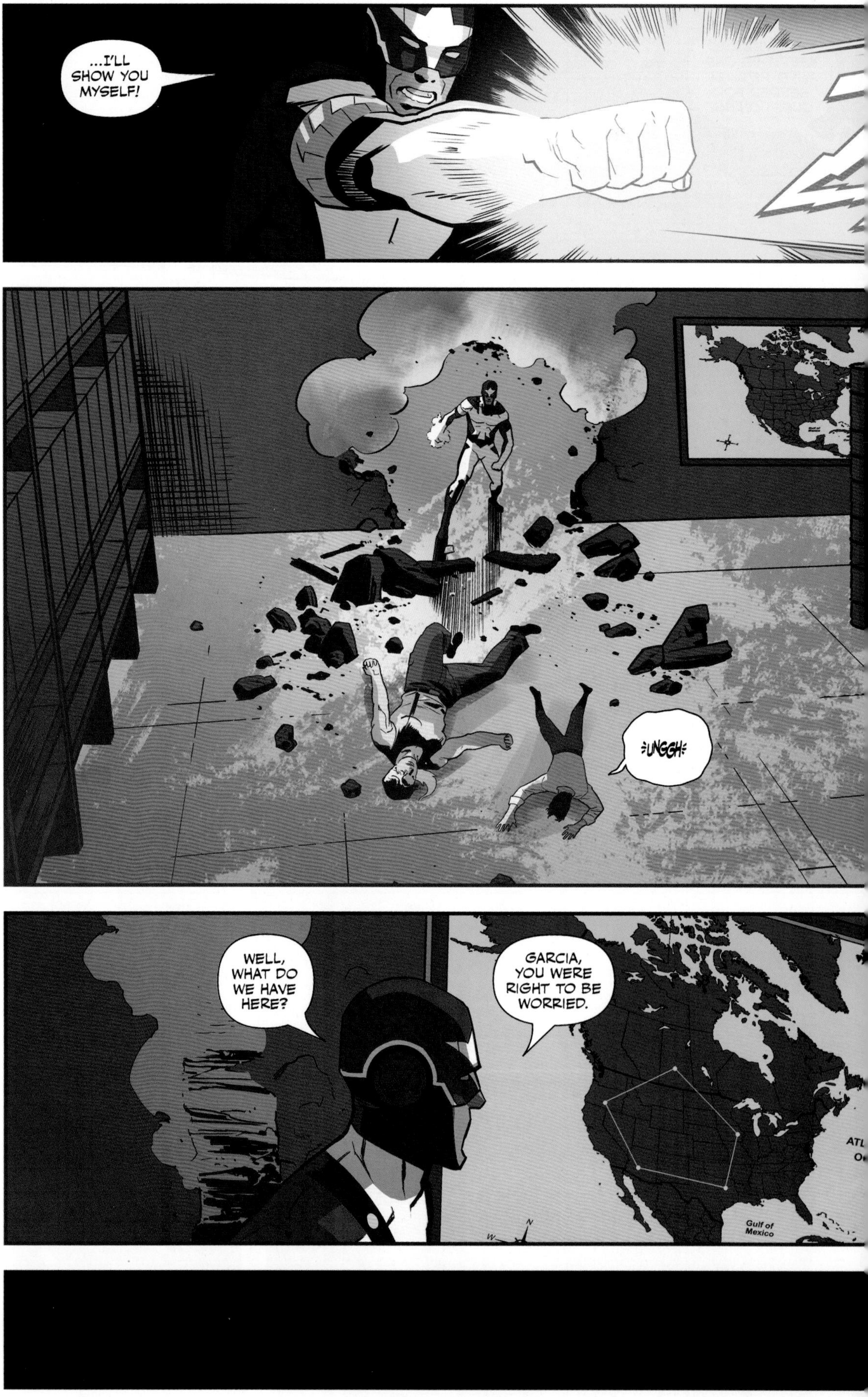
...I'LL SHOW YOU MYSELF!
UNGGH
WELL, WHAT DO WE HAVE HERE?
GARCIA, YOU WERE RIGHT TO BE WORRIED.
Gulf of Mexico

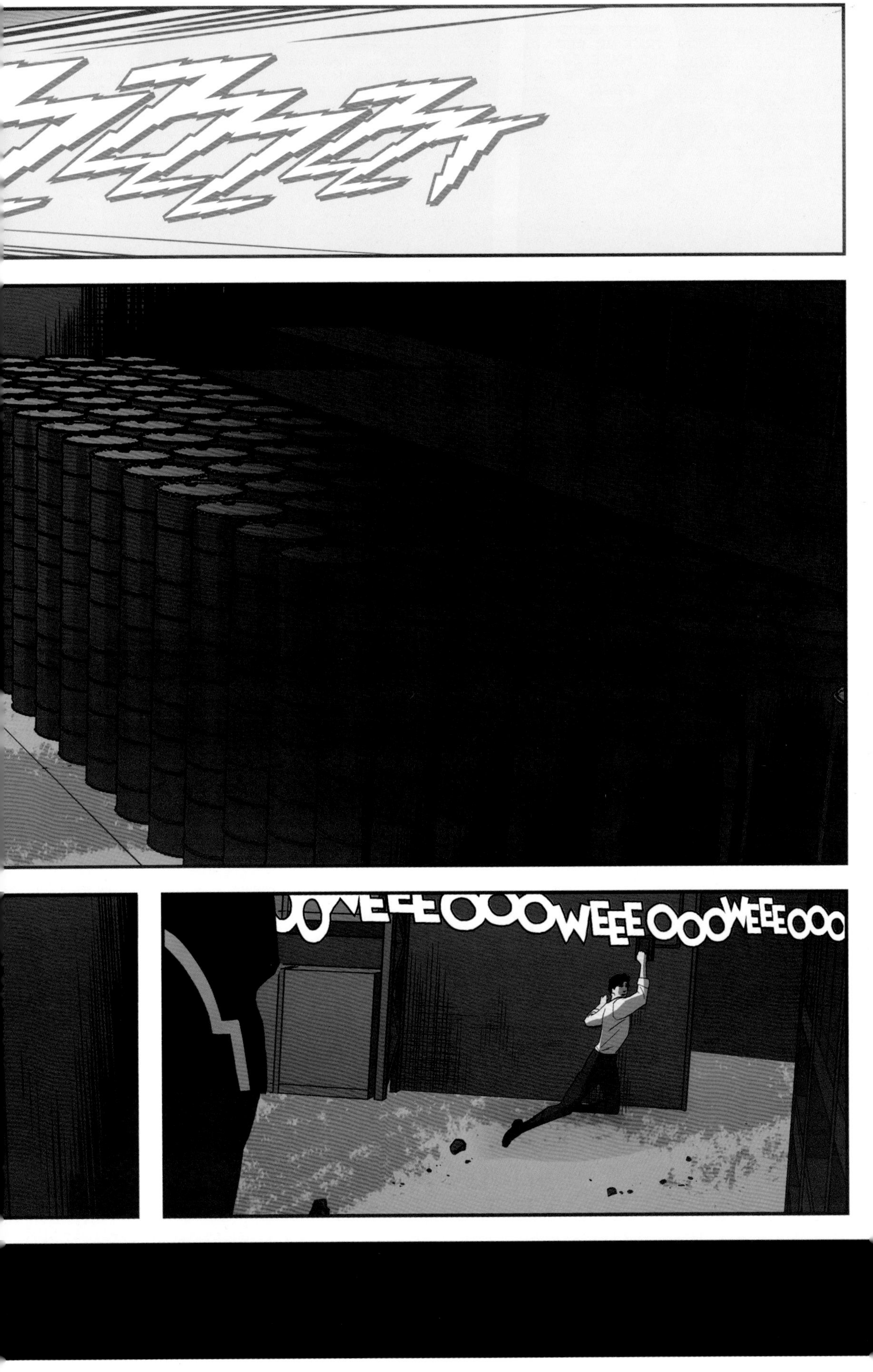
OOOWEEEOOOWEEEOOO

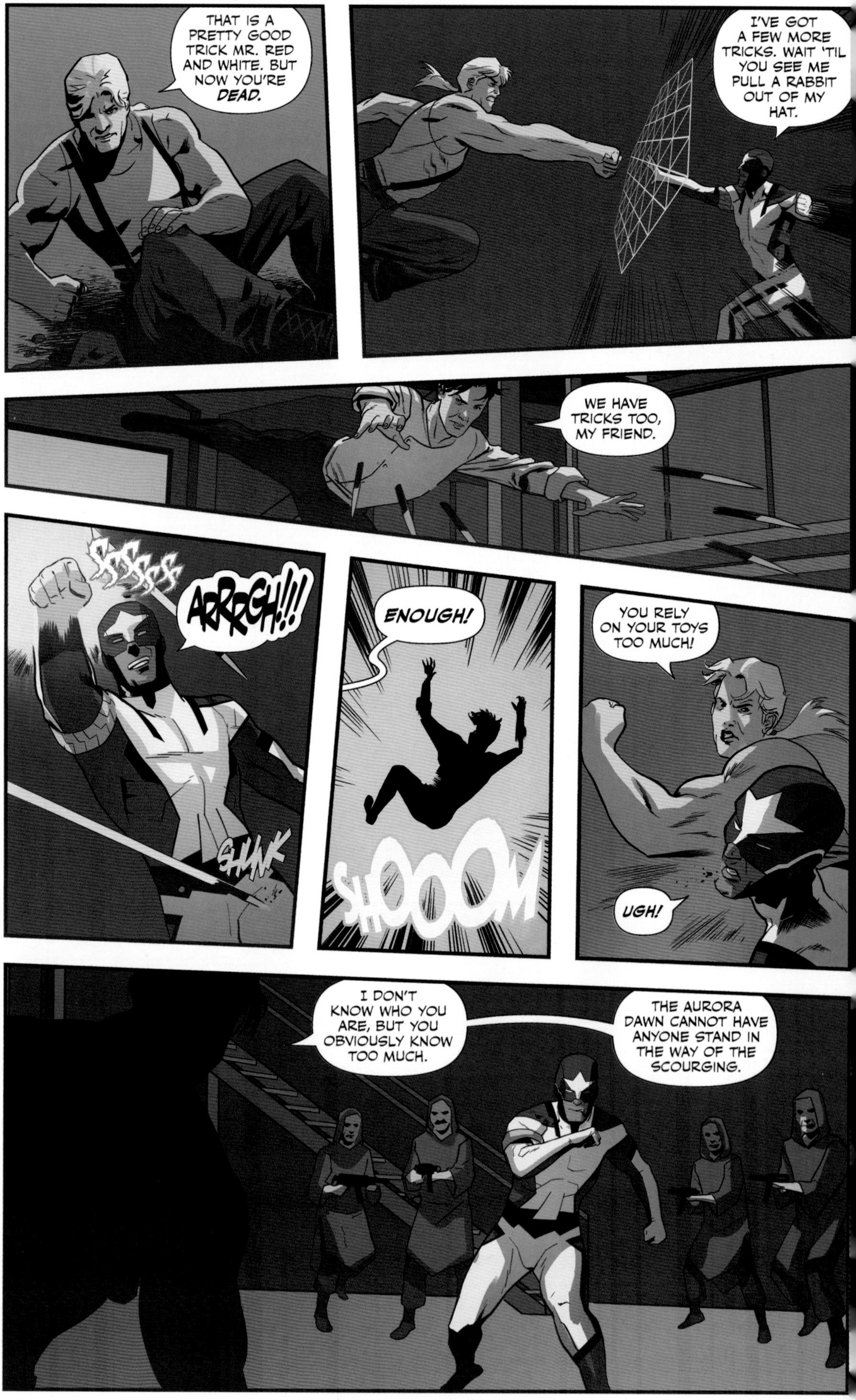
THAT IS A PRETTY GOOD TRICK MR. RED AND WHITE. BUT NOW YOU'RE *DEAD.*
I'VE GOT A FEW MORE TRICKS. WAIT 'TIL YOU SEE ME PULL A RABBIT OUT OF MY HAT.
WE HAVE TRICKS TOO, MY FRIEND.
SSSSS
ARRRGH!!!
SHUNK
ENOUGH!
SHOOOM
YOU RELY ON YOUR TOYS TOO MUCH!
UGH!
I DON'T KNOW WHO YOU ARE, BUT YOU OBVIOUSLY KNOW TOO MUCH.
THE AURORA DAWN CANNOT HAVE ANYONE STAND IN THE WAY OF THE SCOURGING.

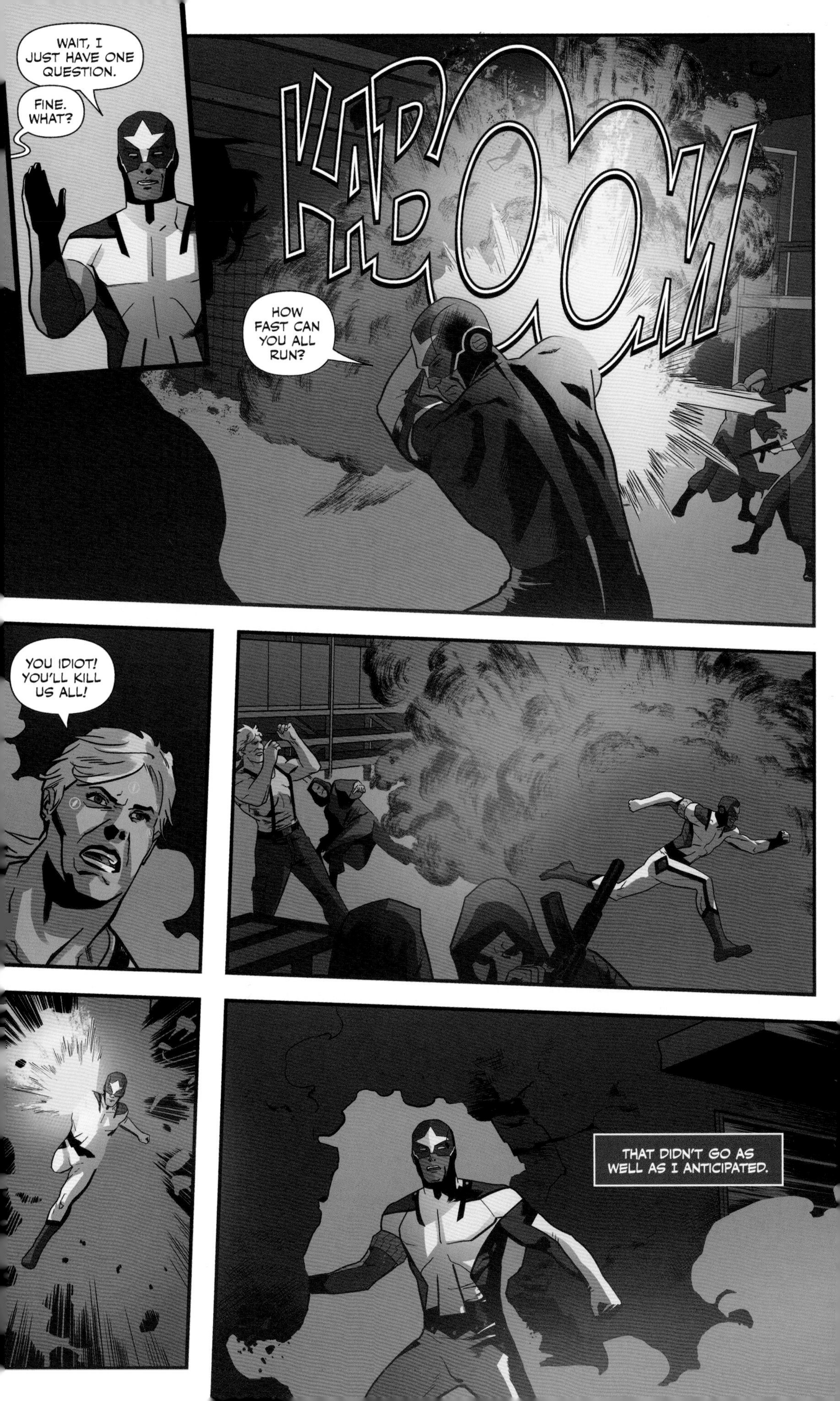
WAIT, I JUST HAVE ONE QUESTION.
FINE. WHAT?
KABOOOM
HOW FAST CAN YOU ALL RUN?
YOU IDIOT! YOU'LL KILL US ALL!
THAT DIDN'T GO AS WELL AS I ANTICIPATED.

YOU HAVE BEEN ABLE TO VERIFY GARCIA'S CONCERNS.

OUR FRIENDS IN WASHINGTON ARE VERY HAPPY WITH YOU.

BREAKING N

I, HOWEVER, AM NOT. WE ARE NOT THE ARMY. WE GO IN, AND GET OUT, WITHOUT BEING NOTICED.

HEY! IT ISN'T MY FAULT THAT YOU SENT ME ON A MISSION WITH AN UNTESTED AND DEADLY PIECE OF TECHNOLOGY!

I KNOW THAT YOU AREN'T RAISING YOUR VOICE AT ME, M. WISE. DO YOU FORGET WHO YOU ARE TALKING TO? I'M NOT SOME BUREAUCRAT FROM OTTAWA.

I KNOW EXACTLY WHAT IT IS LIKE IN THE FIELD.

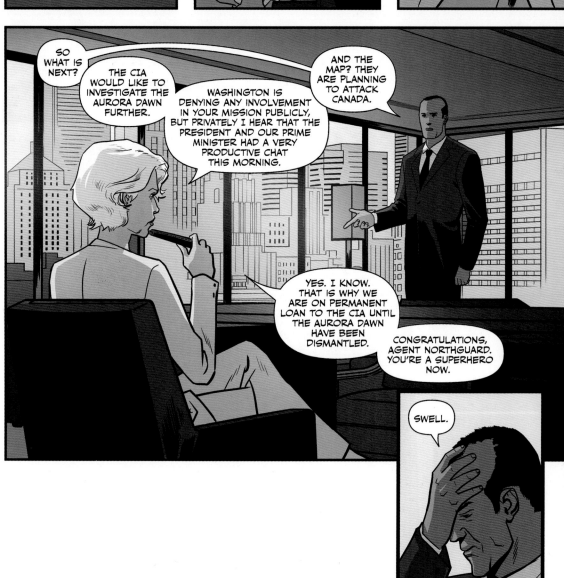

SO WHAT IS NEXT?

THE CIA WOULD LIKE TO INVESTIGATE THE AURORA DAWN FURTHER.

WASHINGTON IS DENYING ANY INVOLVEMENT IN YOUR MISSION PUBLICLY, BUT PRIVATELY I HEAR THAT THE PRESIDENT AND OUR PRIME MINISTER HAD A VERY PRODUCTIVE CHAT THIS MORNING.

AND THE MAP? THEY ARE PLANNING TO ATTACK CANADA.

YES. I KNOW. THAT IS WHY WE ARE ON PERMANENT LOAN TO THE CIA UNTIL THE AURORA DAWN HAVE BEEN DISMANTLED.

CONGRATULATIONS, AGENT NORTHGUARD. YOU'RE A SUPERHERO NOW.

SWELL.

CatC NEWS — Canadian Superhero Blows Up Warehouse

THIS IS UNACCEPTABLE!

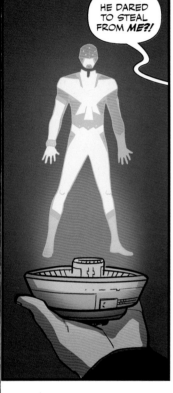

HE DARED TO STEAL FROM *ME?!*

I CAN CREATE ANOTHER WEAPON. AND I APPRECIATE THAT PHIL FOOLED US.

BUT PUTTING ON THAT COSTUME? AND RUNNING AROUND LIKE AN IDIOT? LIKE TOM WOULD?

IT IS INFURIATING.

SO THIS MISSION WILL REQUIRE YOUR SPECIFIC SKILLS. I WANT MY PROPERTY BACK. AND IF PHIL REFUSES...

...ELIMINATE HIM.

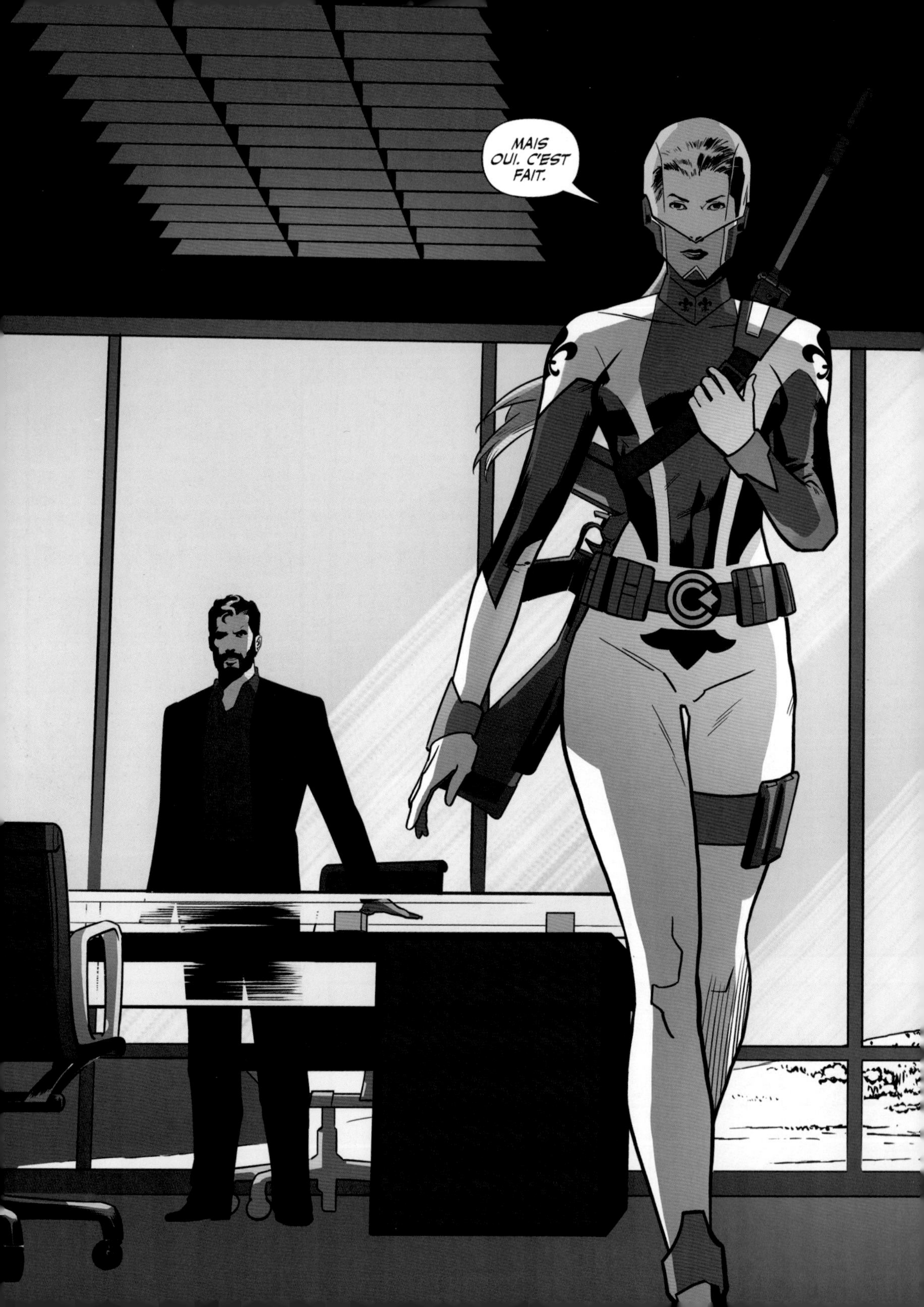
MAIS OUI. C'EST FAIT.

CHAPTER 2
DANGEROUS ENCOUNTER

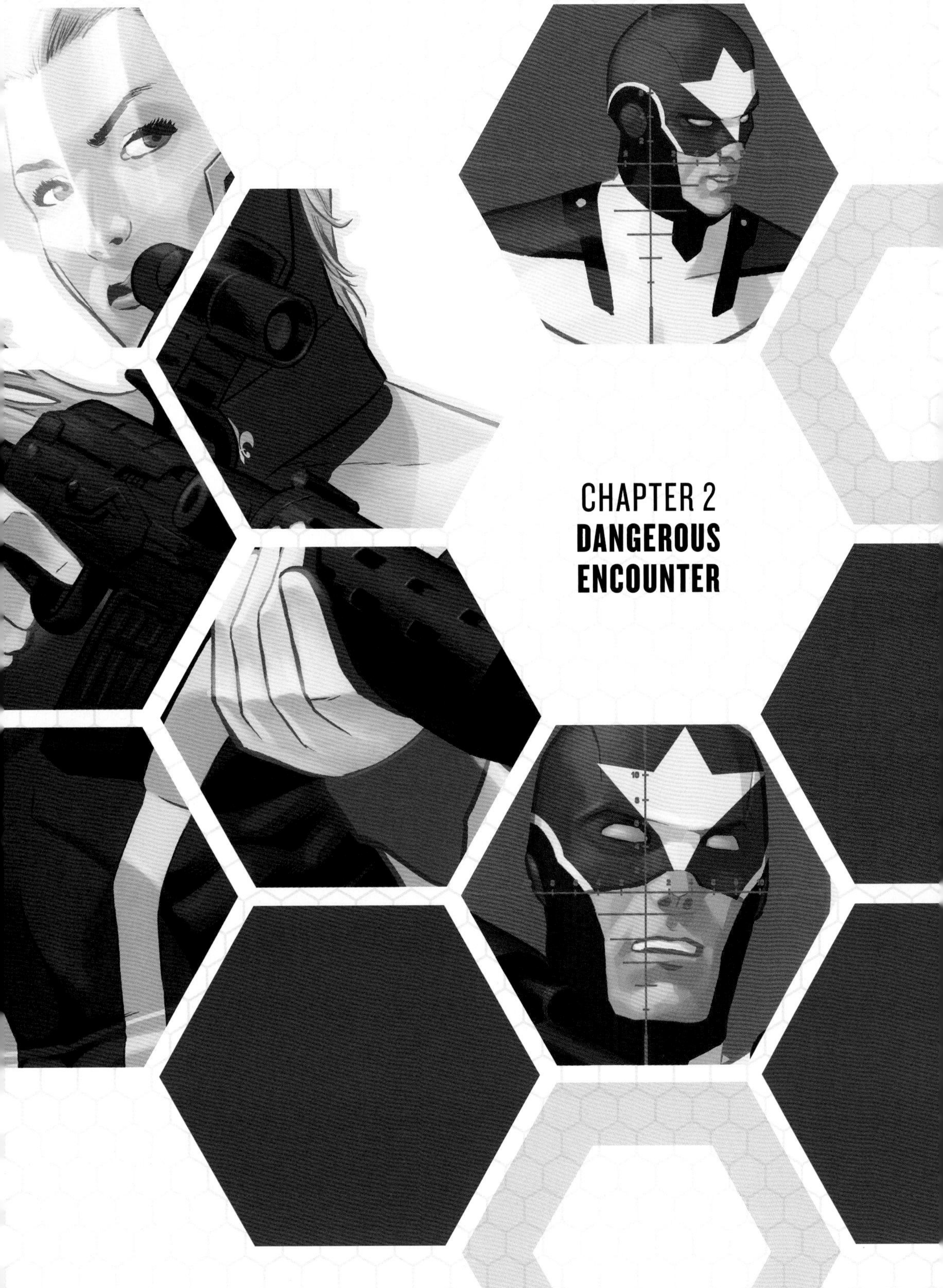

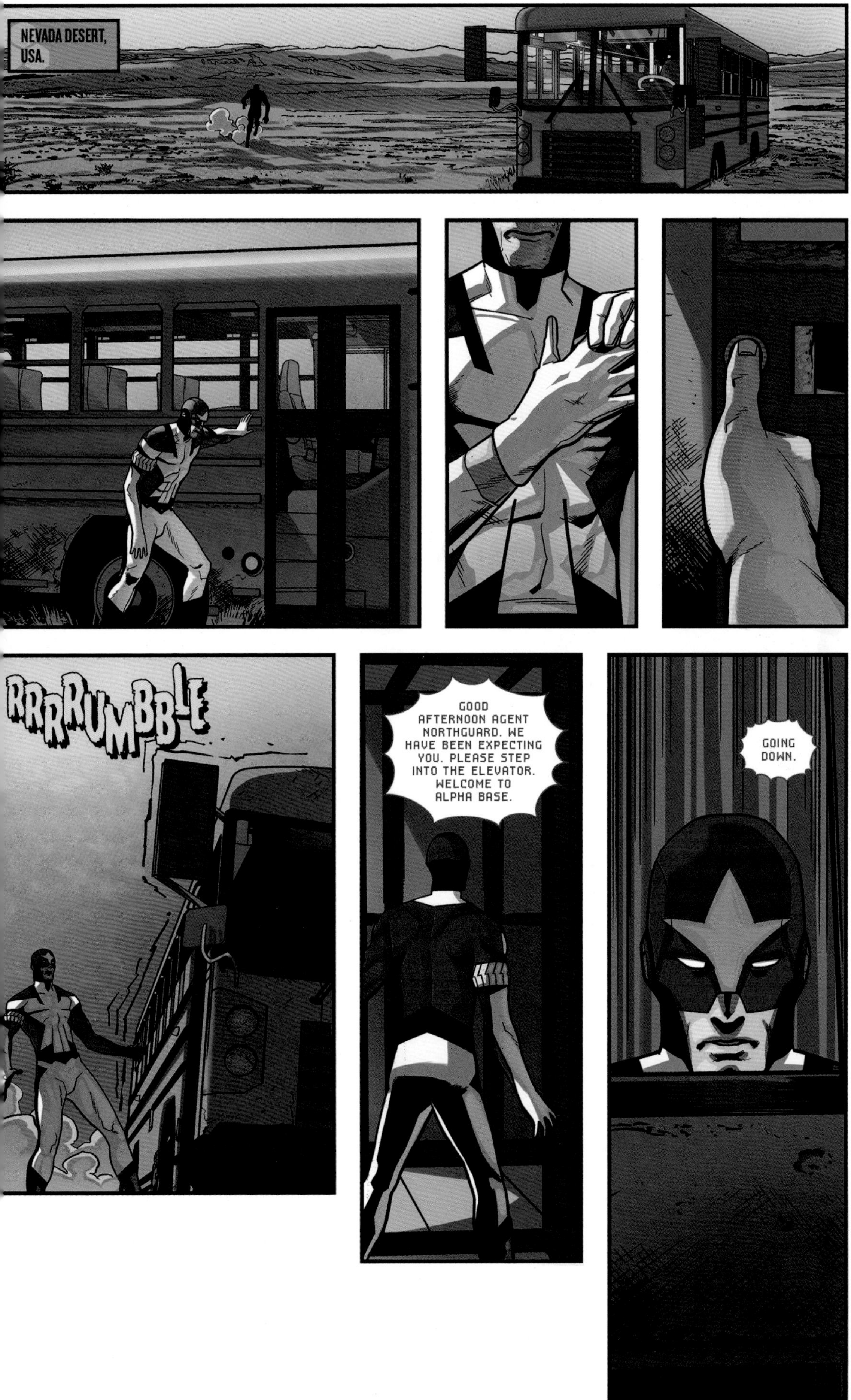
NEVADA DESERT, USA.
RRRRUMBBLE
GOOD AFTERNOON AGENT NORTHGUARD. WE HAVE BEEN EXPECTING YOU. PLEASE STEP INTO THE ELEVATOR. WELCOME TO ALPHA BASE.
GOING DOWN.

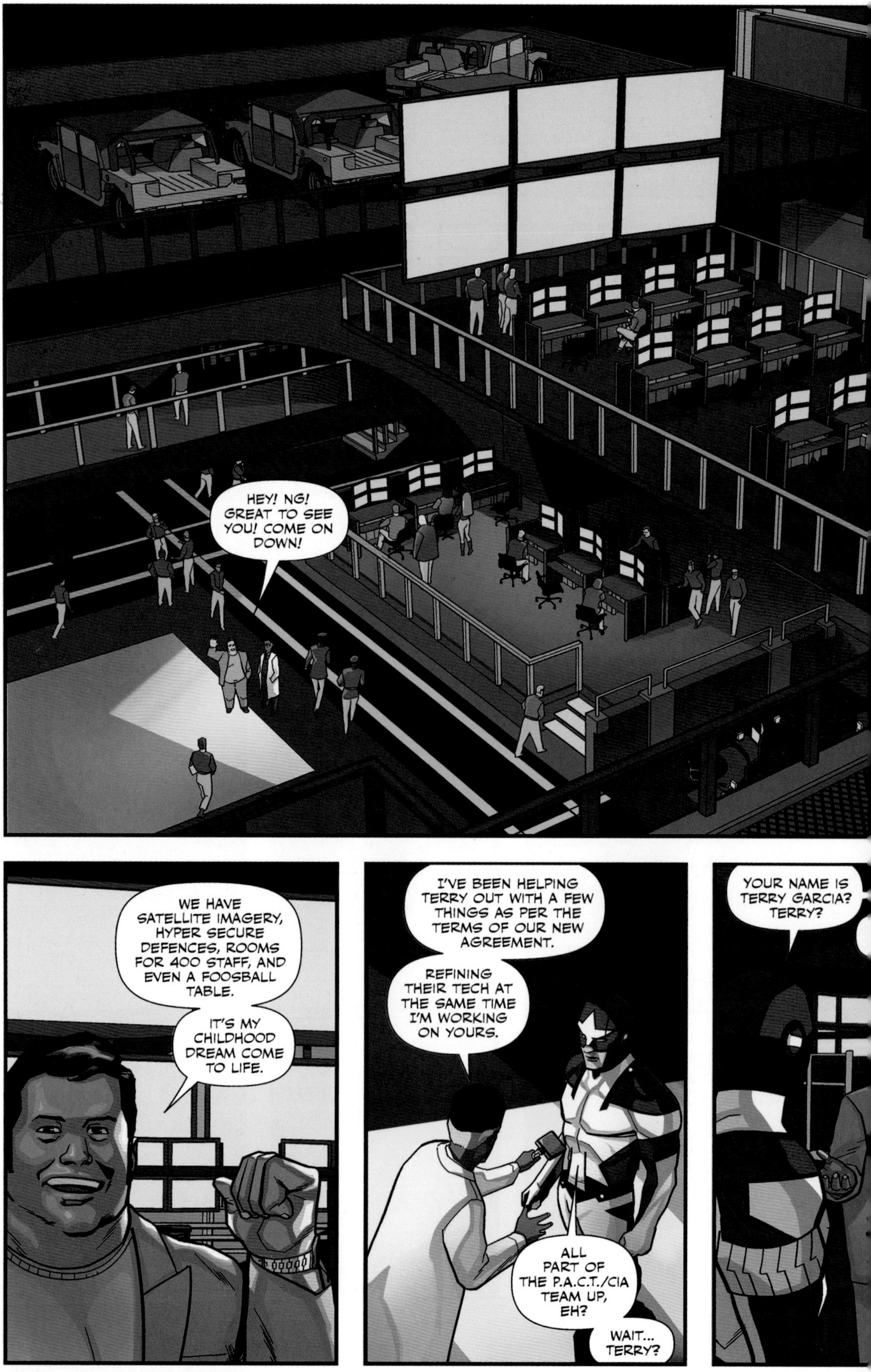
HEY! NG! GREAT TO SEE YOU! COME ON DOWN!
WE HAVE SATELLITE IMAGERY, HYPER SECURE DEFENCES, ROOMS FOR 400 STAFF, AND EVEN A FOOSBALL TABLE.
IT'S MY CHILDHOOD DREAM COME TO LIFE.
I'VE BEEN HELPING TERRY OUT WITH A FEW THINGS AS PER THE TERMS OF OUR NEW AGREEMENT.
REFINING THEIR TECH AT THE SAME TIME I'M WORKING ON YOURS.
ALL PART OF THE P.A.C.T./CIA TEAM UP, EH?
WAIT... TERRY?
YOUR NAME IS TERRY GARCIA? TERRY?

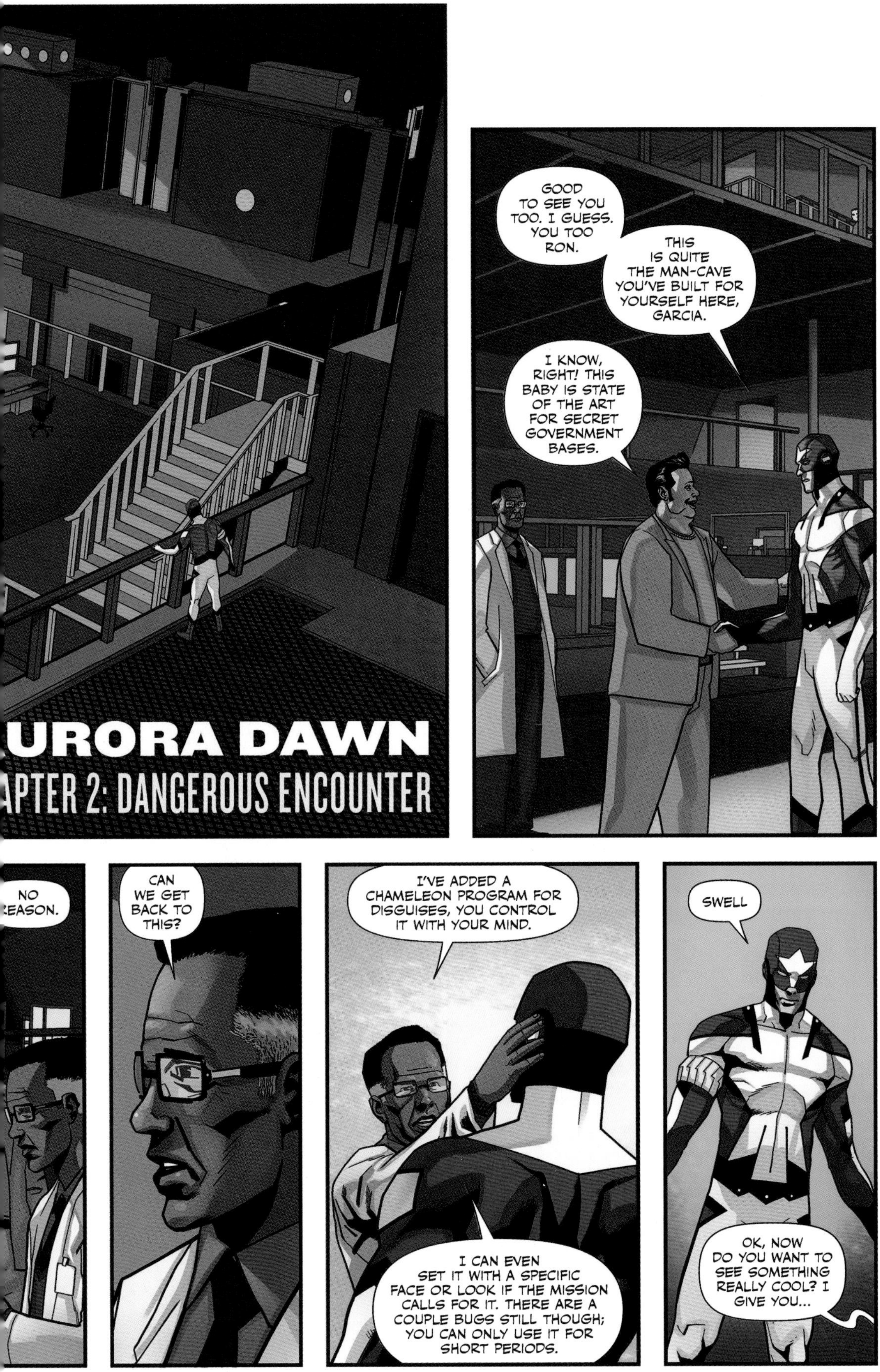

URORA DAWN
APTER 2: DANGEROUS ENCOUNTER
GOOD TO SEE YOU TOO. I GUESS. YOU TOO RON.
THIS IS QUITE THE MAN-CAVE YOU'VE BUILT FOR YOURSELF HERE, GARCIA.
I KNOW, RIGHT! THIS BABY IS STATE OF THE ART FOR SECRET GOVERNMENT BASES.
NO REASON.
CAN WE GET BACK TO THIS?
I'VE ADDED A CHAMELEON PROGRAM FOR DISGUISES, YOU CONTROL IT WITH YOUR MIND.
I CAN EVEN SET IT WITH A SPECIFIC FACE OR LOOK IF THE MISSION CALLS FOR IT. THERE ARE A COUPLE BUGS STILL THOUGH; YOU CAN ONLY USE IT FOR SHORT PERIODS.
SWELL
OK, NOW DO YOU WANT TO SEE SOMETHING REALLY COOL? I GIVE YOU...

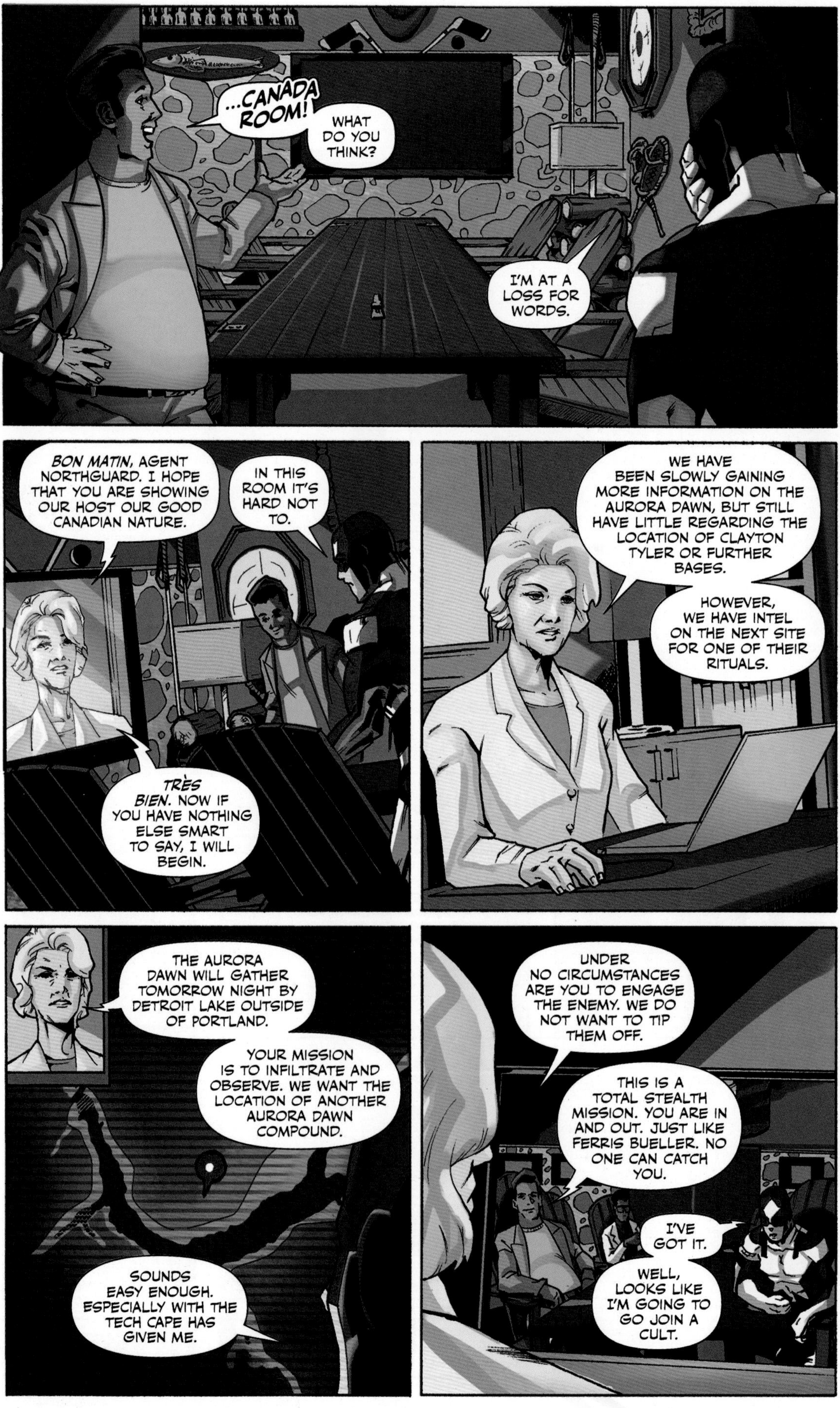
...CANADA ROOM!
WHAT DO YOU THINK?
I'M AT A LOSS FOR WORDS.
BON MATIN, AGENT NORTHGUARD. I HOPE THAT YOU ARE SHOWING OUR HOST OUR GOOD CANADIAN NATURE.
IN THIS ROOM IT'S HARD NOT TO.
TRÈS BIEN. NOW IF YOU HAVE NOTHING ELSE SMART TO SAY, I WILL BEGIN.
WE HAVE BEEN SLOWLY GAINING MORE INFORMATION ON THE AURORA DAWN, BUT STILL HAVE LITTLE REGARDING THE LOCATION OF CLAYTON TYLER OR FURTHER BASES.
HOWEVER, WE HAVE INTEL ON THE NEXT SITE FOR ONE OF THEIR RITUALS.
THE AURORA DAWN WILL GATHER TOMORROW NIGHT BY DETROIT LAKE OUTSIDE OF PORTLAND.
YOUR MISSION IS TO INFILTRATE AND OBSERVE. WE WANT THE LOCATION OF ANOTHER AURORA DAWN COMPOUND.
SOUNDS EASY ENOUGH. ESPECIALLY WITH THE TECH CAPE HAS GIVEN ME.
UNDER NO CIRCUMSTANCES ARE YOU TO ENGAGE THE ENEMY. WE DO NOT WANT TO TIP THEM OFF.
THIS IS A TOTAL STEALTH MISSION. YOU ARE IN AND OUT. JUST LIKE FERRIS BUELLER. NO ONE CAN CATCH YOU.
I'VE GOT IT.
WELL, LOOKS LIKE I'M GOING TO GO JOIN A CULT.

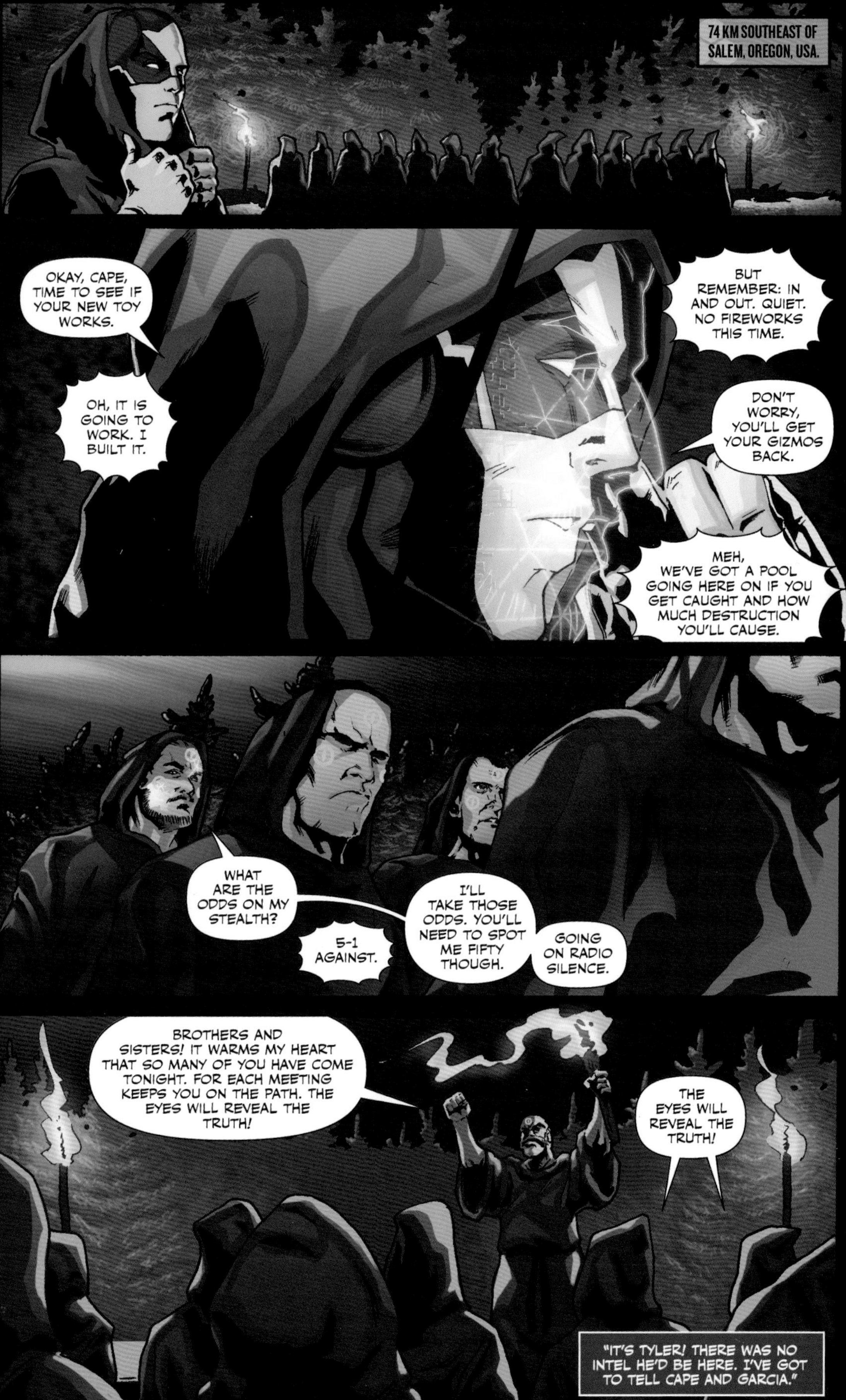
74 KM SOUTHEAST OF SALEM, OREGON, USA.
OKAY, CAPE, TIME TO SEE IF YOUR NEW TOY WORKS.
OH, IT IS GOING TO WORK. I BUILT IT.
BUT REMEMBER: IN AND OUT. QUIET. NO FIREWORKS THIS TIME.
DON'T WORRY, YOU'LL GET YOUR GIZMOS BACK.
MEH, WE'VE GOT A POOL GOING HERE ON IF YOU GET CAUGHT AND HOW MUCH DESTRUCTION YOU'LL CAUSE.
WHAT ARE THE ODDS ON MY STEALTH?
5-1 AGAINST.
I'LL TAKE THOSE ODDS. YOU'LL NEED TO SPOT ME FIFTY THOUGH.
GOING ON RADIO SILENCE.
BROTHERS AND SISTERS! IT WARMS MY HEART THAT SO MANY OF YOU HAVE COME TONIGHT. FOR EACH MEETING KEEPS YOU ON THE PATH. THE EYES WILL REVEAL THE TRUTH!
THE EYES WILL REVEAL THE TRUTH!
"IT'S TYLER! THERE WAS NO INTEL HE'D BE HERE. I'VE GOT TO TELL CAPE AND GARCIA."

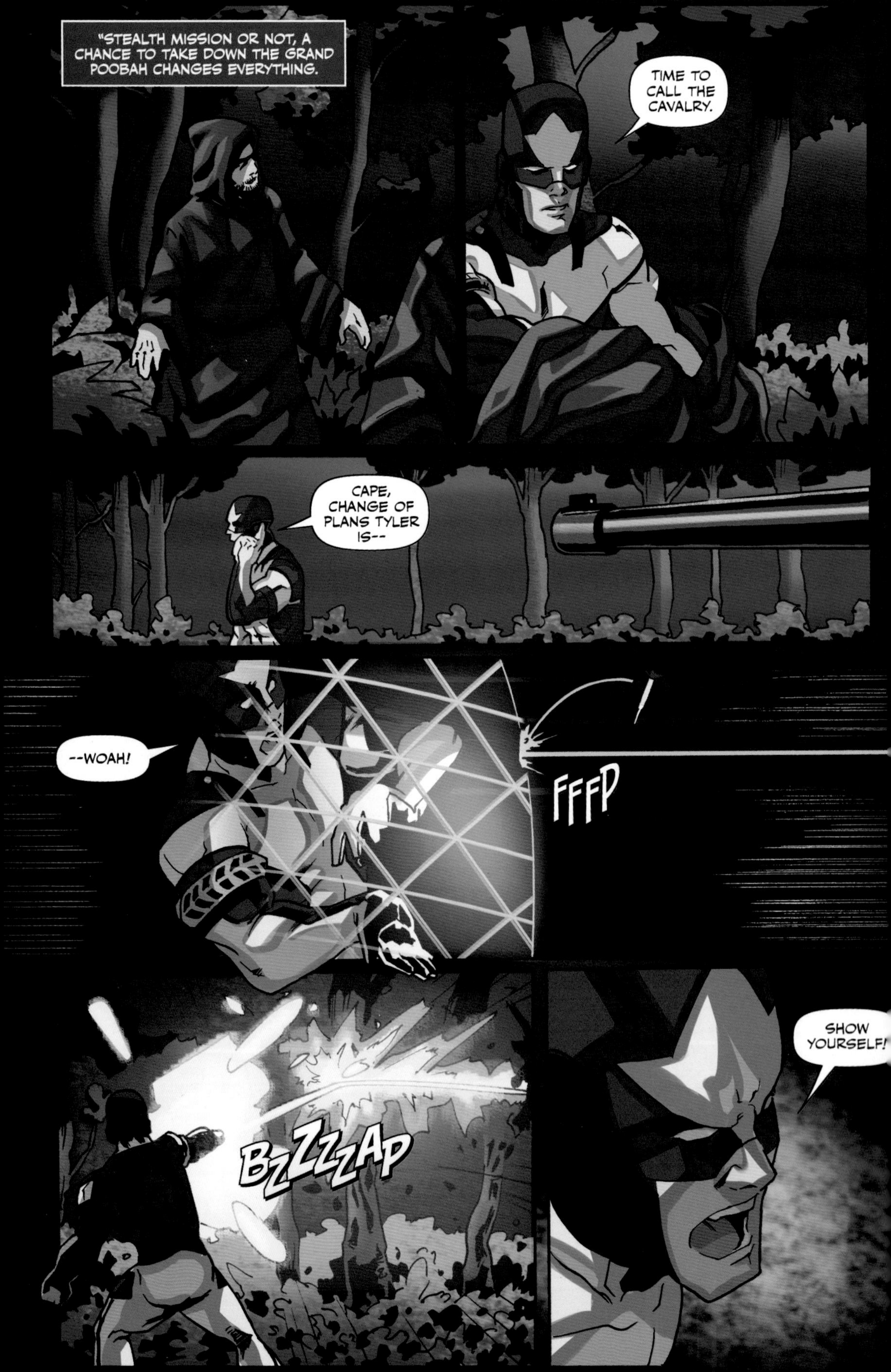
"STEALTH MISSION OR NOT, A CHANCE TO TAKE DOWN THE GRAND POOBAH CHANGES EVERYTHING.
TIME TO CALL THE CAVALRY.
CAPE, CHANGE OF PLANS TYLER IS--
--WOAH!
FFFP
BZZZZAP
SHOW YOURSELF!

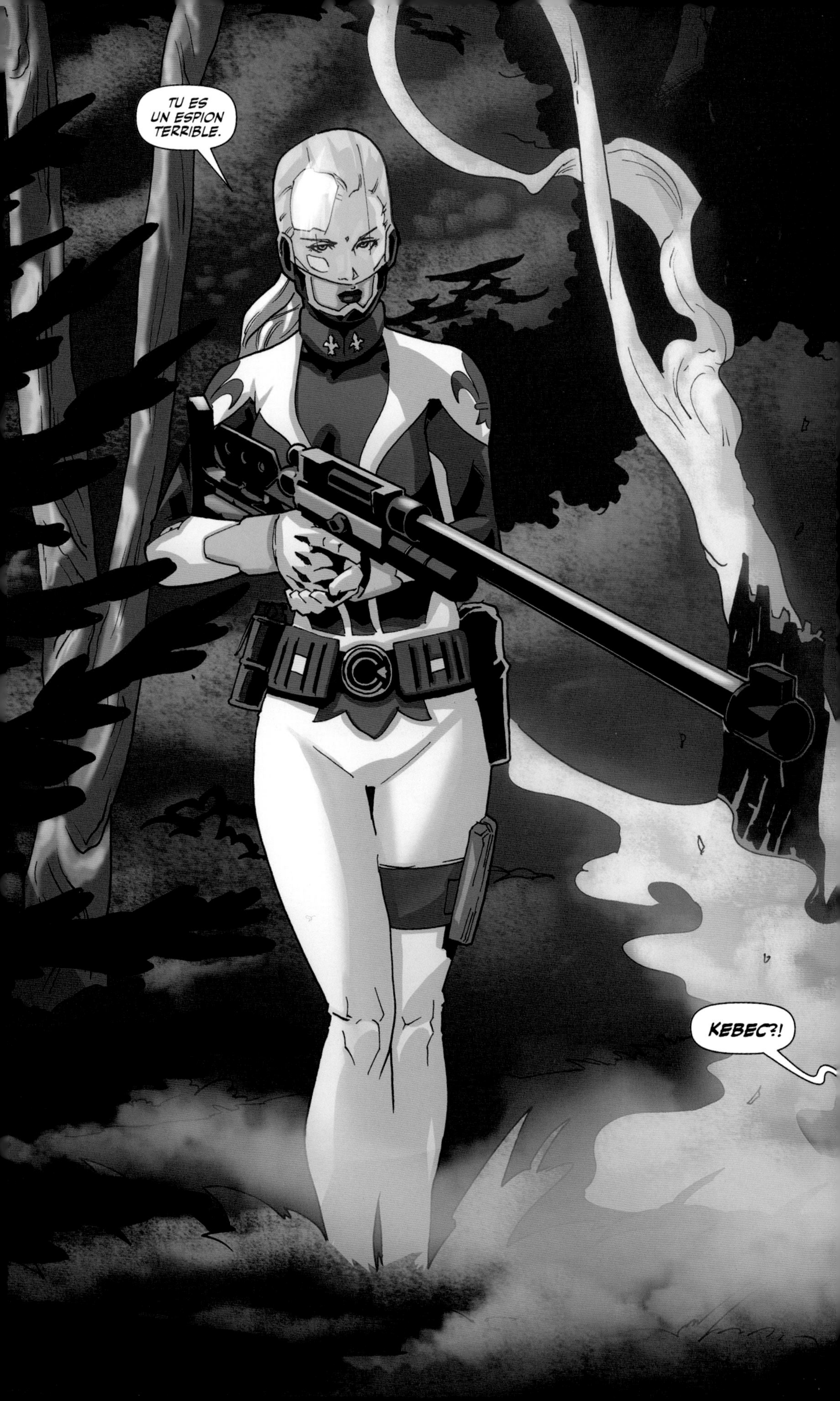
TU ES UN ESPION TERRIBLE.
KEBEC?!

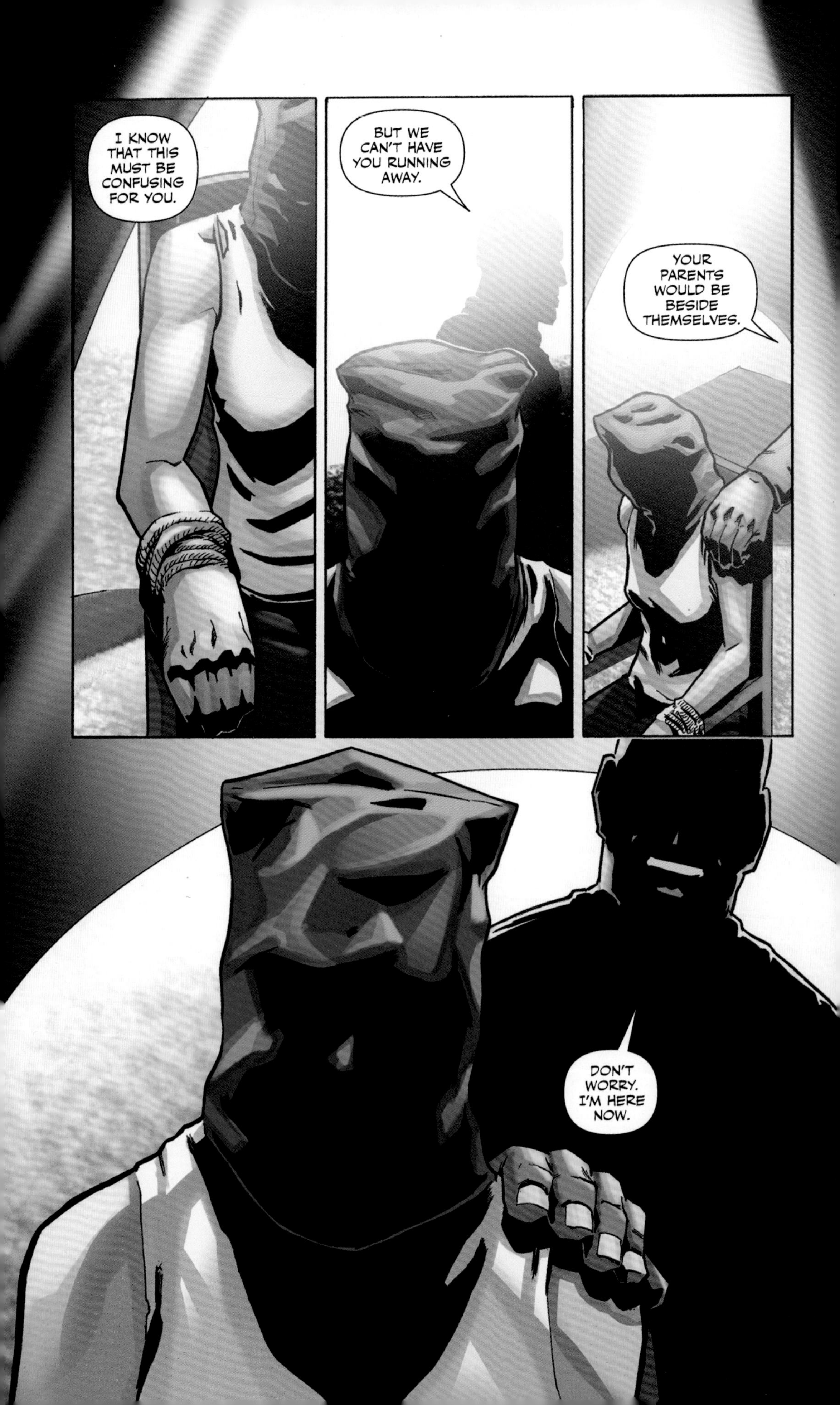
I KNOW THAT THIS MUST BE CONFUSING FOR YOU.
BUT WE CAN'T HAVE YOU RUNNING AWAY.
YOUR PARENTS WOULD BE BESIDE THEMSELVES.
DON'T WORRY. I'M HERE NOW.

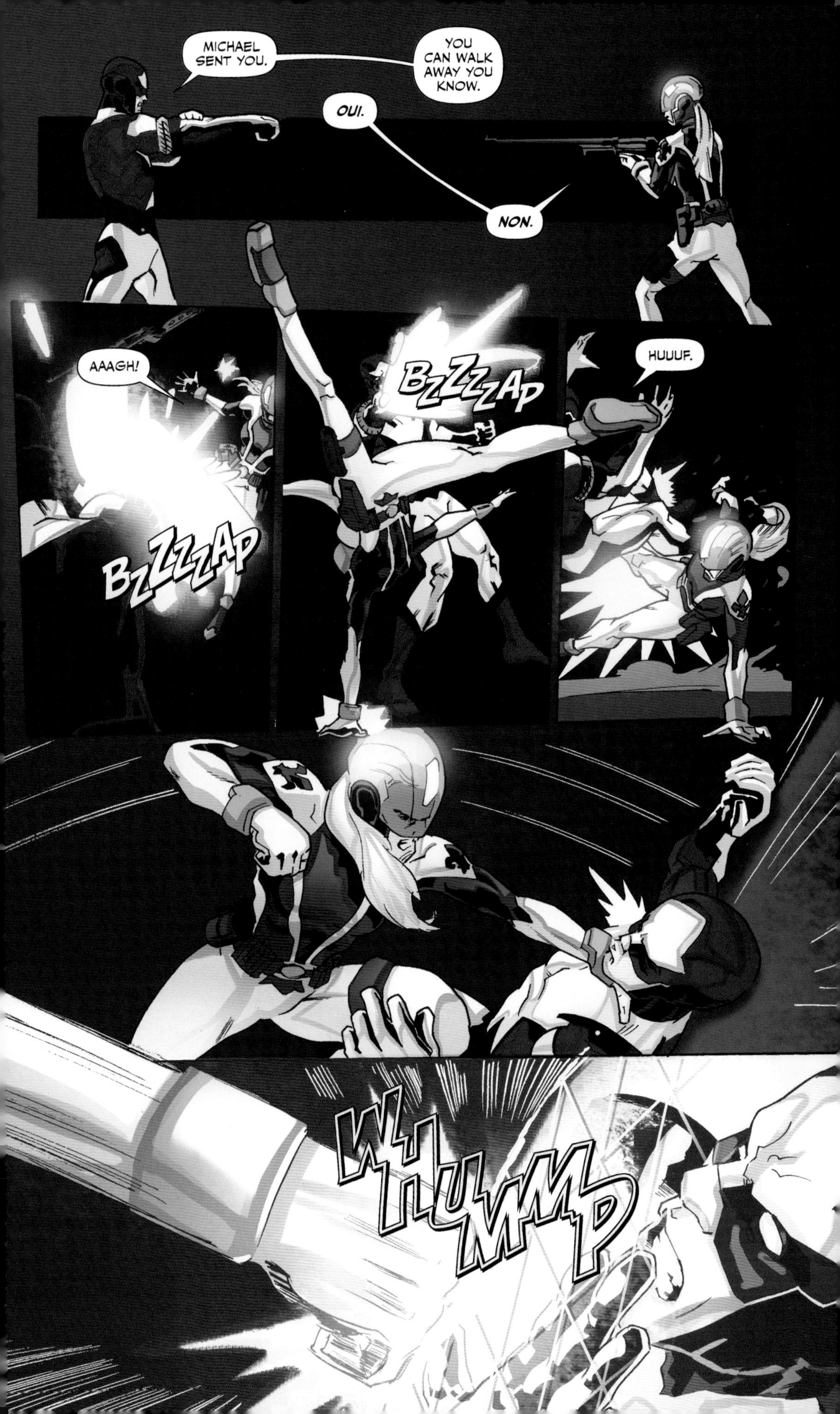
MICHAEL SENT YOU.
YOU CAN WALK AWAY YOU KNOW.
OUI.
NON.
AAAGH!
BZZZZAP
BZZZZAP
HUUUF.
WHUMMP

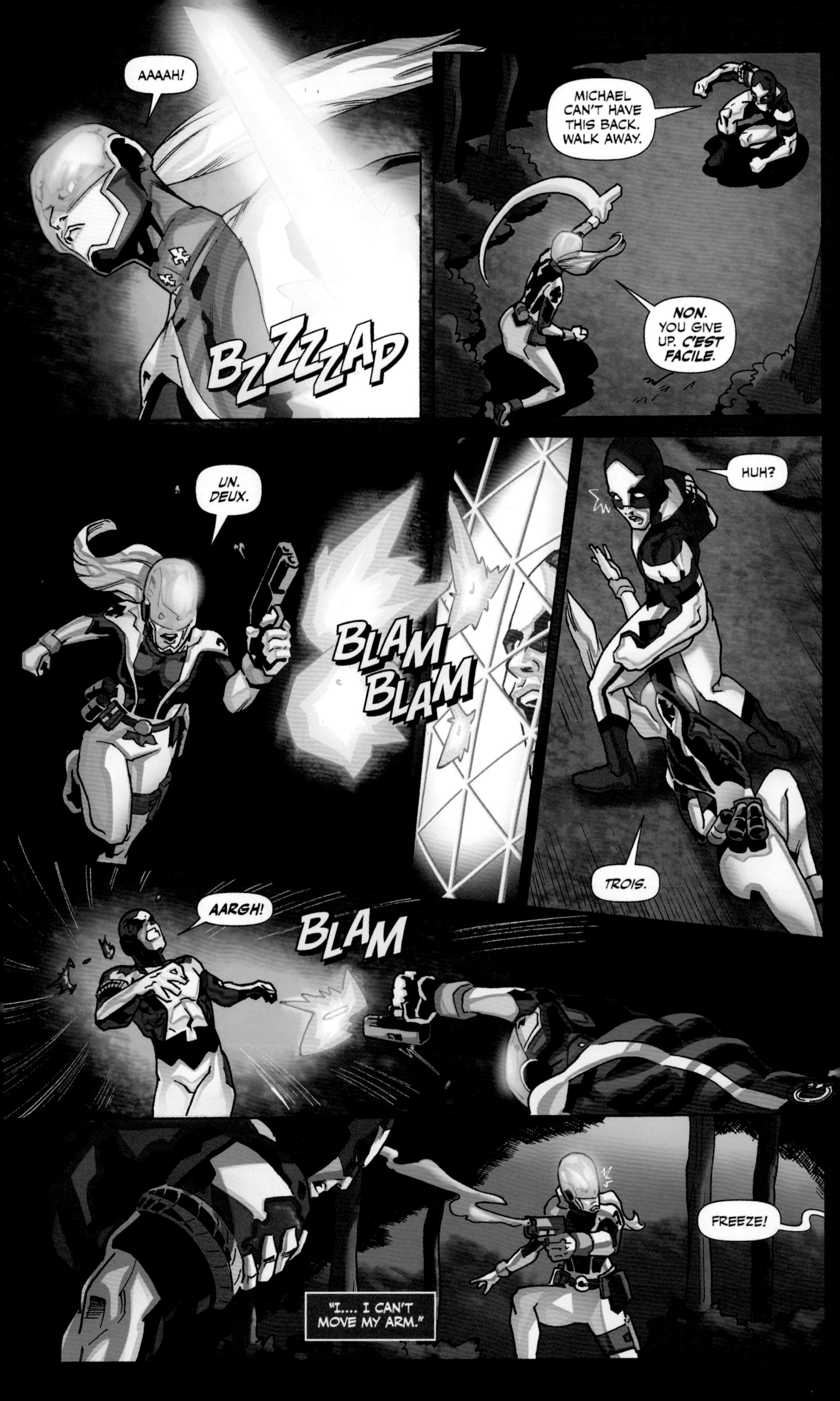
AAAAH!
BZZZZZAP
MICHAEL CAN'T HAVE THIS BACK. WALK AWAY.
NON. YOU GIVE UP. C'EST FACILE.
UN. DEUX.
BLAM BLAM
HUH?
TROIS.
AARGH!
BLAM
FREEZE!
"I.... I CAN'T MOVE MY ARM."

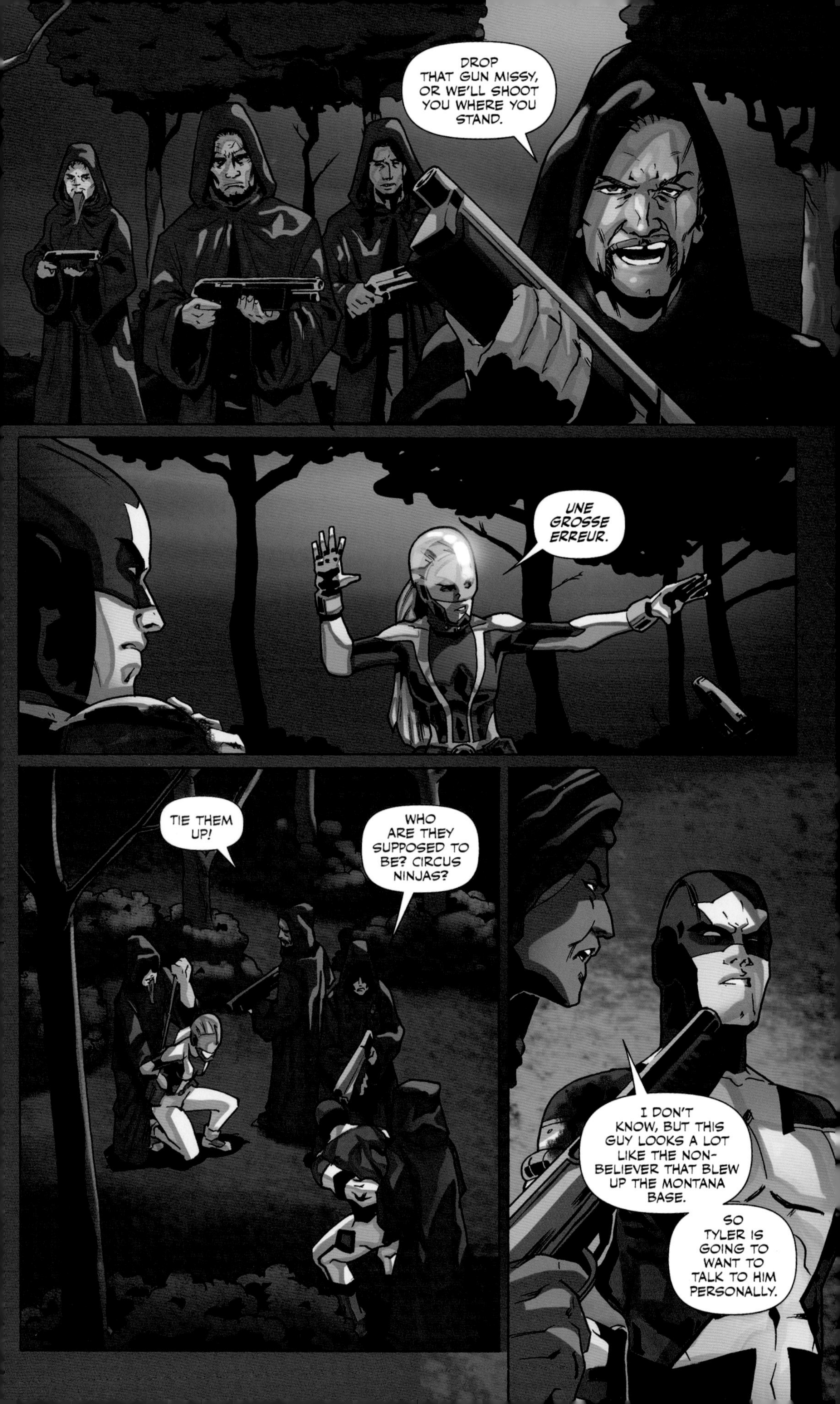
DROP THAT GUN MISSY, OR WE'LL SHOOT YOU WHERE YOU STAND.
UNE GROSSE ERREUR.
TIE THEM UP!
WHO ARE THEY SUPPOSED TO BE? CIRCUS NINJAS?
I DON'T KNOW, BUT THIS GUY LOOKS A LOT LIKE THE NON-BELIEVER THAT BLEW UP THE MONTANA BASE.
SO TYLER IS GOING TO WANT TO TALK TO HIM PERSONALLY.

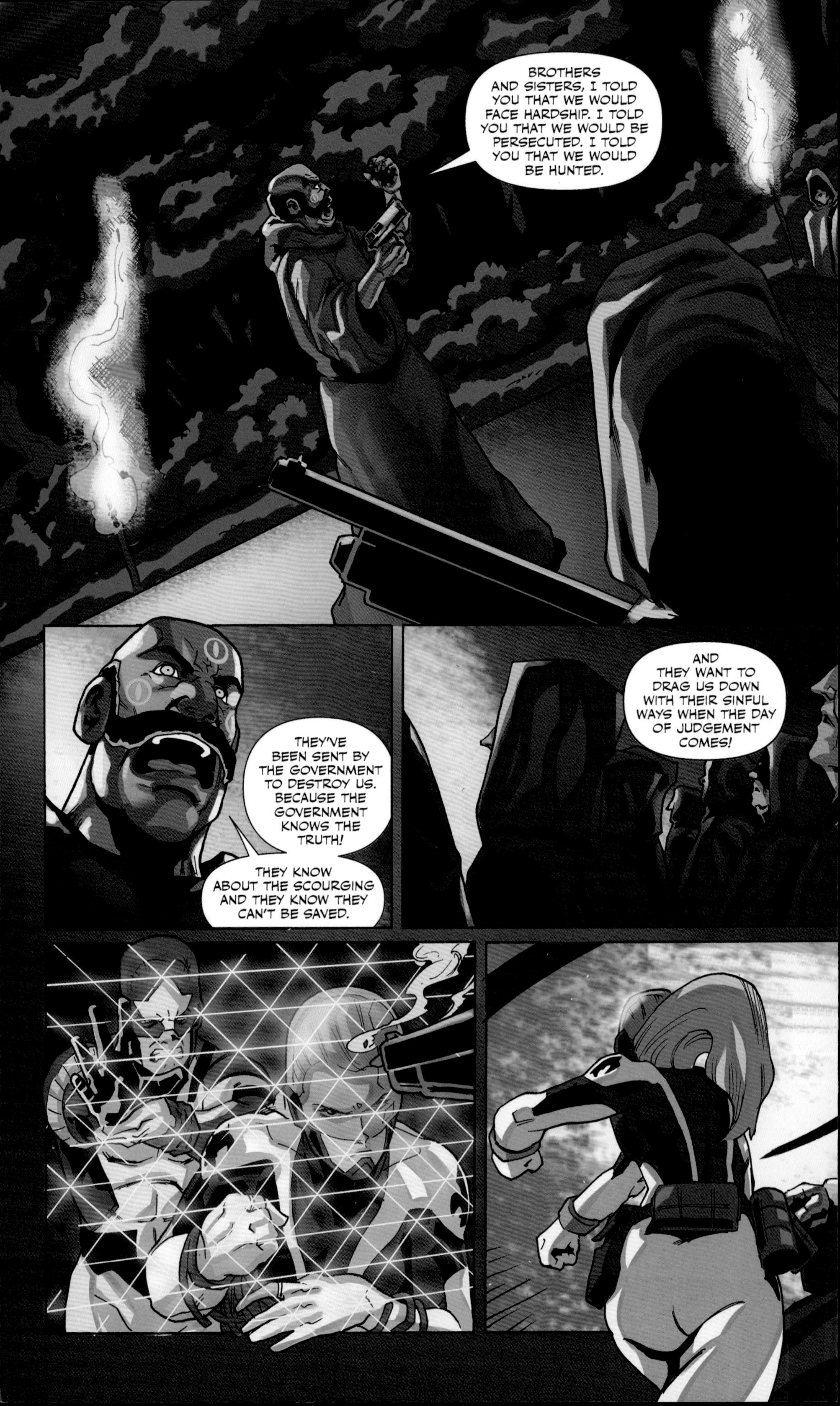

BROTHERS AND SISTERS, I TOLD YOU THAT WE WOULD FACE HARDSHIP. I TOLD YOU THAT WE WOULD BE PERSECUTED. I TOLD YOU THAT WE WOULD BE HUNTED.
THEY'VE BEEN SENT BY THE GOVERNMENT TO DESTROY US. BECAUSE THE GOVERNMENT KNOWS THE TRUTH!
THEY KNOW ABOUT THE SCOURGING AND THEY KNOW THEY CAN'T BE SAVED.
AND THEY WANT TO DRAG US DOWN WITH THEIR SINFUL WAYS WHEN THE DAY OF JUDGEMENT COMES!

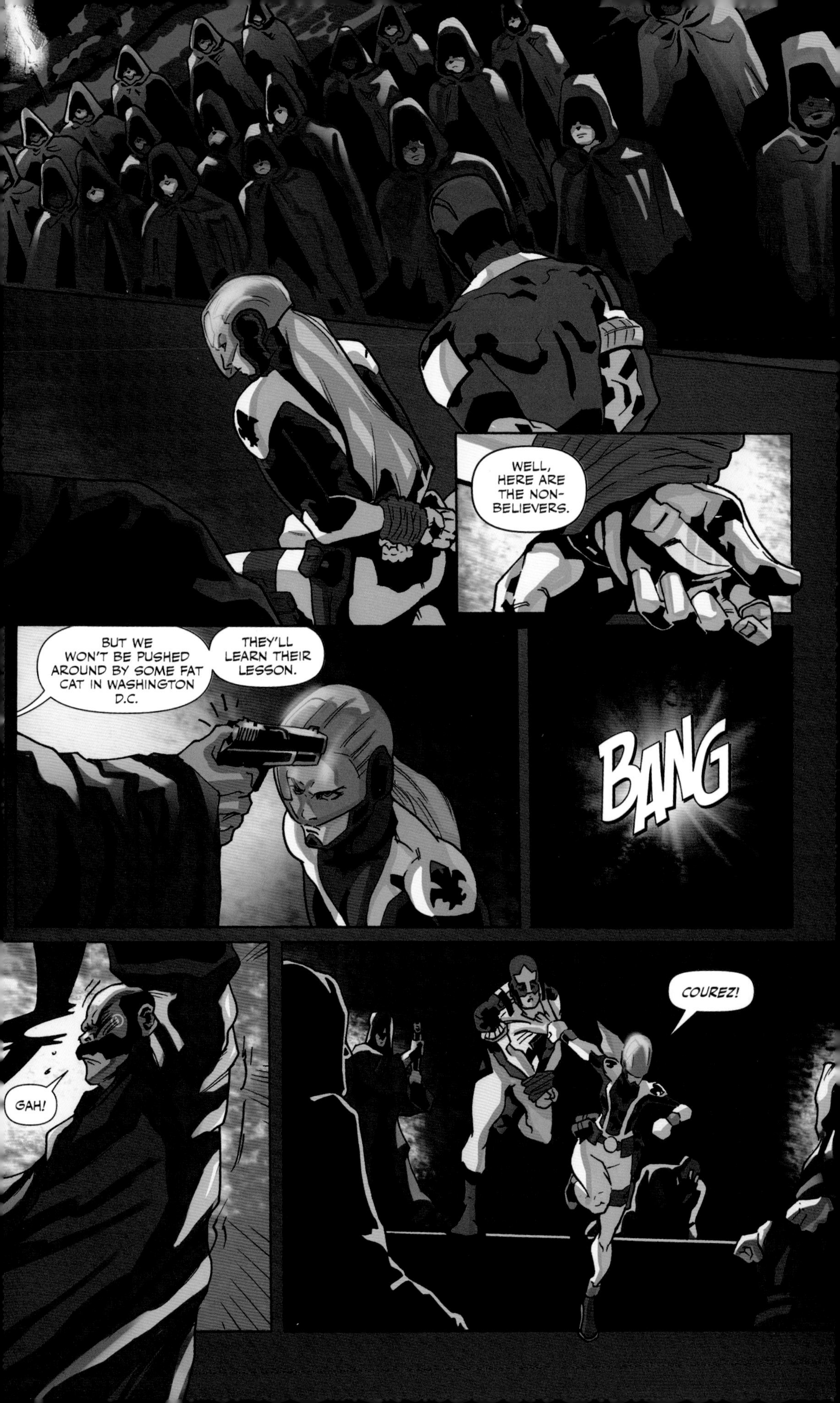
WELL, HERE ARE THE NON-BELIEVERS.
BUT WE WON'T BE PUSHED AROUND BY SOME FAT CAT IN WASHINGTON D.C.
THEY'LL LEARN THEIR LESSON.
BANG
GAH!
COUREZ!

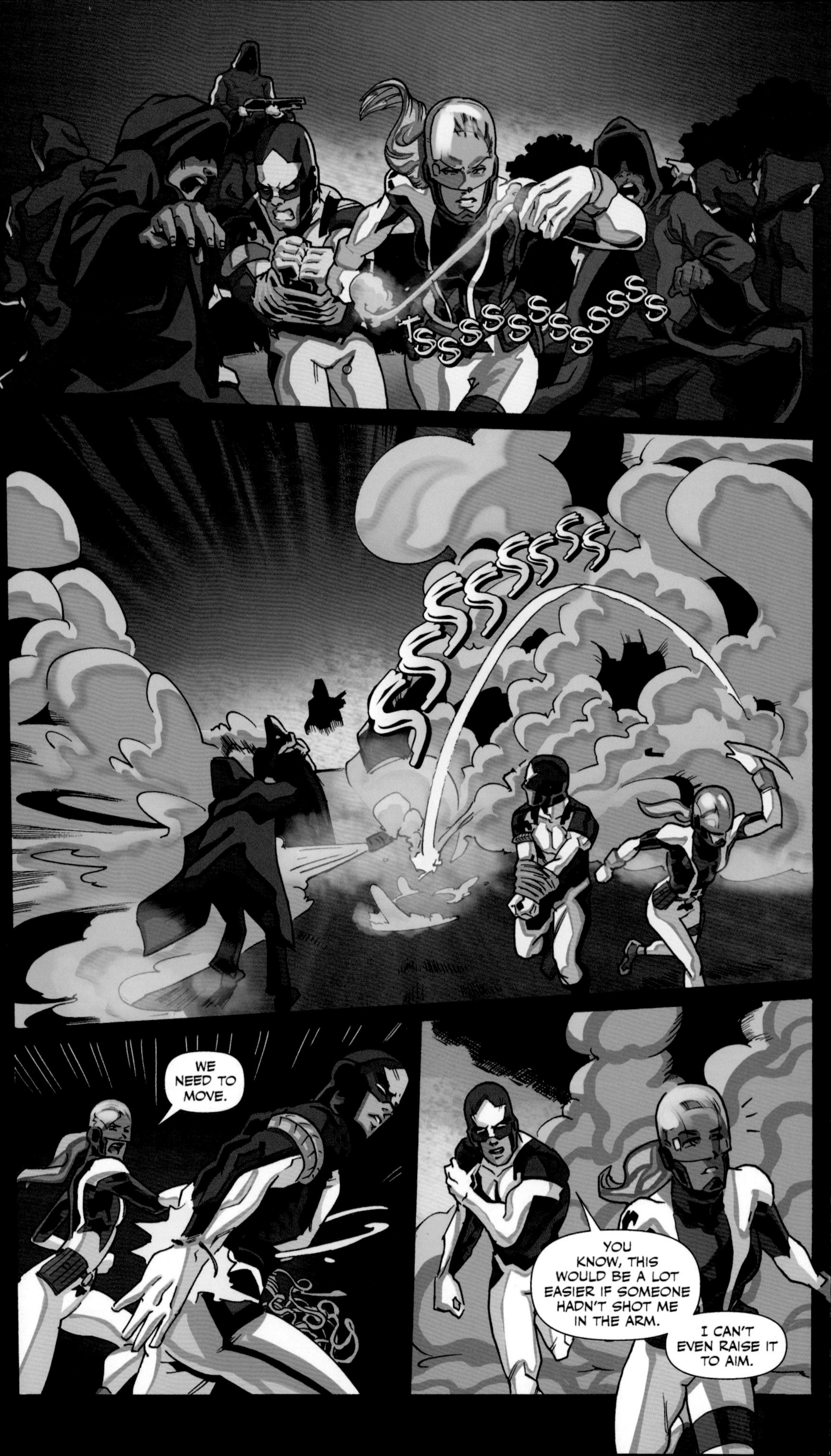
TSSSSSSSSSSSSSS
SSSSSSSSS
WE NEED TO MOVE.
YOU KNOW, THIS WOULD BE A LOT EASIER IF SOMEONE HADN'T SHOT ME IN THE ARM.
I CAN'T EVEN RAISE IT TO AIM.

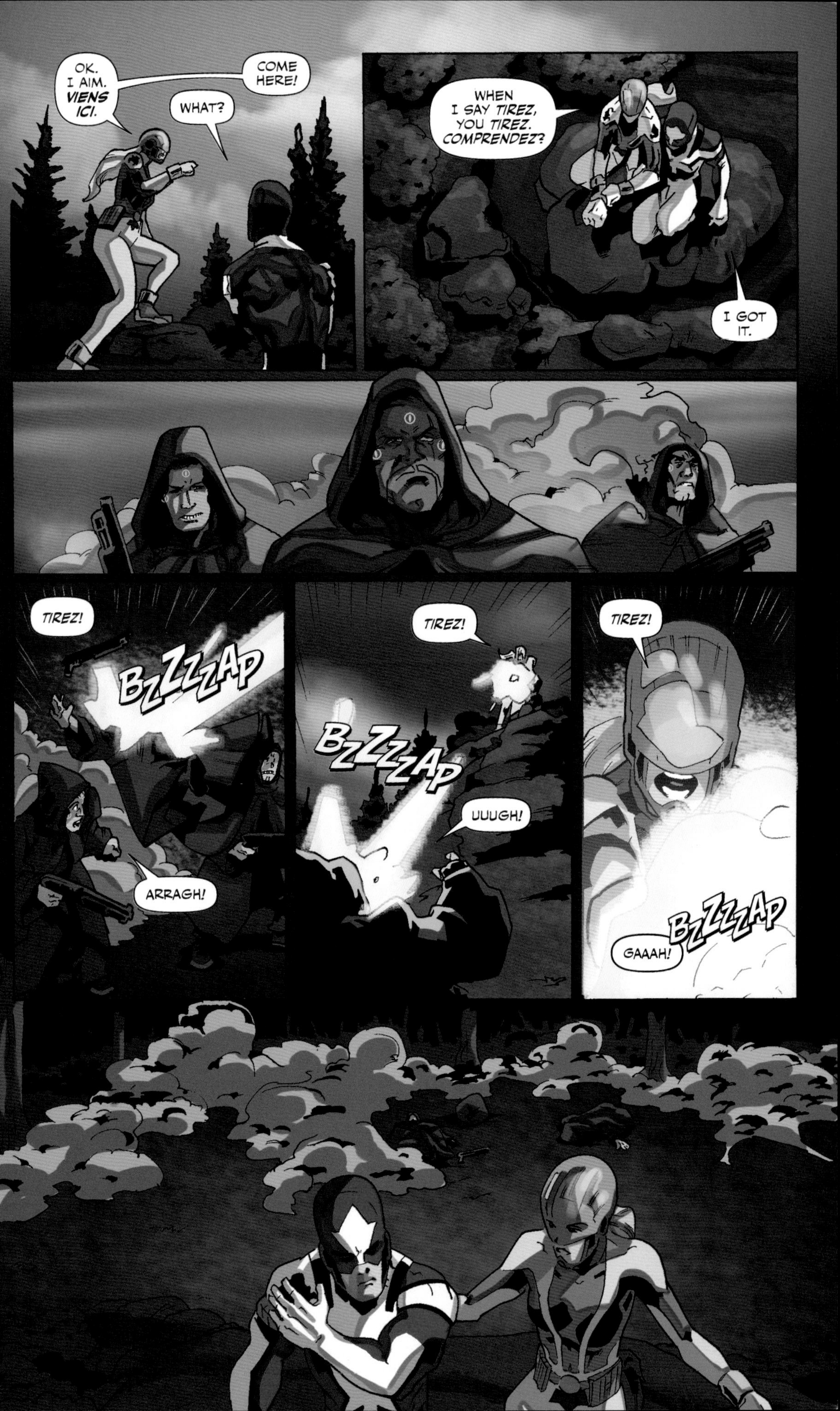
OK. I AIM. *VIENS ICI.*
COME HERE!
WHAT?
WHEN I SAY *TIREZ,* YOU *TIREZ. COMPRENDEZ?*
I GOT IT.
TIREZ!
BZZZZAP
ARRAGH!
TIREZ!
BZZZZAP
UUUGH!
TIREZ!
BZZZZAP
GAAAH!

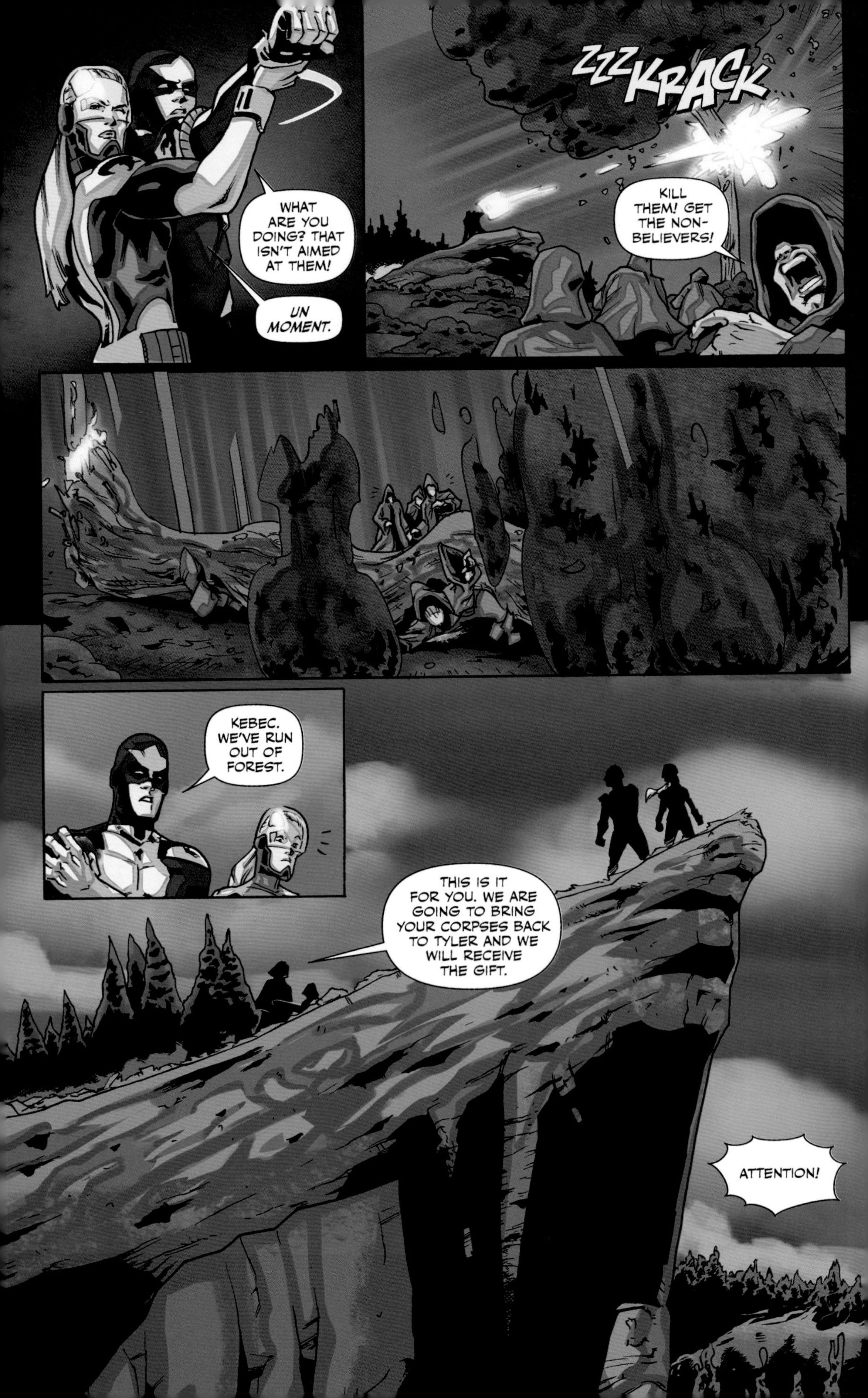
WHAT ARE YOU DOING? THAT ISN'T AIMED AT THEM!
UN MOMENT.
ZZZKRACK
KILL THEM! GET THE NON-BELIEVERS!
KEBEC. WE'VE RUN OUT OF FOREST.
THIS IS IT FOR YOU. WE ARE GOING TO BRING YOUR CORPSES BACK TO TYLER AND WE WILL RECEIVE THE GIFT.
ATTENTION!

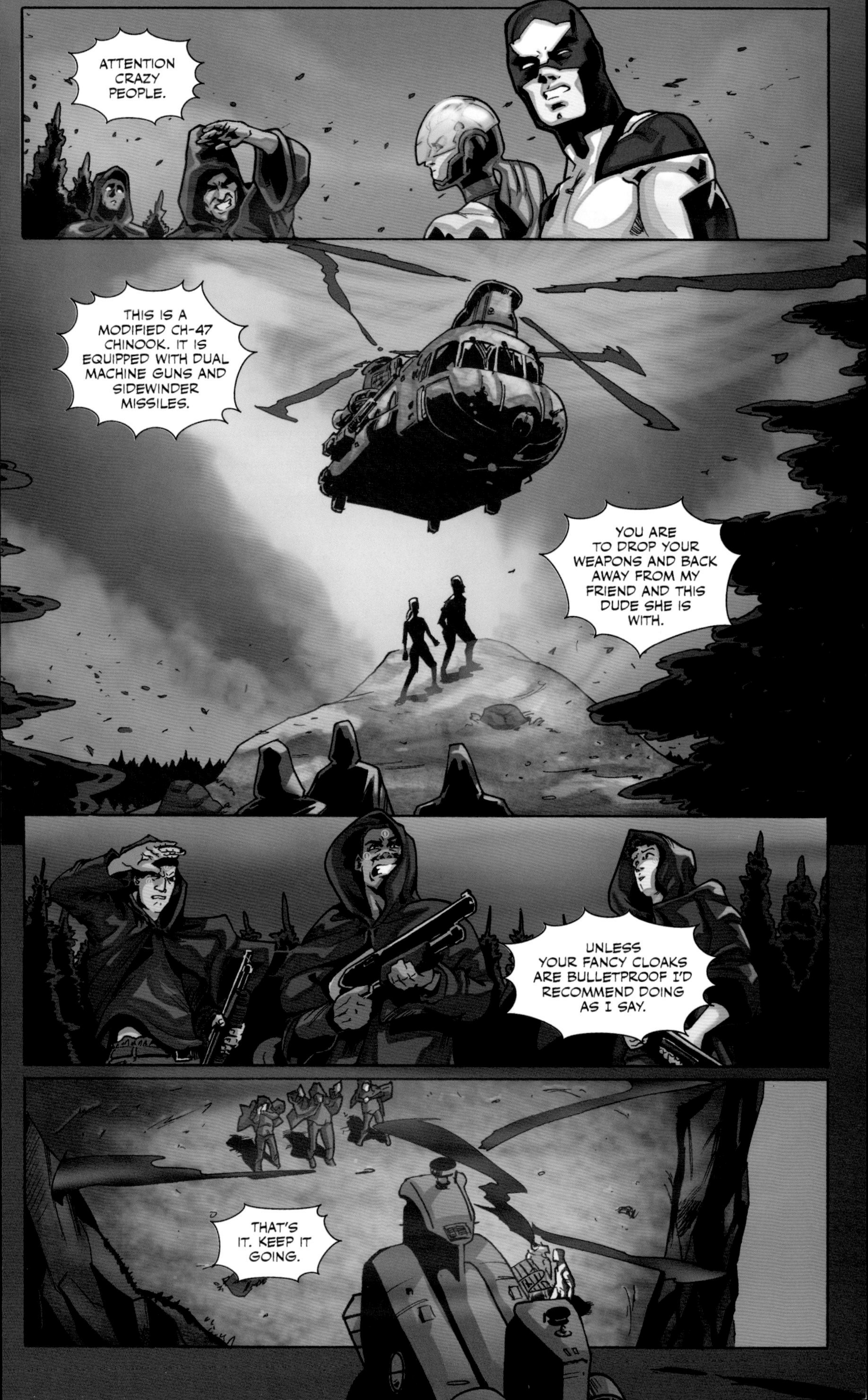
ATTENTION CRAZY PEOPLE.
THIS IS A MODIFIED CH-47 CHINOOK. IT IS EQUIPPED WITH DUAL MACHINE GUNS AND SIDEWINDER MISSILES.
YOU ARE TO DROP YOUR WEAPONS AND BACK AWAY FROM MY FRIEND AND THIS DUDE SHE IS WITH.
UNLESS YOUR FANCY CLOAKS ARE BULLETPROOF I'D RECOMMEND DOING AS I SAY.
THAT'S IT. KEEP IT GOING.

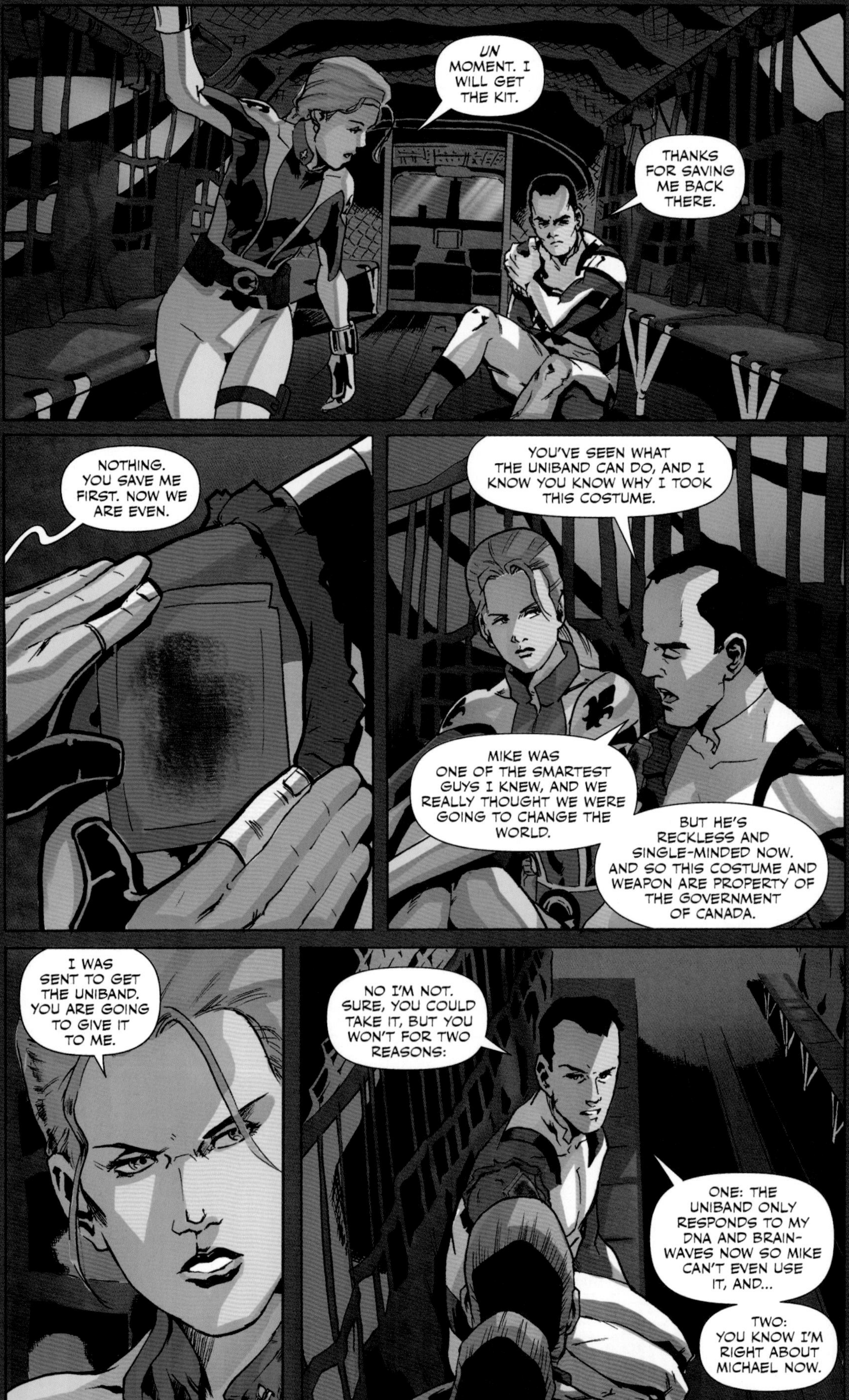
UN MOMENT. I WILL GET THE KIT.
THANKS FOR SAVING ME BACK THERE.
NOTHING. YOU SAVE ME FIRST. NOW WE ARE EVEN.
YOU'VE SEEN WHAT THE UNIBAND CAN DO, AND I KNOW YOU KNOW WHY I TOOK THIS COSTUME.
MIKE WAS ONE OF THE SMARTEST GUYS I KNEW, AND WE REALLY THOUGHT WE WERE GOING TO CHANGE THE WORLD.
BUT HE'S RECKLESS AND SINGLE-MINDED NOW. AND SO THIS COSTUME AND WEAPON ARE PROPERTY OF THE GOVERNMENT OF CANADA.
I WAS SENT TO GET THE UNIBAND. YOU ARE GOING TO GIVE IT TO ME.
NO I'M NOT. SURE, YOU COULD TAKE IT, BUT YOU WON'T FOR TWO REASONS:
ONE: THE UNIBAND ONLY RESPONDS TO MY DNA AND BRAIN-WAVES NOW SO MIKE CAN'T EVEN USE IT, AND...
TWO: YOU KNOW I'M RIGHT ABOUT MICHAEL NOW.

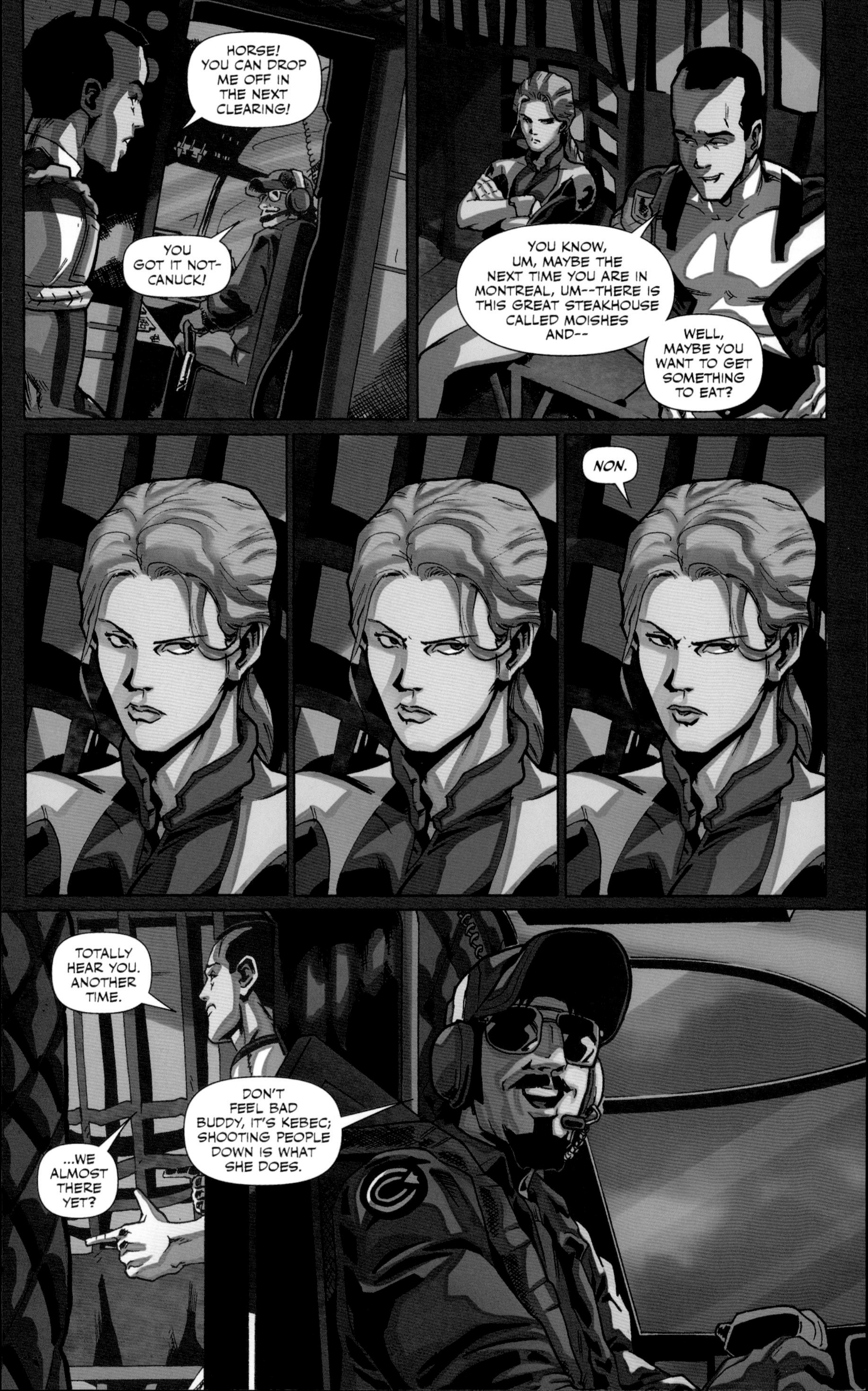
HORSE! YOU CAN DROP ME OFF IN THE NEXT CLEARING!
YOU GOT IT NOT-CANUCK!
YOU KNOW, UM, MAYBE THE NEXT TIME YOU ARE IN MONTREAL, UM--THERE IS THIS GREAT STEAKHOUSE CALLED MOISHES AND--
WELL, MAYBE YOU WANT TO GET SOMETHING TO EAT?
NON.
TOTALLY HEAR YOU. ANOTHER TIME.
...WE ALMOST THERE YET?
DON'T FEEL BAD BUDDY, IT'S KEBEC; SHOOTING PEOPLE DOWN IS WHAT SHE DOES.

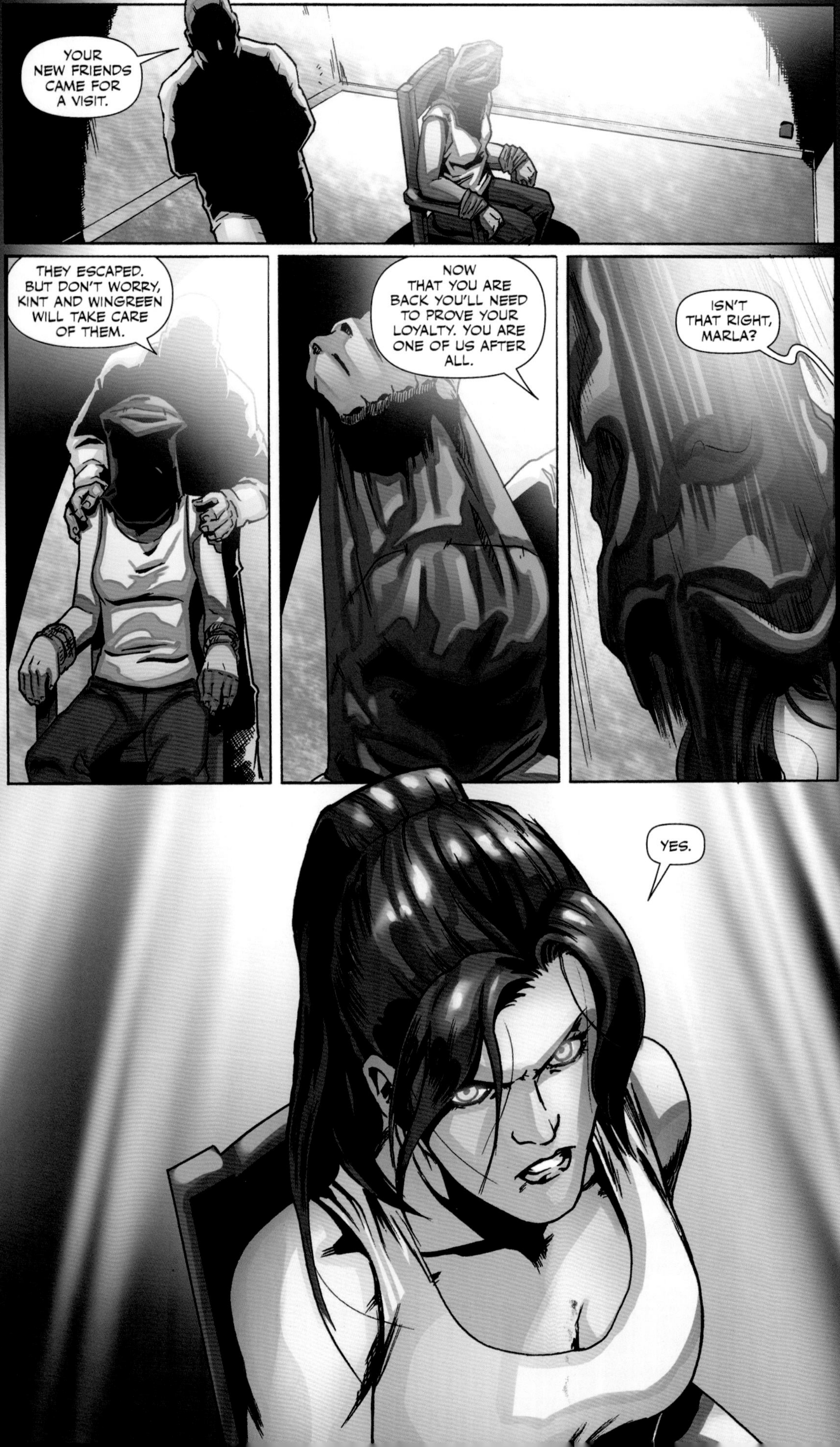
YOUR NEW FRIENDS CAME FOR A VISIT.
THEY ESCAPED. BUT DON'T WORRY, KINT AND WINGREEN WILL TAKE CARE OF THEM.
NOW THAT YOU ARE BACK YOU'LL NEED TO PROVE YOUR LOYALTY. YOU ARE ONE OF US AFTER ALL.
ISN'T THAT RIGHT, MARLA?
YES.

CHAPTER 3
THE EYES ARE WATCHING

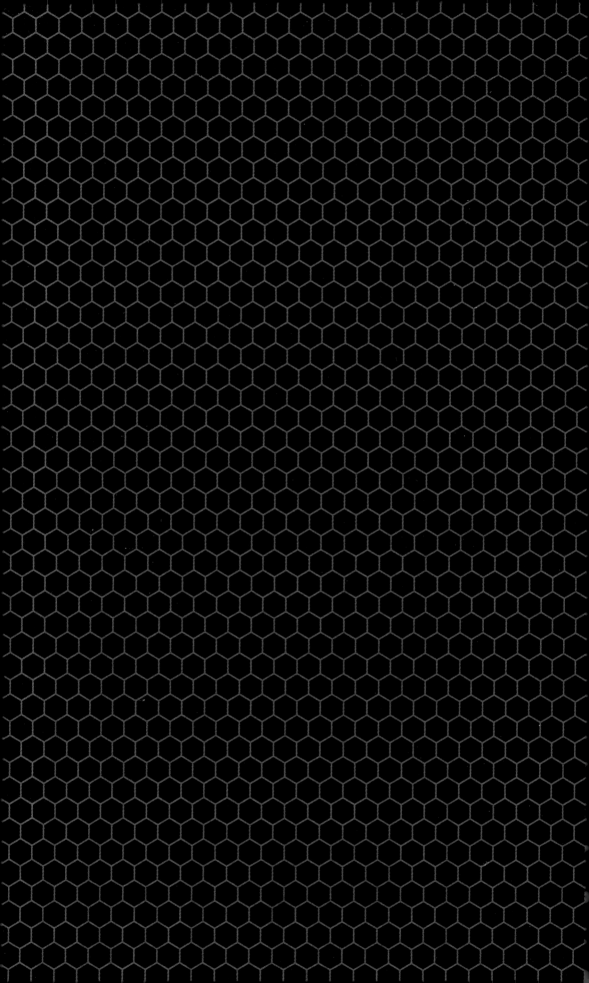

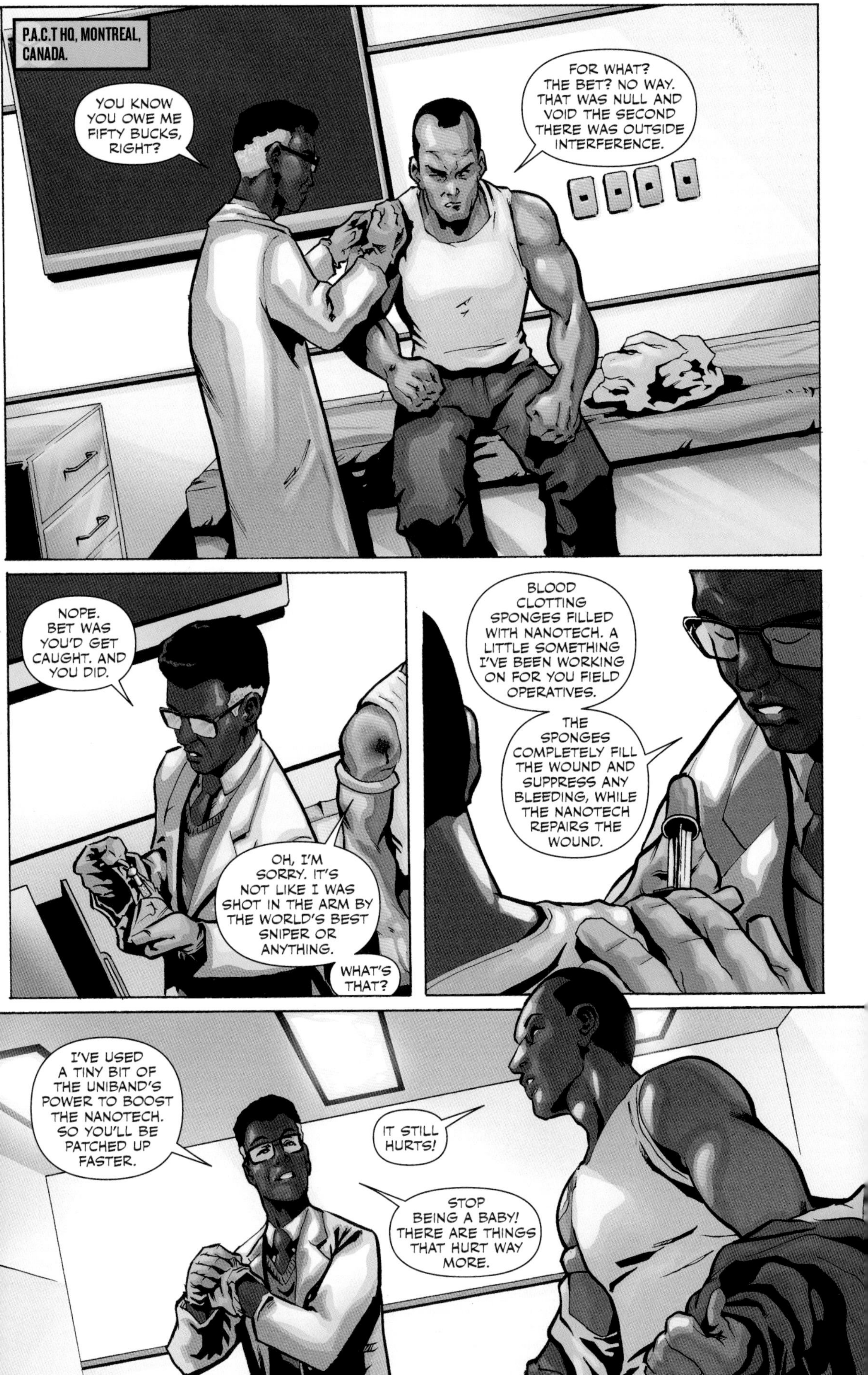
P.A.C.T HQ, MONTREAL, CANADA.
YOU KNOW YOU OWE ME FIFTY BUCKS, RIGHT?
FOR WHAT? THE BET? NO WAY. THAT WAS NULL AND VOID THE SECOND THERE WAS OUTSIDE INTERFERENCE.
NOPE. BET WAS YOU'D GET CAUGHT. AND YOU DID.
OH, I'M SORRY. IT'S NOT LIKE I WAS SHOT IN THE ARM BY THE WORLD'S BEST SNIPER OR ANYTHING.
WHAT'S THAT?
BLOOD CLOTTING SPONGES FILLED WITH NANOTECH. A LITTLE SOMETHING I'VE BEEN WORKING ON FOR YOU FIELD OPERATIVES.
THE SPONGES COMPLETELY FILL THE WOUND AND SUPPRESS ANY BLEEDING, WHILE THE NANOTECH REPAIRS THE WOUND.
I'VE USED A TINY BIT OF THE UNIBAND'S POWER TO BOOST THE NANOTECH. SO YOU'LL BE PATCHED UP FASTER.
IT STILL HURTS!
STOP BEING A BABY! THERE ARE THINGS THAT HURT WAY MORE.

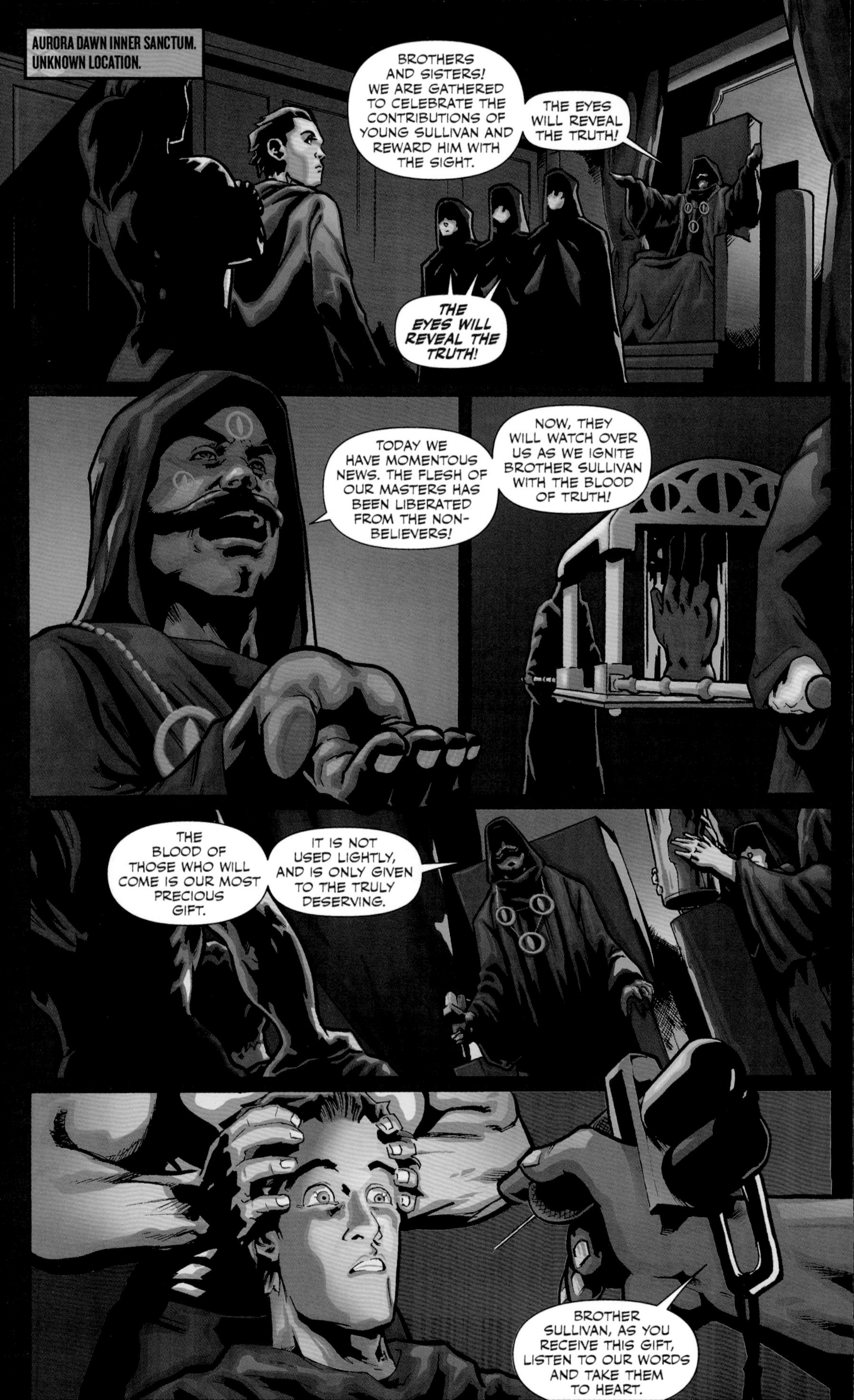
AURORA DAWN INNER SANCTUM. UNKNOWN LOCATION.
BROTHERS AND SISTERS! WE ARE GATHERED TO CELEBRATE THE CONTRIBUTIONS OF YOUNG SULLIVAN AND REWARD HIM WITH THE SIGHT.
THE EYES WILL REVEAL THE TRUTH!
THE EYES WILL REVEAL THE TRUTH!
TODAY WE HAVE MOMENTOUS NEWS. THE FLESH OF OUR MASTERS HAS BEEN LIBERATED FROM THE NON-BELIEVERS!
NOW, THEY WILL WATCH OVER US AS WE IGNITE BROTHER SULLIVAN WITH THE BLOOD OF TRUTH!
THE BLOOD OF THOSE WHO WILL COME IS OUR MOST PRECIOUS GIFT.
IT IS NOT USED LIGHTLY, AND IS ONLY GIVEN TO THE TRULY DESERVING.
BROTHER SULLIVAN, AS YOU RECEIVE THIS GIFT, LISTEN TO OUR WORDS AND TAKE THEM TO HEART.

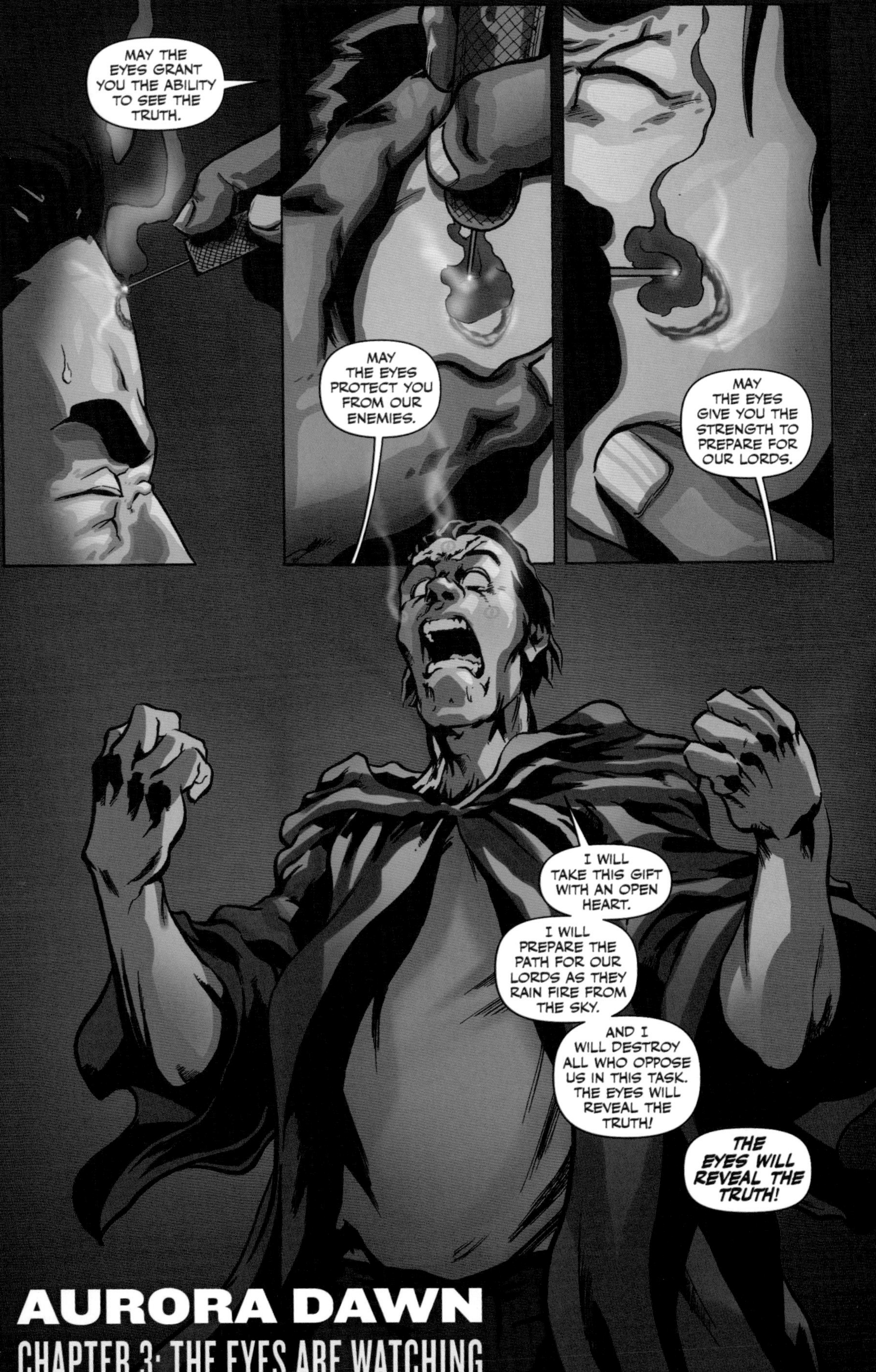

AURORA DAWN

CHAPTER 3: THE EYES ARE WATCHING

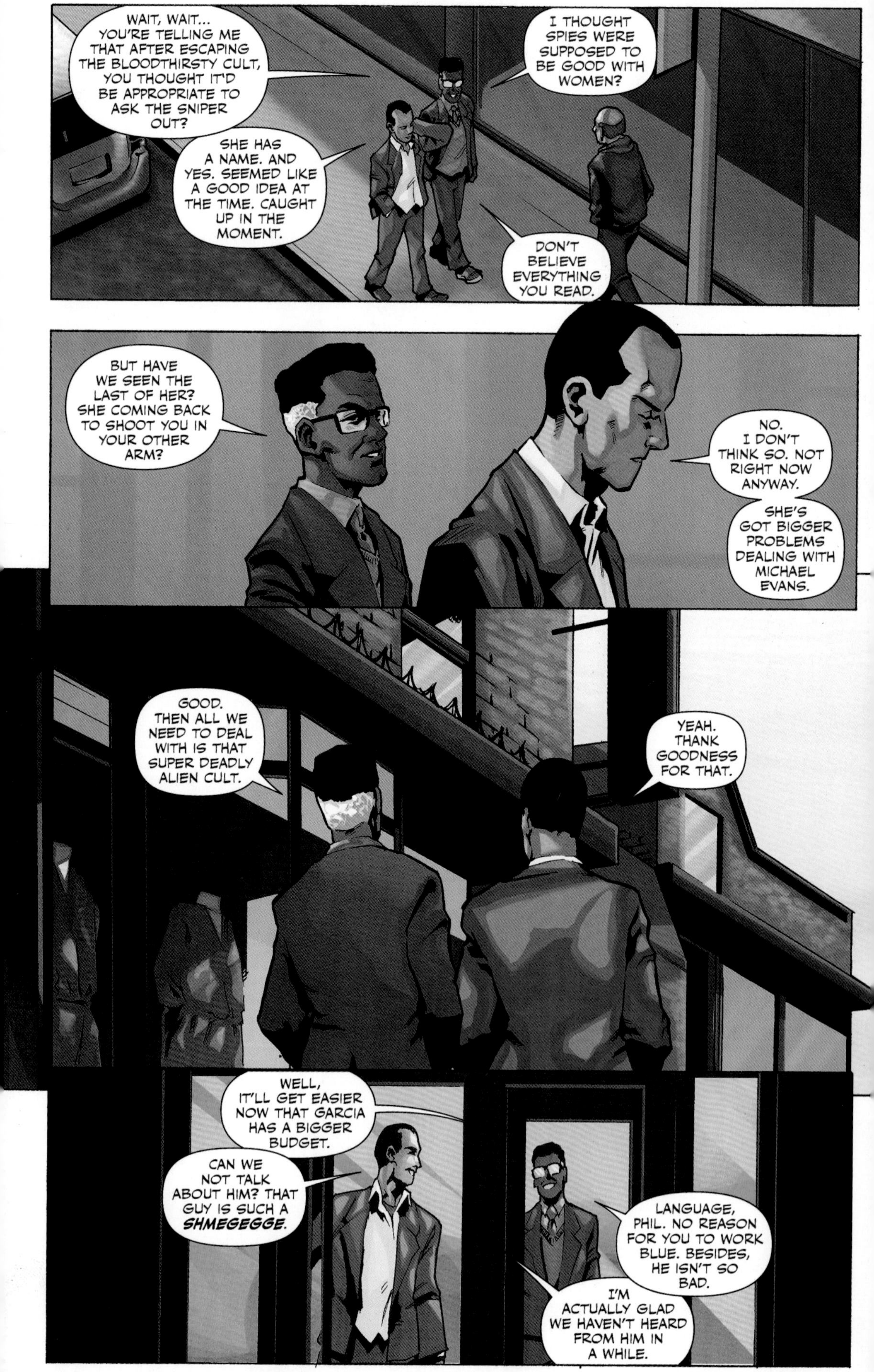
WAIT, WAIT... YOU'RE TELLING ME THAT AFTER ESCAPING THE BLOODTHIRSTY CULT, YOU THOUGHT IT'D BE APPROPRIATE TO ASK THE SNIPER OUT?
SHE HAS A NAME. AND YES. SEEMED LIKE A GOOD IDEA AT THE TIME. CAUGHT UP IN THE MOMENT.
I THOUGHT SPIES WERE SUPPOSED TO BE GOOD WITH WOMEN?
DON'T BELIEVE EVERYTHING YOU READ.
BUT HAVE WE SEEN THE LAST OF HER? SHE COMING BACK TO SHOOT YOU IN YOUR OTHER ARM?
NO. I DON'T THINK SO. NOT RIGHT NOW ANYWAY.
SHE'S GOT BIGGER PROBLEMS DEALING WITH MICHAEL EVANS.
GOOD. THEN ALL WE NEED TO DEAL WITH IS THAT SUPER DEADLY ALIEN CULT.
YEAH. THANK GOODNESS FOR THAT.
WELL, IT'LL GET EASIER NOW THAT GARCIA HAS A BIGGER BUDGET.
CAN WE NOT TALK ABOUT HIM? THAT GUY IS SUCH A ***SHMEGEGGE***.
LANGUAGE, PHIL. NO REASON FOR YOU TO WORK BLUE. BESIDES, HE ISN'T SO BAD.
I'M ACTUALLY GLAD WE HAVEN'T HEARD FROM HIM IN A WHILE.

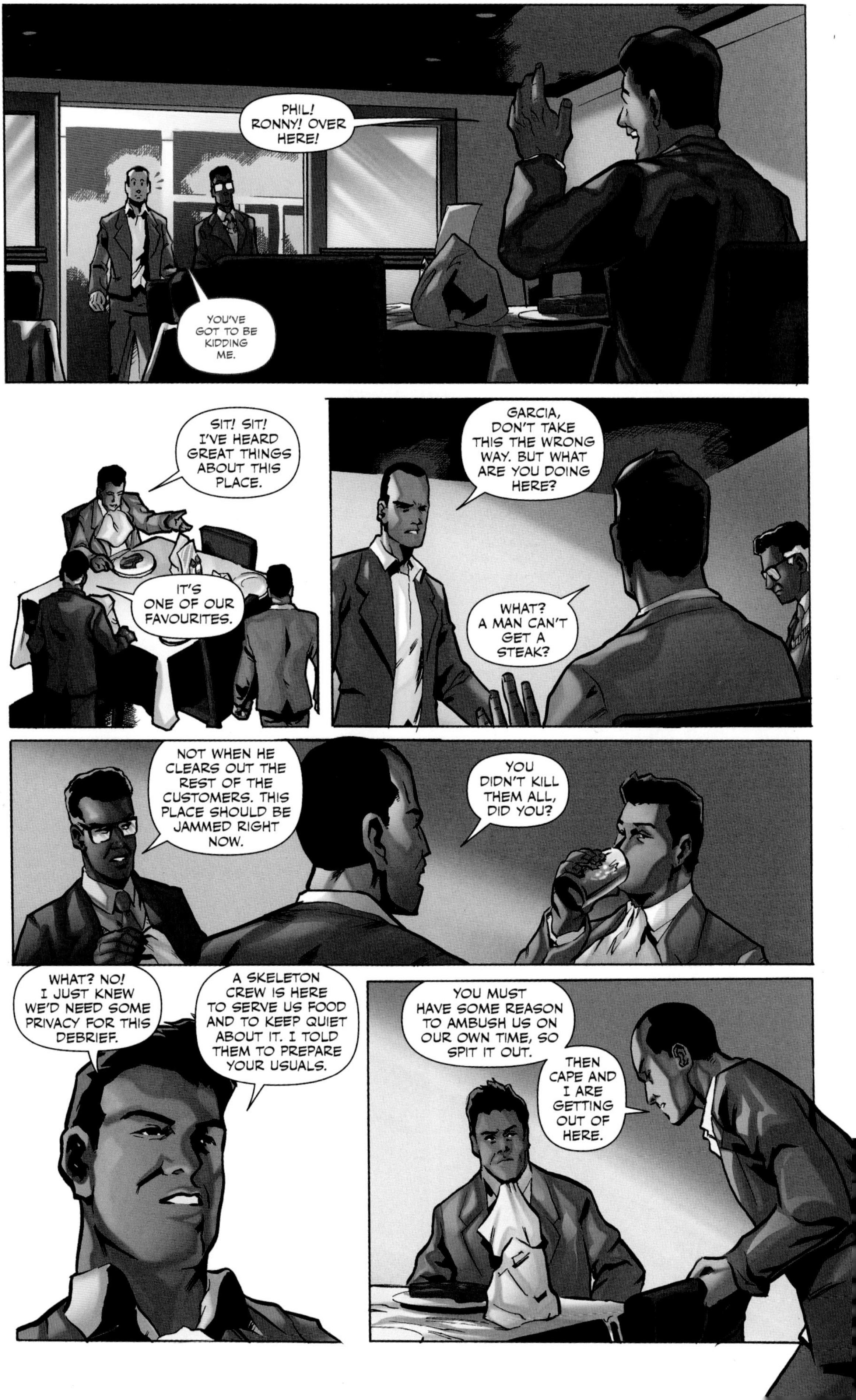
PHIL! RONNY! OVER HERE!
YOU'VE GOT TO BE KIDDING ME.
SIT! SIT! I'VE HEARD GREAT THINGS ABOUT THIS PLACE.
IT'S ONE OF OUR FAVOURITES.
GARCIA, DON'T TAKE THIS THE WRONG WAY. BUT WHAT ARE YOU DOING HERE?
WHAT? A MAN CAN'T GET A STEAK?
NOT WHEN HE CLEARS OUT THE REST OF THE CUSTOMERS. THIS PLACE SHOULD BE JAMMED RIGHT NOW.
YOU DIDN'T KILL THEM ALL, DID YOU?
WHAT? NO! I JUST KNEW WE'D NEED SOME PRIVACY FOR THIS DEBRIEF.
A SKELETON CREW IS HERE TO SERVE US FOOD AND TO KEEP QUIET ABOUT IT. I TOLD THEM TO PREPARE YOUR USUALS.
YOU MUST HAVE SOME REASON TO AMBUSH US ON OUR OWN TIME, SO SPIT IT OUT.
THEN CAPE AND I ARE GETTING OUT OF HERE.

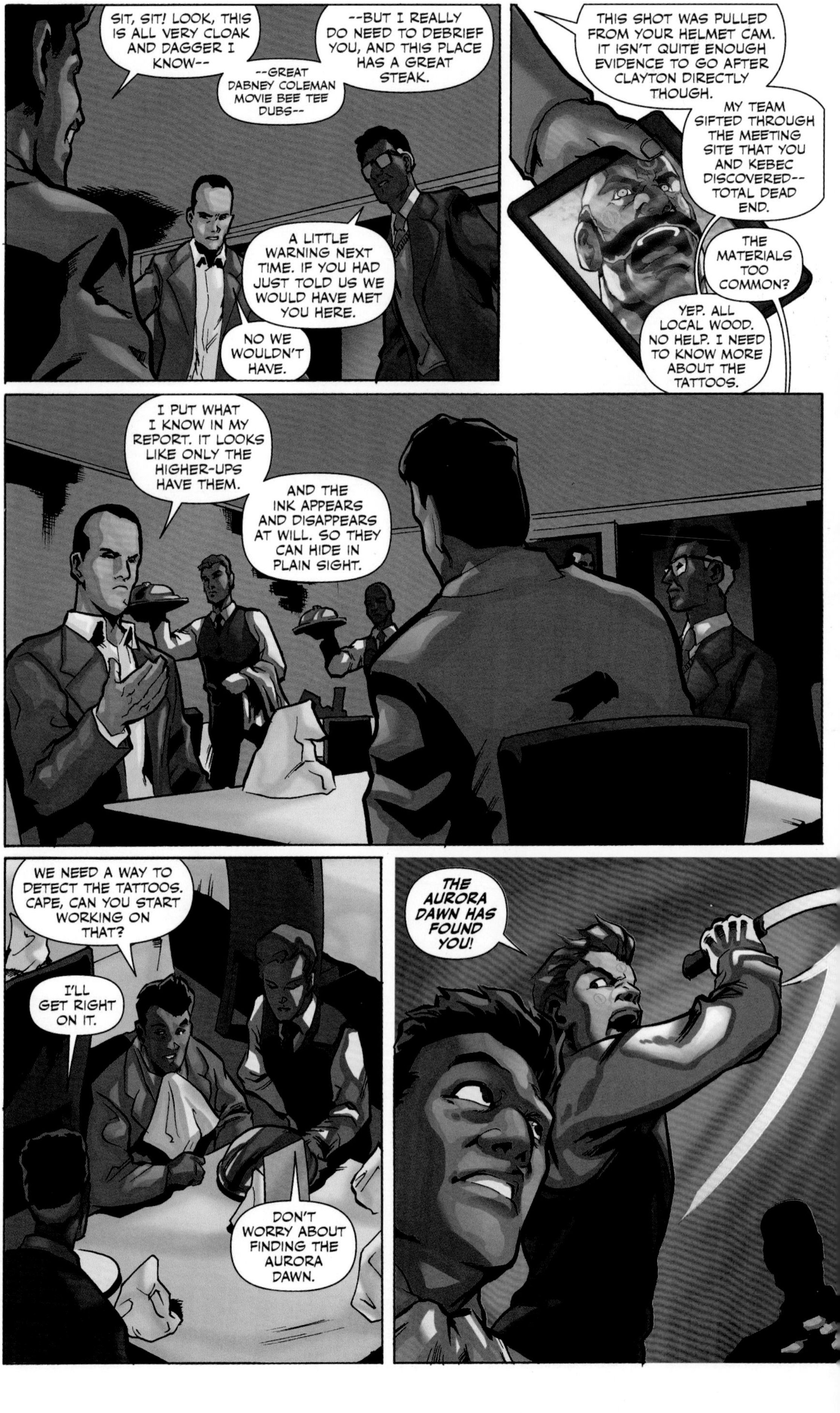
SIT, SIT! LOOK, THIS IS ALL VERY CLOAK AND DAGGER I KNOW--
--GREAT DABNEY COLEMAN MOVIE BEE TEE DUBS--
--BUT I REALLY DO NEED TO DEBRIEF YOU, AND THIS PLACE HAS A GREAT STEAK.
A LITTLE WARNING NEXT TIME. IF YOU HAD JUST TOLD US WE WOULD HAVE MET YOU HERE.
NO WE WOULDN'T HAVE.
THIS SHOT WAS PULLED FROM YOUR HELMET CAM. IT ISN'T QUITE ENOUGH EVIDENCE TO GO AFTER CLAYTON DIRECTLY THOUGH.
MY TEAM SIFTED THROUGH THE MEETING SITE THAT YOU AND KEBEC DISCOVERED-- TOTAL DEAD END.
THE MATERIALS TOO COMMON?
YEP. ALL LOCAL WOOD. NO HELP. I NEED TO KNOW MORE ABOUT THE TATTOOS.
I PUT WHAT I KNOW IN MY REPORT. IT LOOKS LIKE ONLY THE HIGHER-UPS HAVE THEM.
AND THE INK APPEARS AND DISAPPEARS AT WILL. SO THEY CAN HIDE IN PLAIN SIGHT.
WE NEED A WAY TO DETECT THE TATTOOS. CAPE, CAN YOU START WORKING ON THAT?
I'LL GET RIGHT ON IT.
DON'T WORRY ABOUT FINDING THE AURORA DAWN.
THE AURORA DAWN HAS FOUND YOU!

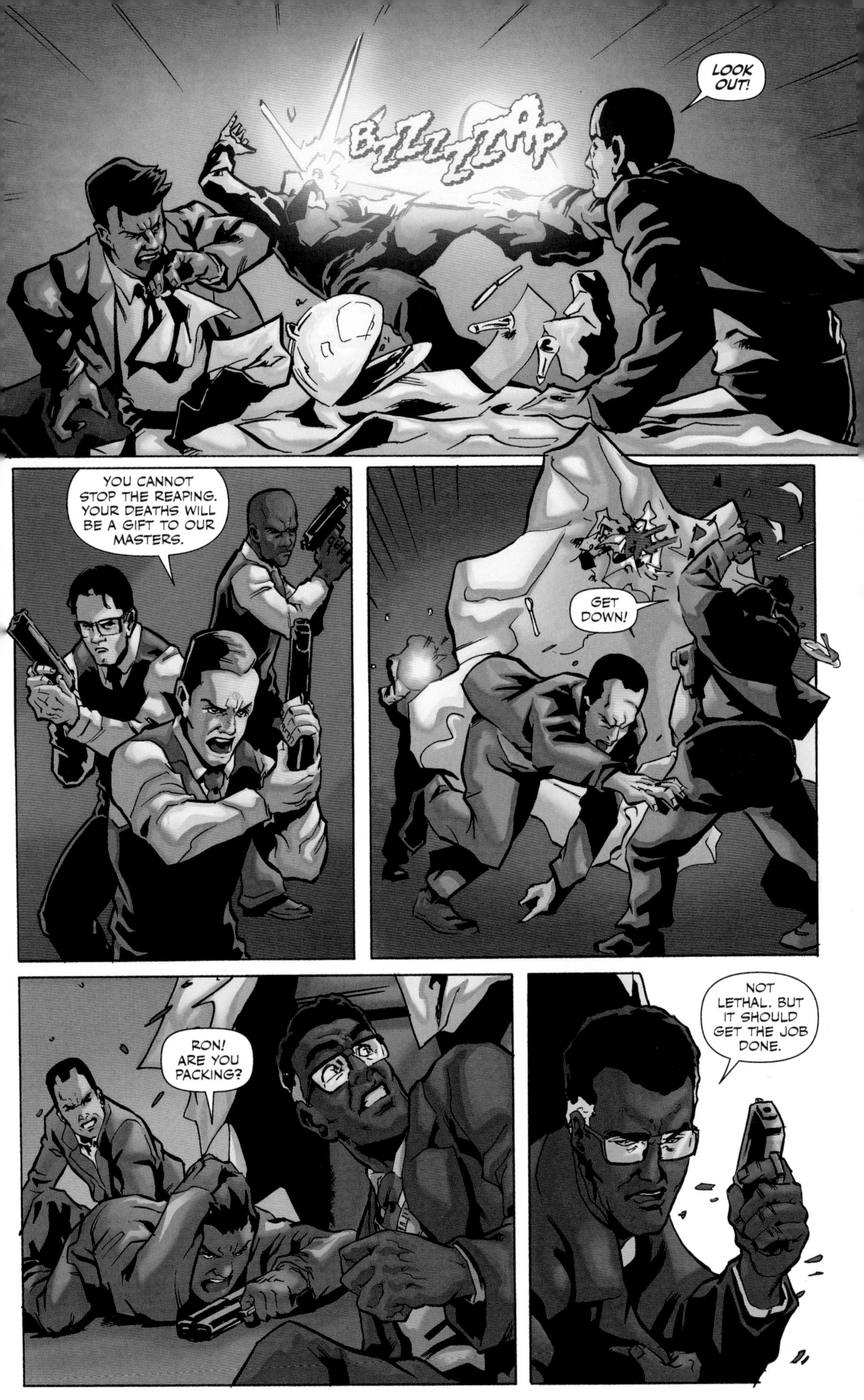
BZZZZAP
LOOK OUT!
YOU CANNOT STOP THE REAPING. YOUR DEATHS WILL BE A GIFT TO OUR MASTERS.
GET DOWN!
RON! ARE YOU PACKING?
NOT LETHAL. BUT IT SHOULD GET THE JOB DONE.

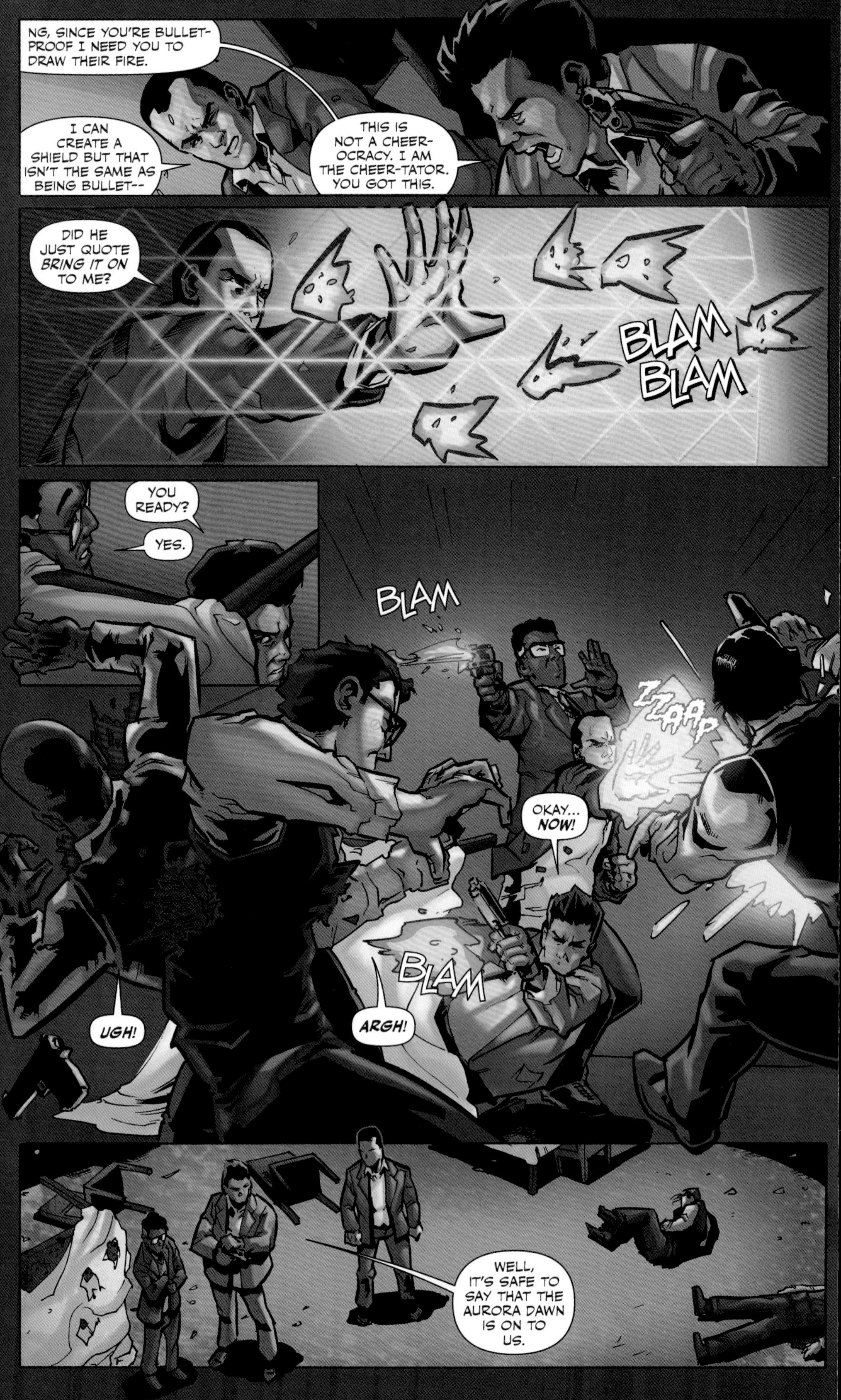
NG, SINCE YOU'RE BULLET-PROOF I NEED YOU TO DRAW THEIR FIRE.
I CAN CREATE A SHIELD BUT THAT ISN'T THE SAME AS BEING BULLET--
THIS IS NOT A CHEER-OCRACY. I AM THE CHEER-TATOR. YOU GOT THIS.
DID HE JUST QUOTE *BRING IT ON* TO ME?
BLAM BLAM
YOU READY?
YES.
BLAM
ZZAAP
OKAY... **NOW!**
BLAM
UGH!
ARGH!
WELL, IT'S SAFE TO SAY THAT THE AURORA DAWN IS ON TO US.

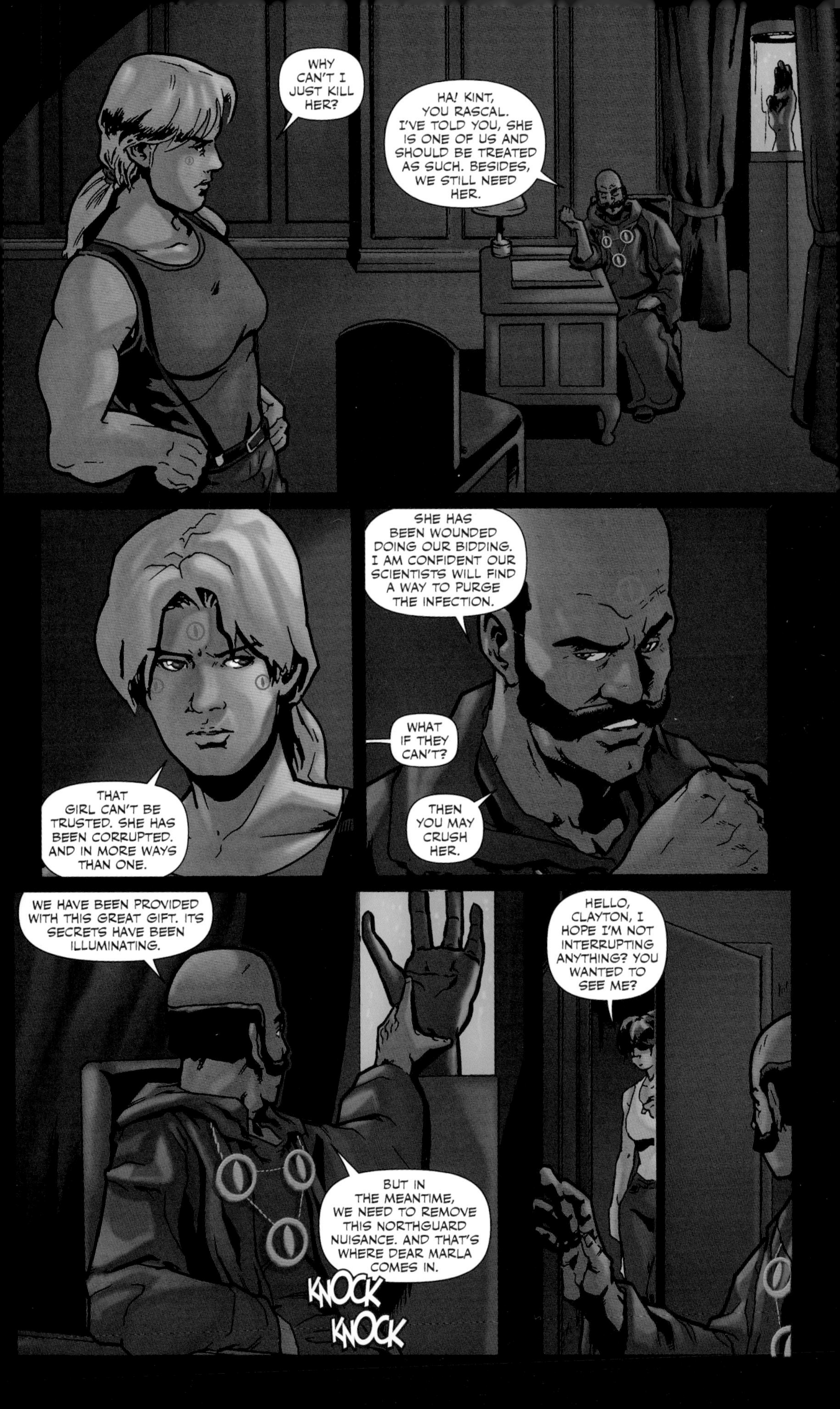
WHY CAN'T I JUST KILL HER?
HA! KINT, YOU RASCAL. I'VE TOLD YOU, SHE IS ONE OF US AND SHOULD BE TREATED AS SUCH. BESIDES, WE STILL NEED HER.
THAT GIRL CAN'T BE TRUSTED. SHE HAS BEEN CORRUPTED. AND IN MORE WAYS THAN ONE.
SHE HAS BEEN WOUNDED DOING OUR BIDDING. I AM CONFIDENT OUR SCIENTISTS WILL FIND A WAY TO PURGE THE INFECTION.
WHAT IF THEY CAN'T?
THEN YOU MAY CRUSH HER.
WE HAVE BEEN PROVIDED WITH THIS GREAT GIFT. ITS SECRETS HAVE BEEN ILLUMINATING.
BUT IN THE MEANTIME, WE NEED TO REMOVE THIS NORTHGUARD NUISANCE. AND THAT'S WHERE DEAR MARLA COMES IN.
KNOCK KNOCK
HELLO, CLAYTON, I HOPE I'M NOT INTERRUPTING ANYTHING? YOU WANTED TO SEE ME?

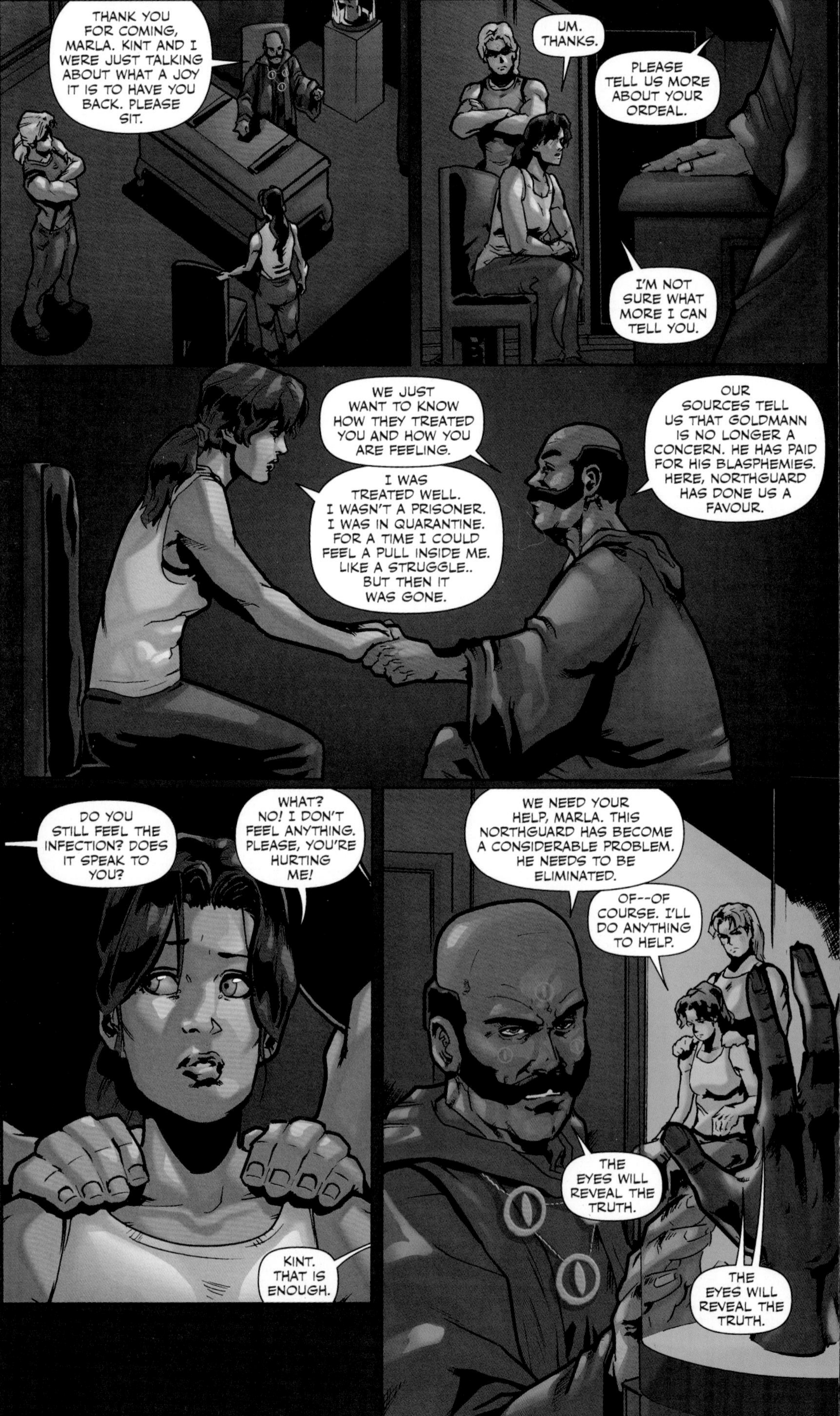
THANK YOU FOR COMING, MARLA. KINT AND I WERE JUST TALKING ABOUT WHAT A JOY IT IS TO HAVE YOU BACK. PLEASE SIT.
UM. THANKS.
PLEASE TELL US MORE ABOUT YOUR ORDEAL.
I'M NOT SURE WHAT MORE I CAN TELL YOU.
WE JUST WANT TO KNOW HOW THEY TREATED YOU AND HOW YOU ARE FEELING.
I WAS TREATED WELL. I WASN'T A PRISONER. I WAS IN QUARANTINE. FOR A TIME I COULD FEEL A PULL INSIDE ME. LIKE A STRUGGLE.. BUT THEN IT WAS GONE.
OUR SOURCES TELL US THAT GOLDMANN IS NO LONGER A CONCERN. HE HAS PAID FOR HIS BLASPHEMIES. HERE, NORTHGUARD HAS DONE US A FAVOUR.
DO YOU STILL FEEL THE INFECTION? DOES IT SPEAK TO YOU?
WHAT? NO! I DON'T FEEL ANYTHING. PLEASE, YOU'RE HURTING ME!
KINT. THAT IS ENOUGH.
WE NEED YOUR HELP, MARLA. THIS NORTHGUARD HAS BECOME A CONSIDERABLE PROBLEM. HE NEEDS TO BE ELIMINATED.
OF--OF COURSE. I'LL DO ANYTHING TO HELP.
THE EYES WILL REVEAL THE TRUTH.
THE EYES WILL REVEAL THE TRUTH.

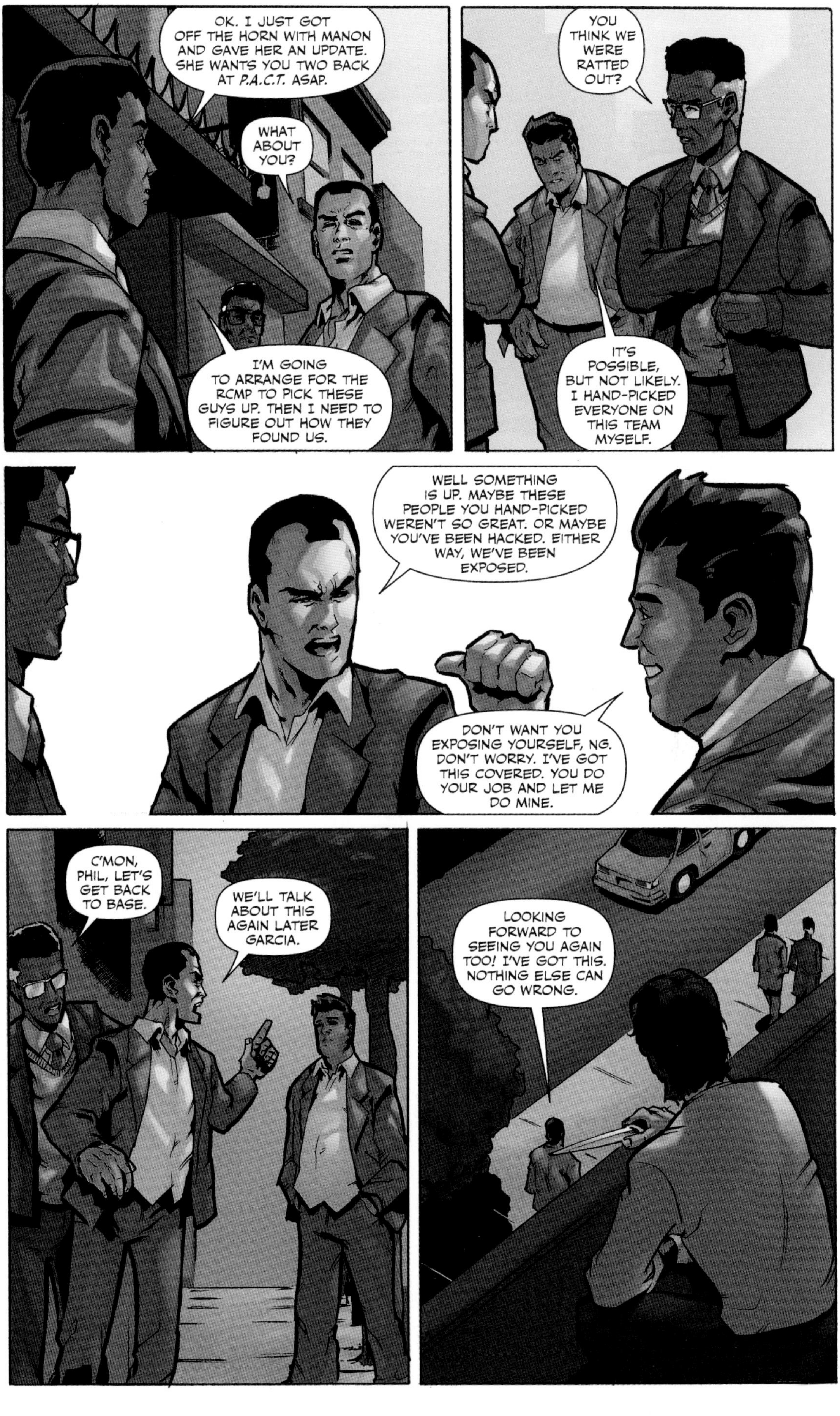
OK. I JUST GOT OFF THE HORN WITH MANON AND GAVE HER AN UPDATE. SHE WANTS YOU TWO BACK AT *P.A.C.T.* ASAP.
WHAT ABOUT YOU?
I'M GOING TO ARRANGE FOR THE RCMP TO PICK THESE GUYS UP. THEN I NEED TO FIGURE OUT HOW THEY FOUND US.
YOU THINK WE WERE RATTED OUT?
IT'S POSSIBLE, BUT NOT LIKELY. I HAND-PICKED EVERYONE ON THIS TEAM MYSELF.
WELL SOMETHING IS UP. MAYBE THESE PEOPLE YOU HAND-PICKED WEREN'T SO GREAT. OR MAYBE YOU'VE BEEN HACKED. EITHER WAY, WE'VE BEEN EXPOSED.
DON'T WANT YOU EXPOSING YOURSELF, NG. DON'T WORRY. I'VE GOT THIS COVERED. YOU DO YOUR JOB AND LET ME DO MINE.
C'MON, PHIL, LET'S GET BACK TO BASE.
WE'LL TALK ABOUT THIS AGAIN LATER GARCIA.
LOOKING FORWARD TO SEEING YOU AGAIN TOO! I'VE GOT THIS. NOTHING ELSE CAN GO WRONG.

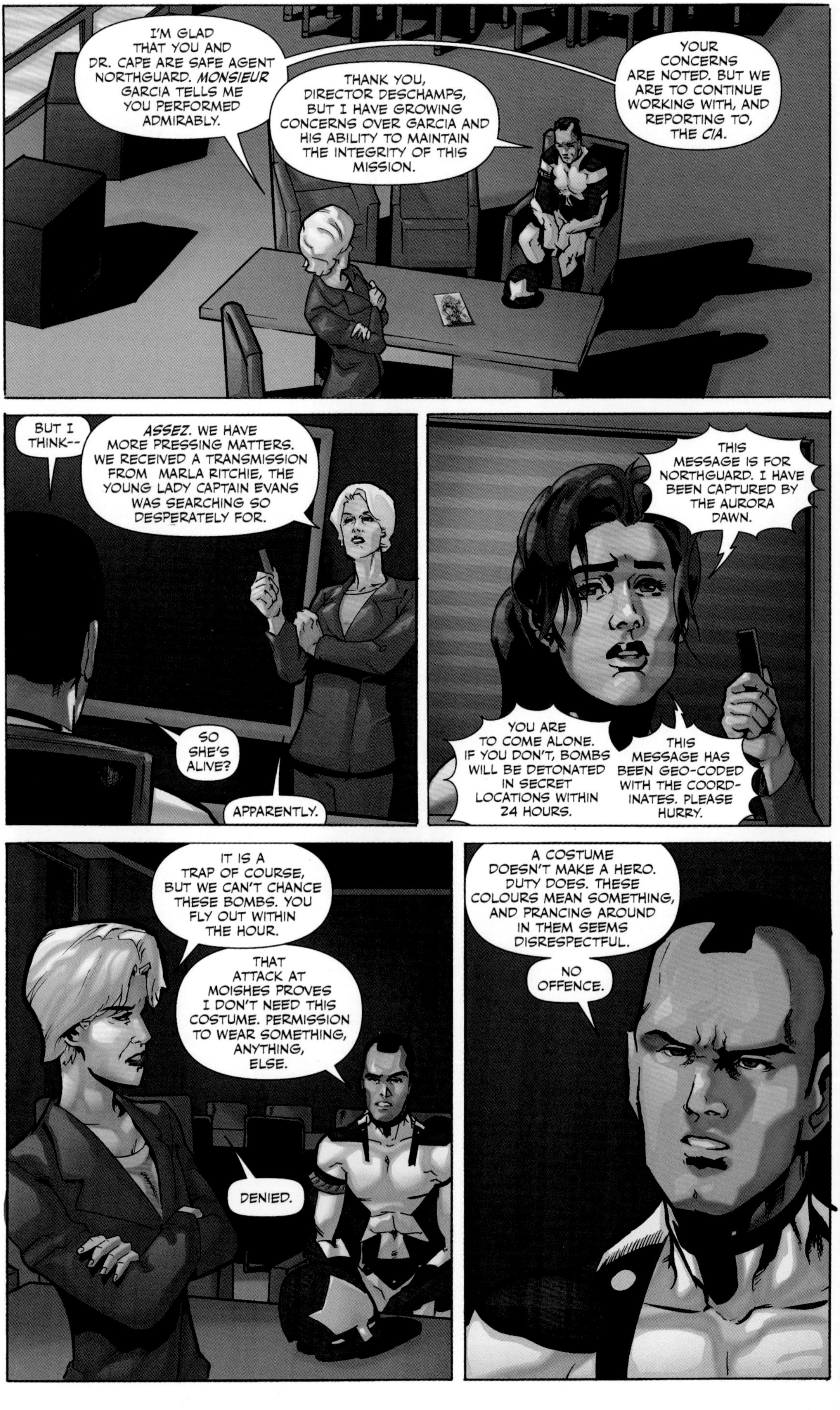
I'M GLAD THAT YOU AND DR. CAPE ARE SAFE AGENT NORTHGUARD. *MONSIEUR* GARCIA TELLS ME YOU PERFORMED ADMIRABLY.
THANK YOU, DIRECTOR DESCHAMPS, BUT I HAVE GROWING CONCERNS OVER GARCIA AND HIS ABILITY TO MAINTAIN THE INTEGRITY OF THIS MISSION.
YOUR CONCERNS ARE NOTED. BUT WE ARE TO CONTINUE WORKING WITH, AND REPORTING TO, THE *CIA*.
BUT I THINK--
ASSEZ. WE HAVE MORE PRESSING MATTERS. WE RECEIVED A TRANSMISSION FROM MARLA RITCHIE, THE YOUNG LADY CAPTAIN EVANS WAS SEARCHING SO DESPERATELY FOR.
SO SHE'S ALIVE?
APPARENTLY.
THIS MESSAGE IS FOR NORTHGUARD. I HAVE BEEN CAPTURED BY THE AURORA DAWN.
YOU ARE TO COME ALONE. IF YOU DON'T, BOMBS WILL BE DETONATED IN SECRET LOCATIONS WITHIN 24 HOURS.
THIS MESSAGE HAS BEEN GEO-CODED WITH THE COORD-INATES. PLEASE HURRY.
IT IS A TRAP OF COURSE, BUT WE CAN'T CHANCE THESE BOMBS. YOU FLY OUT WITHIN THE HOUR.
THAT ATTACK AT MOISHES PROVES I DON'T NEED THIS COSTUME. PERMISSION TO WEAR SOMETHING, ANYTHING, ELSE.
DENIED.
A COSTUME DOESN'T MAKE A HERO. DUTY DOES. THESE COLOURS MEAN SOMETHING, AND PRANCING AROUND IN THEM SEEMS DISRESPECTFUL.
NO OFFENCE.

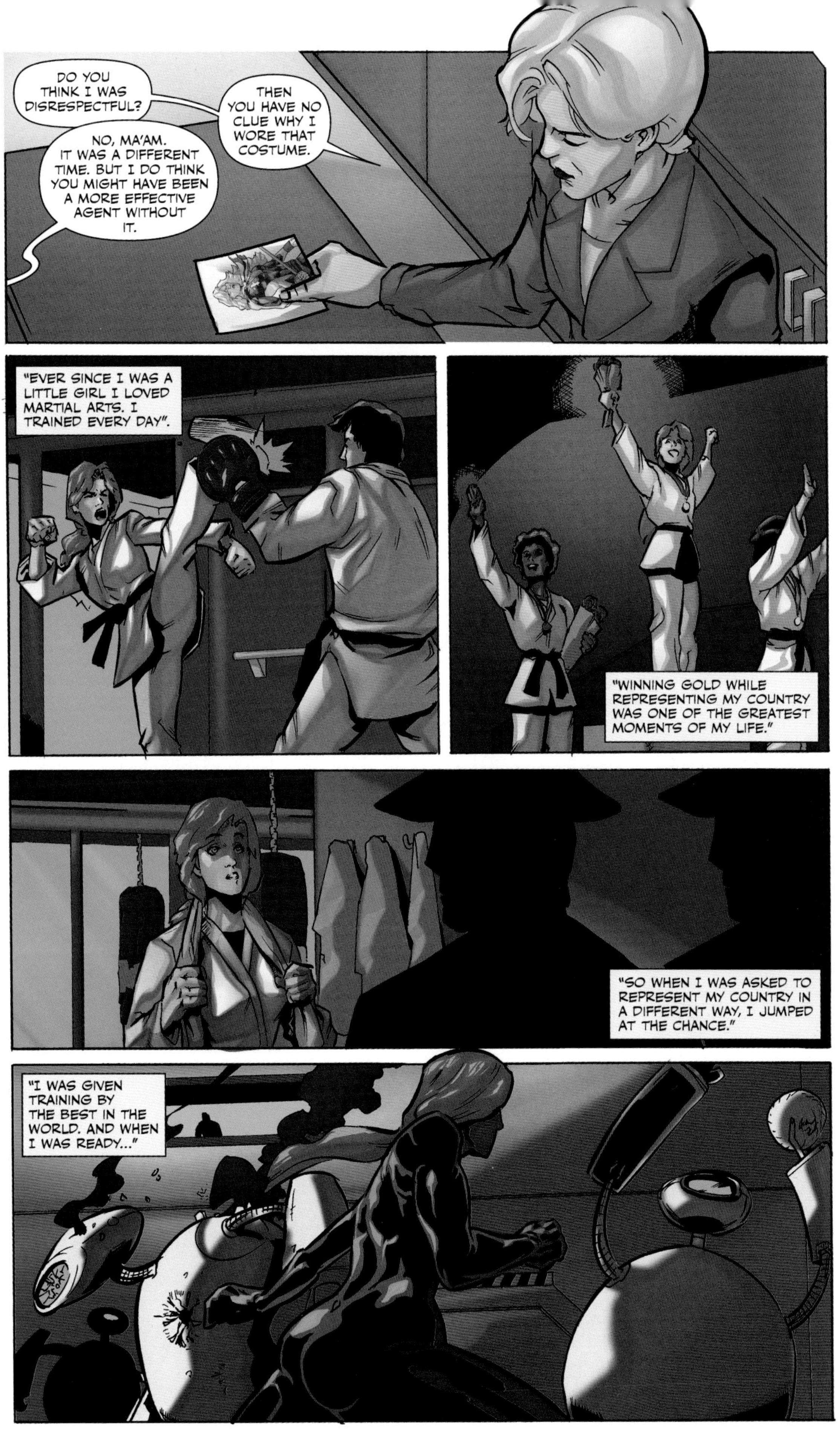

DO YOU THINK I WAS DISRESPECTFUL?
NO, MA'AM. IT WAS A DIFFERENT TIME. BUT I DO THINK YOU MIGHT HAVE BEEN A MORE EFFECTIVE AGENT WITHOUT IT.
THEN YOU HAVE NO CLUE WHY I WORE THAT COSTUME.
"EVER SINCE I WAS A LITTLE GIRL I LOVED MARTIAL ARTS. I TRAINED EVERY DAY".
"WINNING GOLD WHILE REPRESENTING MY COUNTRY WAS ONE OF THE GREATEST MOMENTS OF MY LIFE."
"SO WHEN I WAS ASKED TO REPRESENT MY COUNTRY IN A DIFFERENT WAY, I JUMPED AT THE CHANCE."
"I WAS GIVEN TRAINING BY THE BEST IN THE WORLD. AND WHEN I WAS READY..."

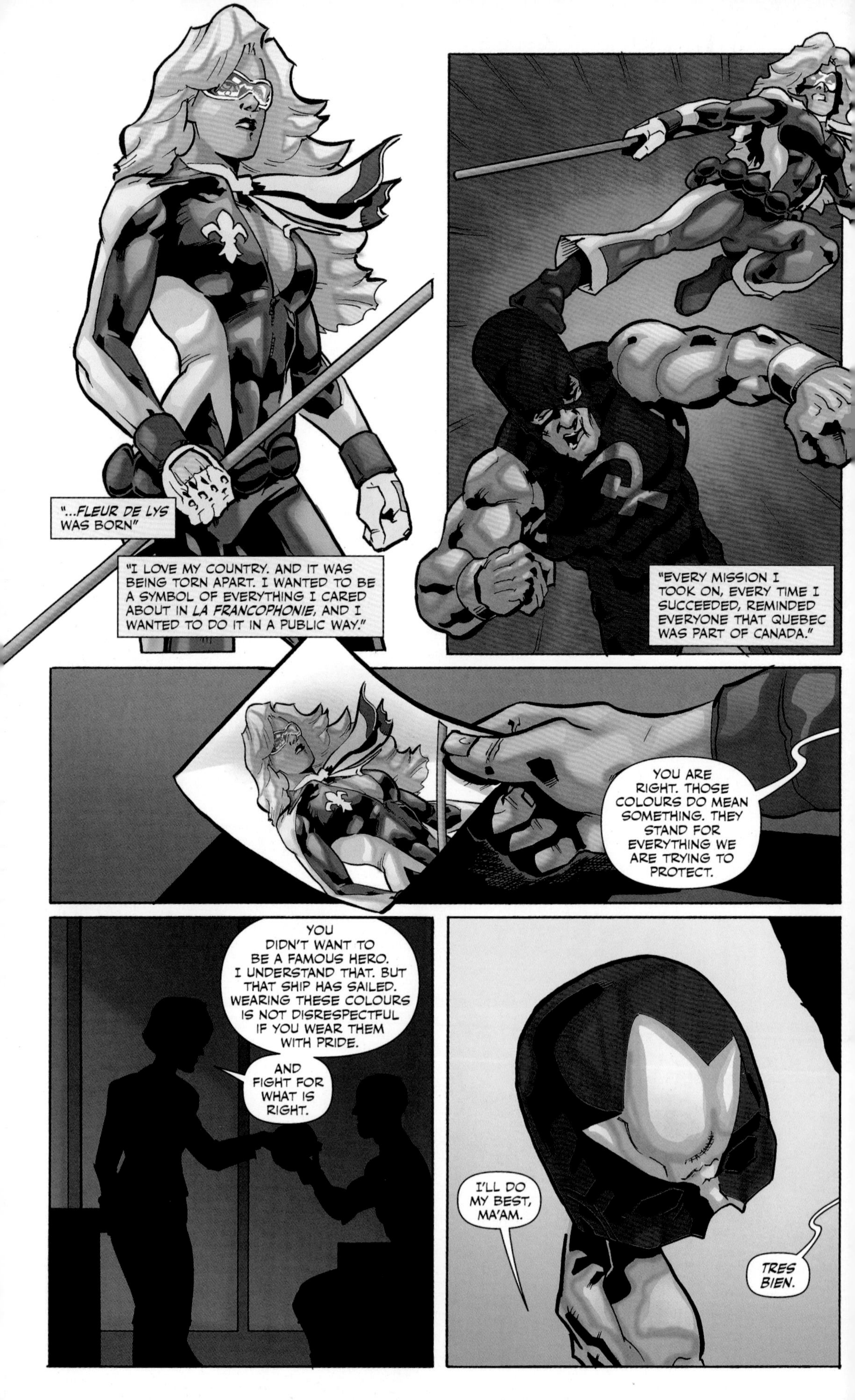
"...FLEUR DE LYS WAS BORN"
"I LOVE MY COUNTRY. AND IT WAS BEING TORN APART. I WANTED TO BE A SYMBOL OF EVERYTHING I CARED ABOUT IN LA FRANCOPHONIE, AND I WANTED TO DO IT IN A PUBLIC WAY."
"EVERY MISSION I TOOK ON, EVERY TIME I SUCCEEDED, REMINDED EVERYONE THAT QUEBEC WAS PART OF CANADA."
YOU ARE RIGHT. THOSE COLOURS DO MEAN SOMETHING. THEY STAND FOR EVERYTHING WE ARE TRYING TO PROTECT.
YOU DIDN'T WANT TO BE A FAMOUS HERO. I UNDERSTAND THAT. BUT THAT SHIP HAS SAILED. WEARING THESE COLOURS IS NOT DISRESPECTFUL IF YOU WEAR THEM WITH PRIDE.
AND FIGHT FOR WHAT IS RIGHT.
I'LL DO MY BEST, MA'AM.
TRES BIEN.

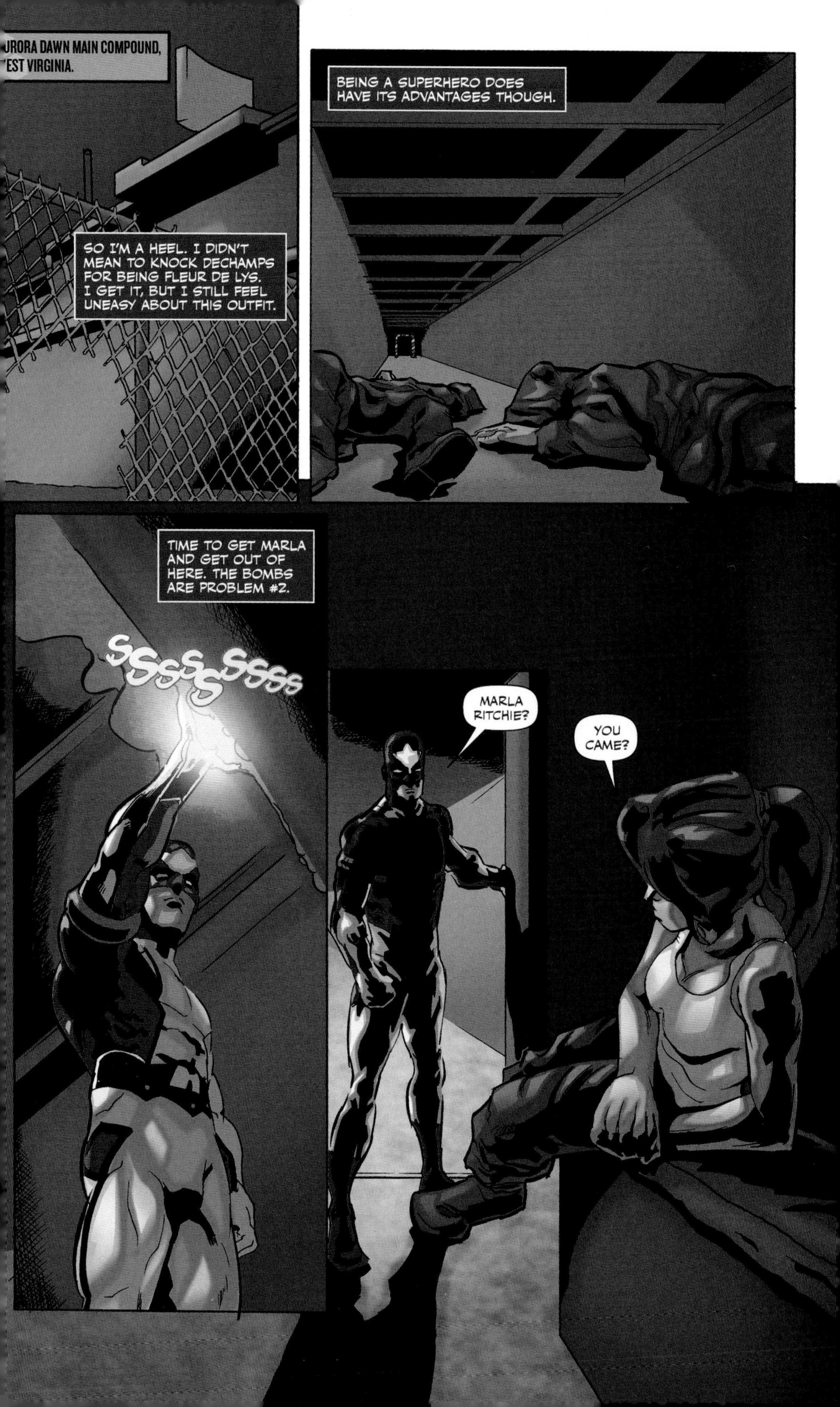
URORA DAWN MAIN COMPOUND,
'EST VIRGINIA.
SO I'M A HEEL. I DIDN'T MEAN TO KNOCK DECHAMPS FOR BEING FLEUR DE LYS. I GET IT, BUT I STILL FEEL UNEASY ABOUT THIS OUTFIT.
BEING A SUPERHERO DOES HAVE ITS ADVANTAGES THOUGH.
TIME TO GET MARLA AND GET OUT OF HERE. THE BOMBS ARE PROBLEM #2.
SSSSSSSSS
MARLA RITCHIE?
YOU CAME?

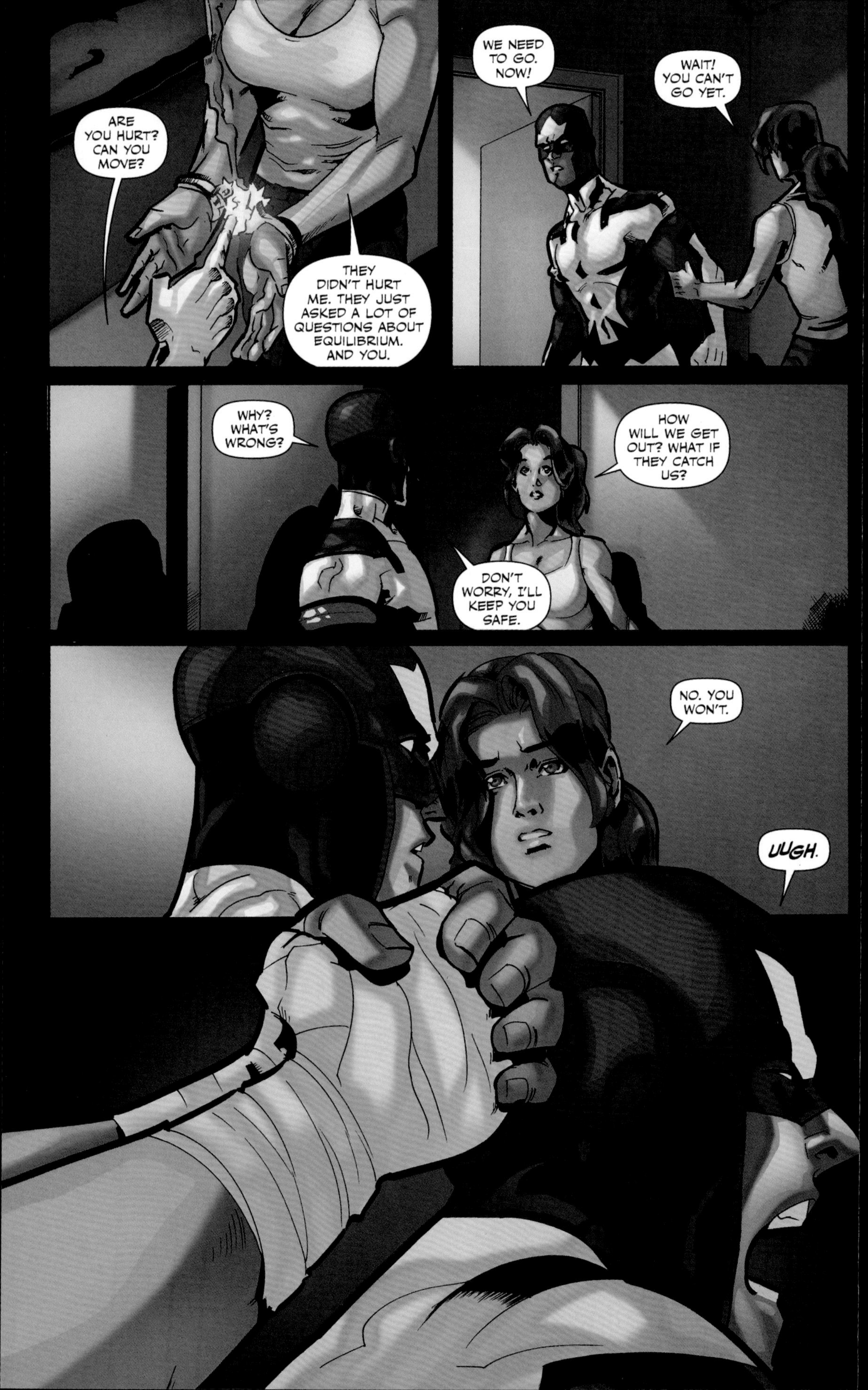
ARE YOU HURT? CAN YOU MOVE?
THEY DIDN'T HURT ME. THEY JUST ASKED A LOT OF QUESTIONS ABOUT EQUILIBRIUM. AND YOU.
WE NEED TO GO. NOW!
WAIT! YOU CAN'T GO YET.
WHY? WHAT'S WRONG?
HOW WILL WE GET OUT? WHAT IF THEY CATCH US?
DON'T WORRY, I'LL KEEP YOU SAFE.
NO. YOU WON'T.
UUGH.

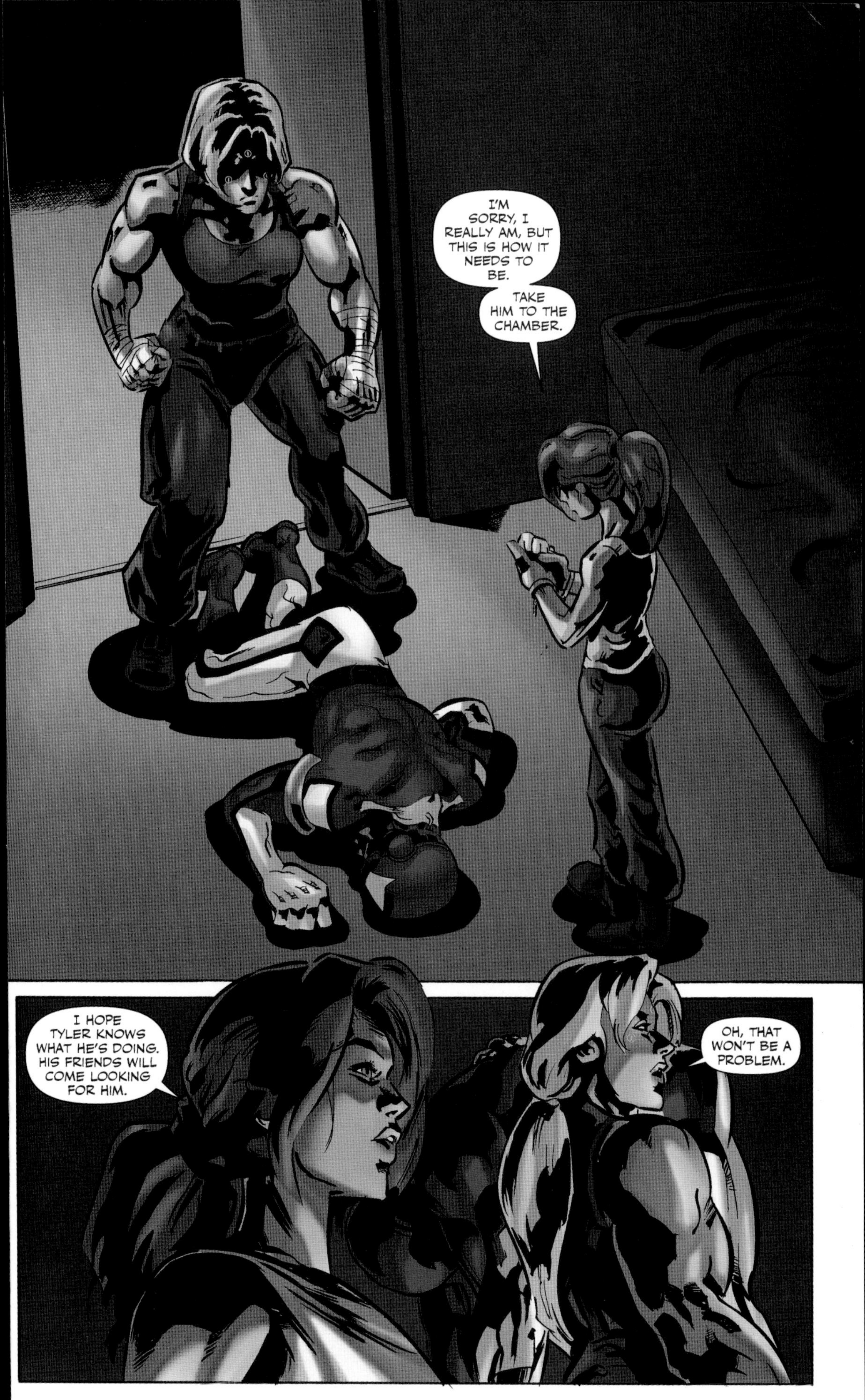
I'M SORRY, I REALLY AM, BUT THIS IS HOW IT NEEDS TO BE.
TAKE HIM TO THE CHAMBER.
I HOPE TYLER KNOWS WHAT HE'S DOING. HIS FRIENDS WILL COME LOOKING FOR HIM.
OH, THAT WON'T BE A PROBLEM.

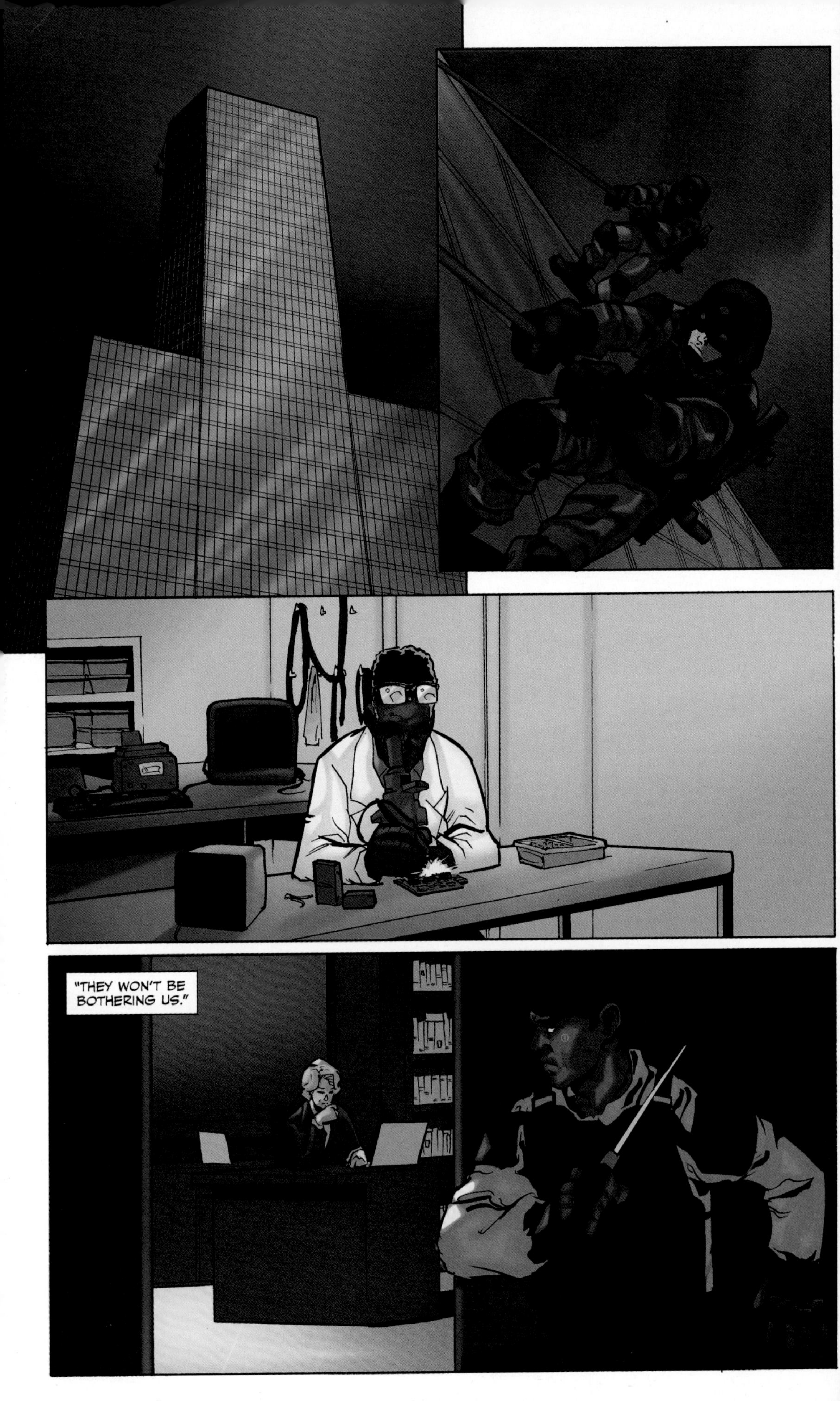
"THEY WON'T BE BOTHERING US."

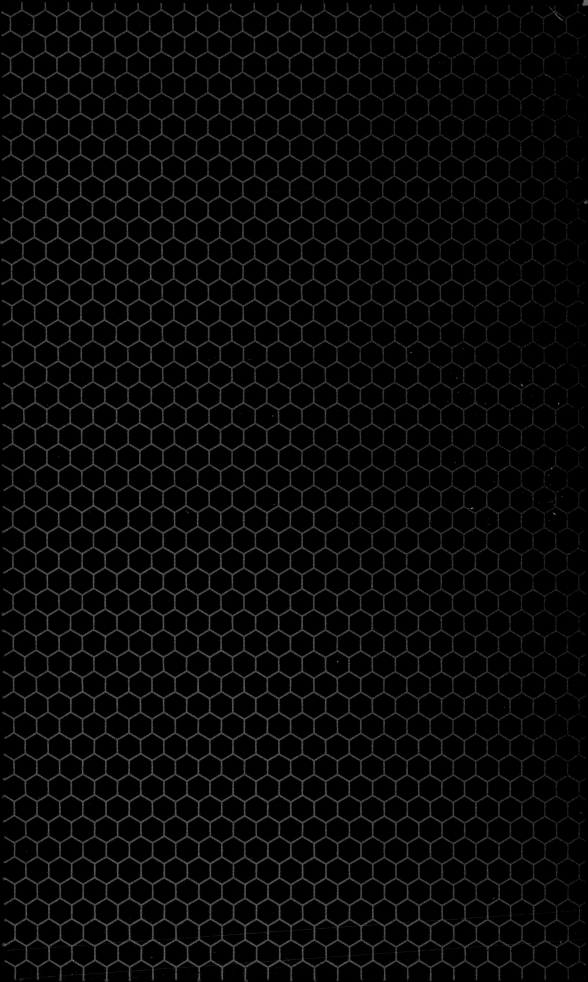

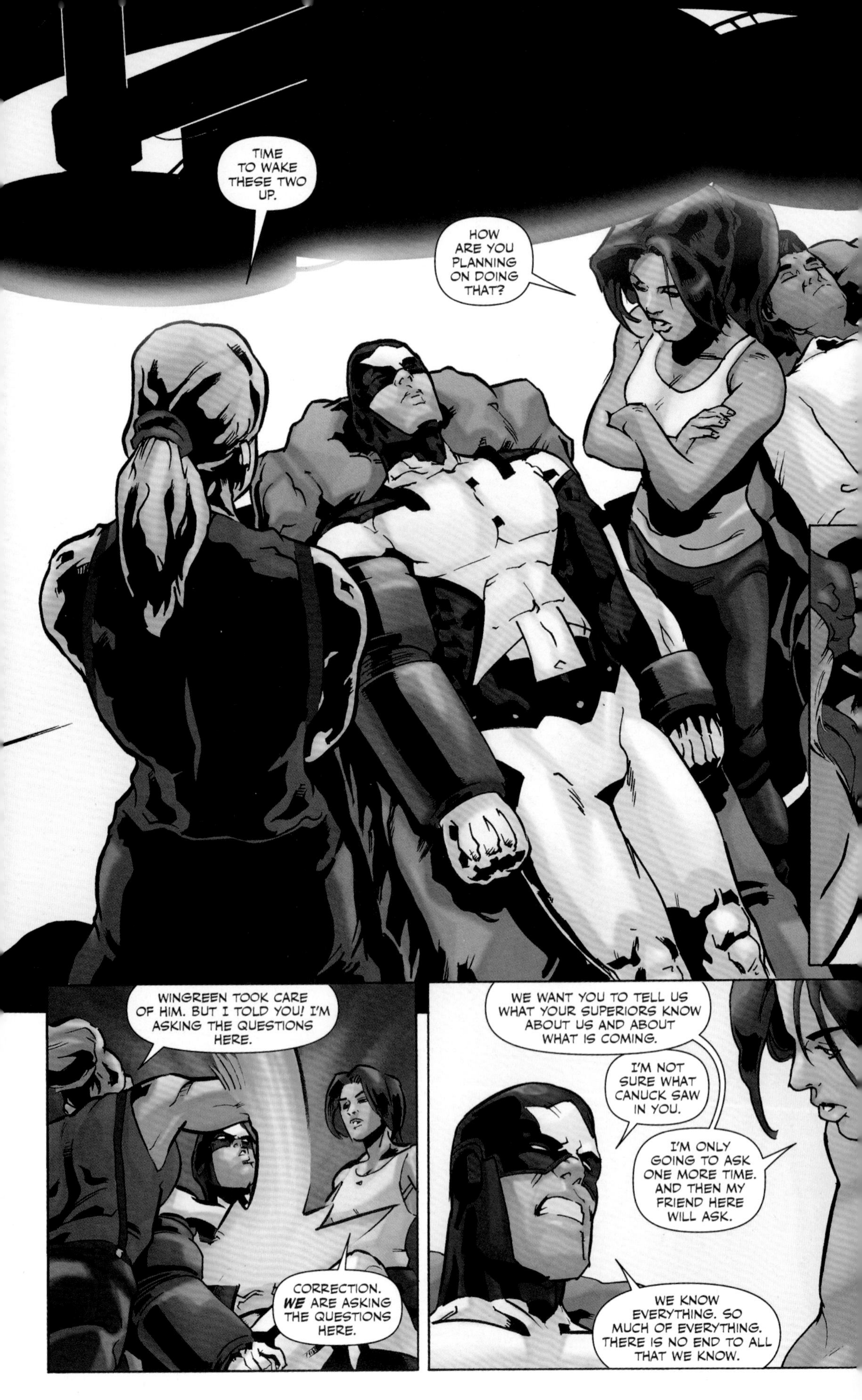
TIME TO WAKE THESE TWO UP.
HOW ARE YOU PLANNING ON DOING THAT?
WINGREEN TOOK CARE OF HIM. BUT I TOLD YOU! I'M ASKING THE QUESTIONS HERE.
CORRECTION. *WE* ARE ASKING THE QUESTIONS HERE.
WE WANT YOU TO TELL US WHAT YOUR SUPERIORS KNOW ABOUT US AND ABOUT WHAT IS COMING.
I'M NOT SURE WHAT CANUCK SAW IN YOU.
I'M ONLY GOING TO ASK ONE MORE TIME. AND THEN MY FRIEND HERE WILL ASK.
WE KNOW EVERYTHING. SO MUCH OF EVERYTHING. THERE IS NO END TO ALL THAT WE KNOW.

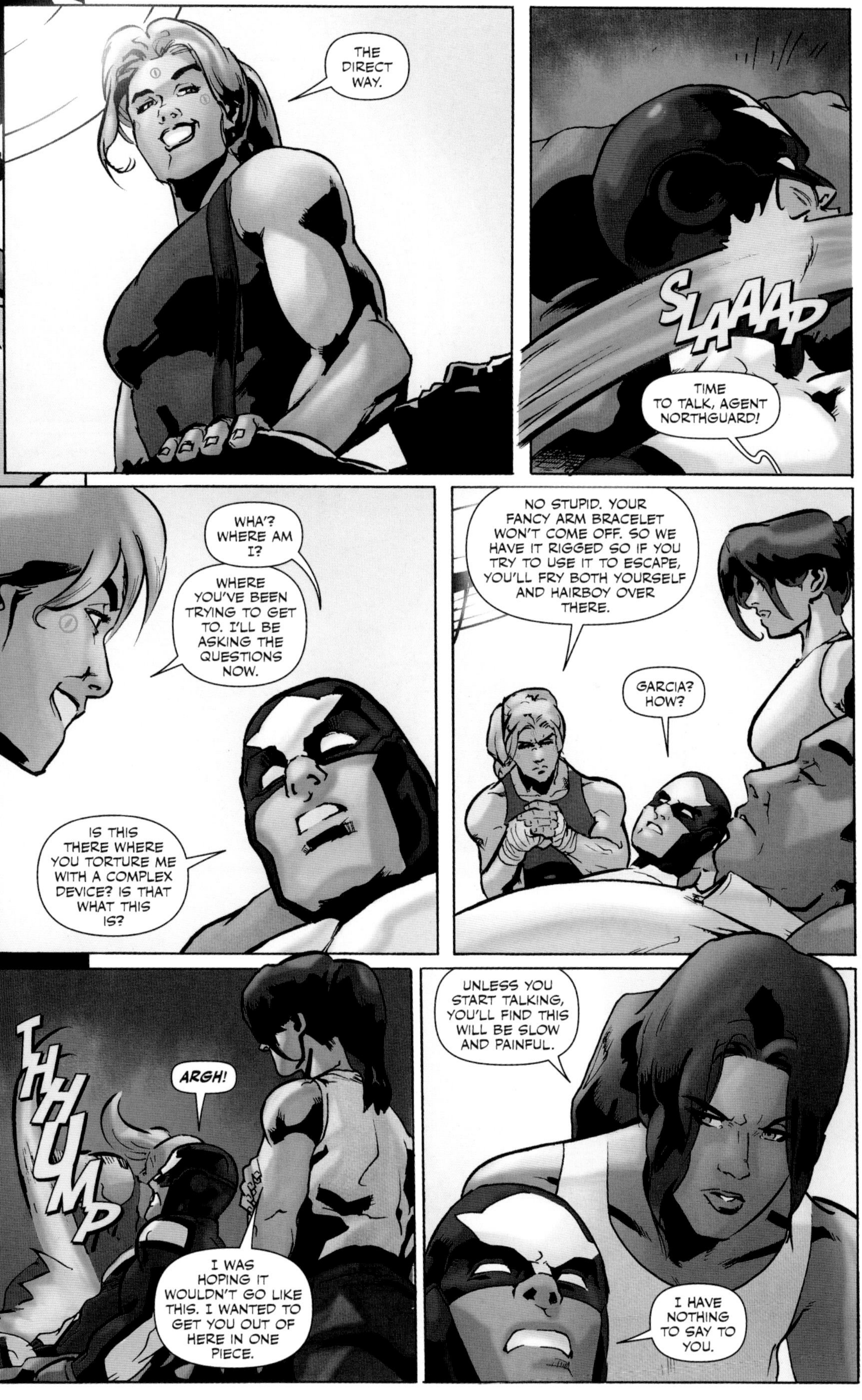
THE DIRECT WAY.
SLAAAP
TIME TO TALK, AGENT NORTHGUARD!
WHA'? WHERE AM I?
WHERE YOU'VE BEEN TRYING TO GET TO. I'LL BE ASKING THE QUESTIONS NOW.
IS THIS THERE WHERE YOU TORTURE ME WITH A COMPLEX DEVICE? IS THAT WHAT THIS IS?
NO STUPID. YOUR FANCY ARM BRACELET WON'T COME OFF. SO WE HAVE IT RIGGED SO IF YOU TRY TO USE IT TO ESCAPE, YOU'LL FRY BOTH YOURSELF AND HAIRBOY OVER THERE.
GARCIA? HOW?
THHUMP
ARGH!
I WAS HOPING IT WOULDN'T GO LIKE THIS. I WANTED TO GET YOU OUT OF HERE IN ONE PIECE.
UNLESS YOU START TALKING, YOU'LL FIND THIS WILL BE SLOW AND PAINFUL.
I HAVE NOTHING TO SAY TO YOU.

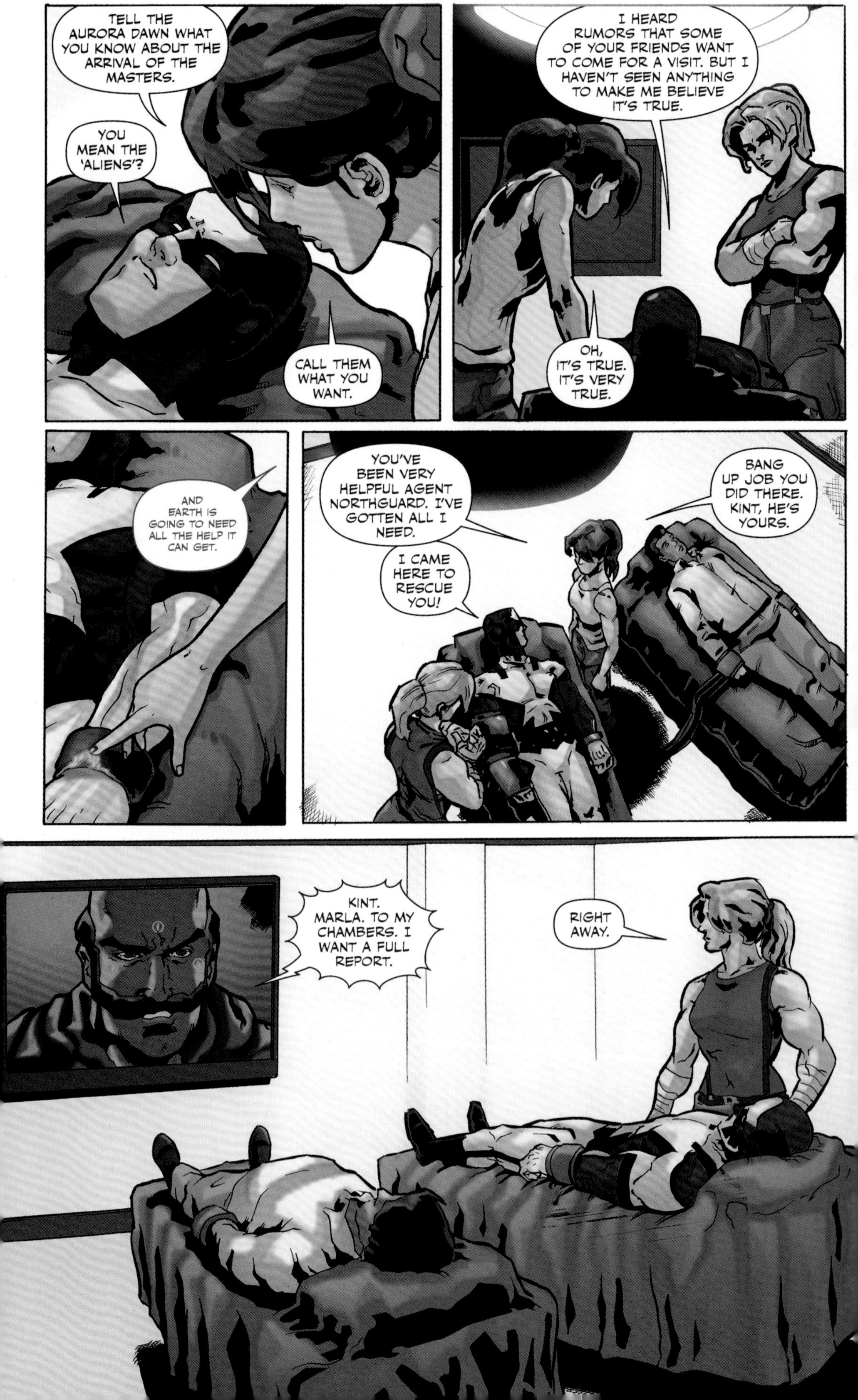
TELL THE AURORA DAWN WHAT YOU KNOW ABOUT THE ARRIVAL OF THE MASTERS.
YOU MEAN THE 'ALIENS'?
CALL THEM WHAT YOU WANT.
I HEARD RUMORS THAT SOME OF YOUR FRIENDS WANT TO COME FOR A VISIT. BUT I HAVEN'T SEEN ANYTHING TO MAKE ME BELIEVE IT'S TRUE.
OH, IT'S TRUE. IT'S VERY TRUE.
AND EARTH IS GOING TO NEED ALL THE HELP IT CAN GET.
YOU'VE BEEN VERY HELPFUL AGENT NORTHGUARD. I'VE GOTTEN ALL I NEED.
I CAME HERE TO RESCUE YOU!
BANG UP JOB YOU DID THERE. KINT, HE'S YOURS.
KINT. MARLA. TO MY CHAMBERS. I WANT A FULL REPORT.
RIGHT AWAY.

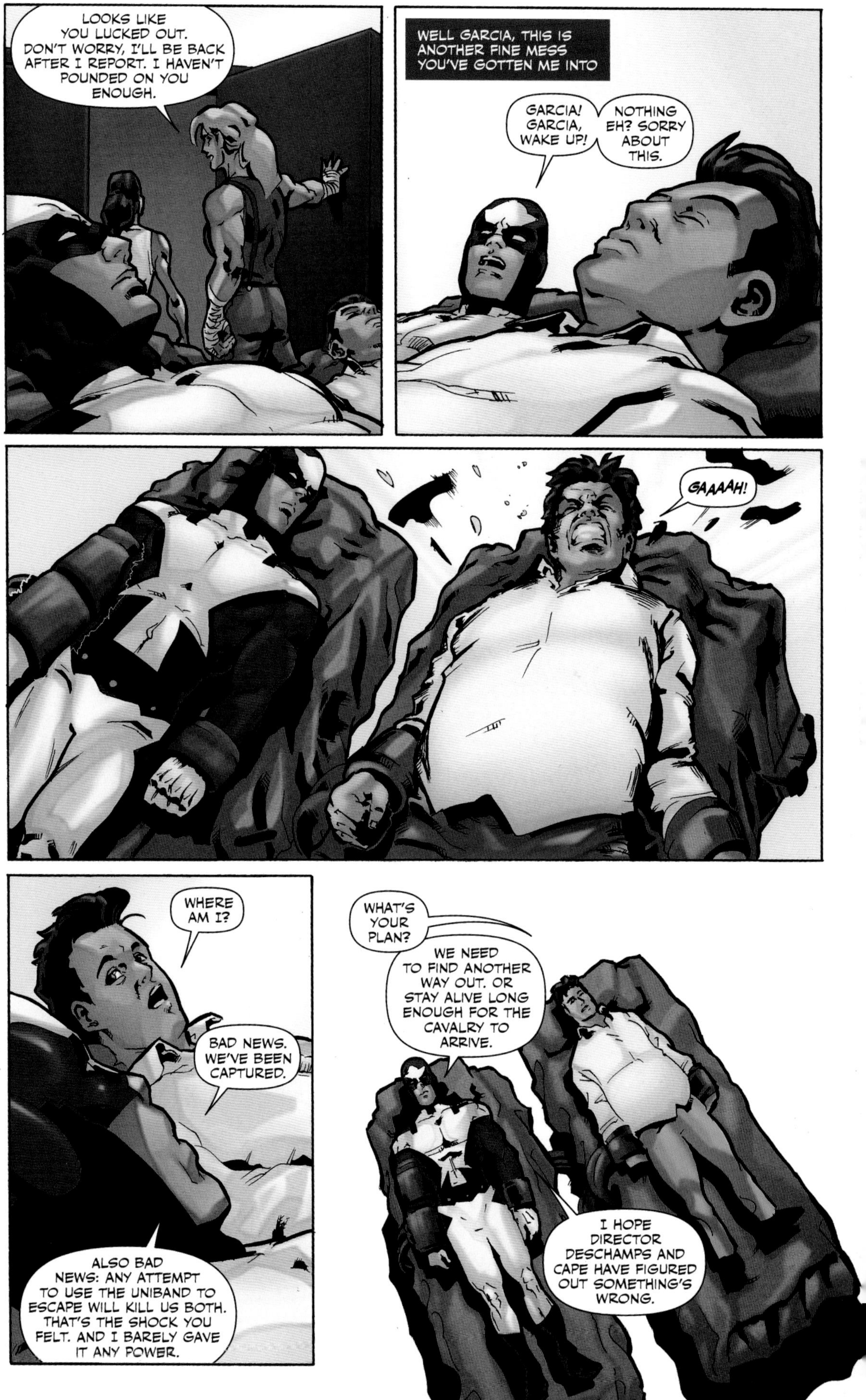
LOOKS LIKE YOU LUCKED OUT. DON'T WORRY, I'LL BE BACK AFTER I REPORT. I HAVEN'T POUNDED ON YOU ENOUGH.
WELL GARCIA, THIS IS ANOTHER FINE MESS YOU'VE GOTTEN ME INTO
GARCIA! GARCIA, WAKE UP!
NOTHING EH? SORRY ABOUT THIS.
GAAAAH!
WHERE AM I?
BAD NEWS. WE'VE BEEN CAPTURED.
ALSO BAD NEWS: ANY ATTEMPT TO USE THE UNIBAND TO ESCAPE WILL KILL US BOTH. THAT'S THE SHOCK YOU FELT. AND I BARELY GAVE IT ANY POWER.
WHAT'S YOUR PLAN?
WE NEED TO FIND ANOTHER WAY OUT. OR STAY ALIVE LONG ENOUGH FOR THE CAVALRY TO ARRIVE.
I HOPE DIRECTOR DESCHAMPS AND CAPE HAVE FIGURED OUT SOMETHING'S WRONG.

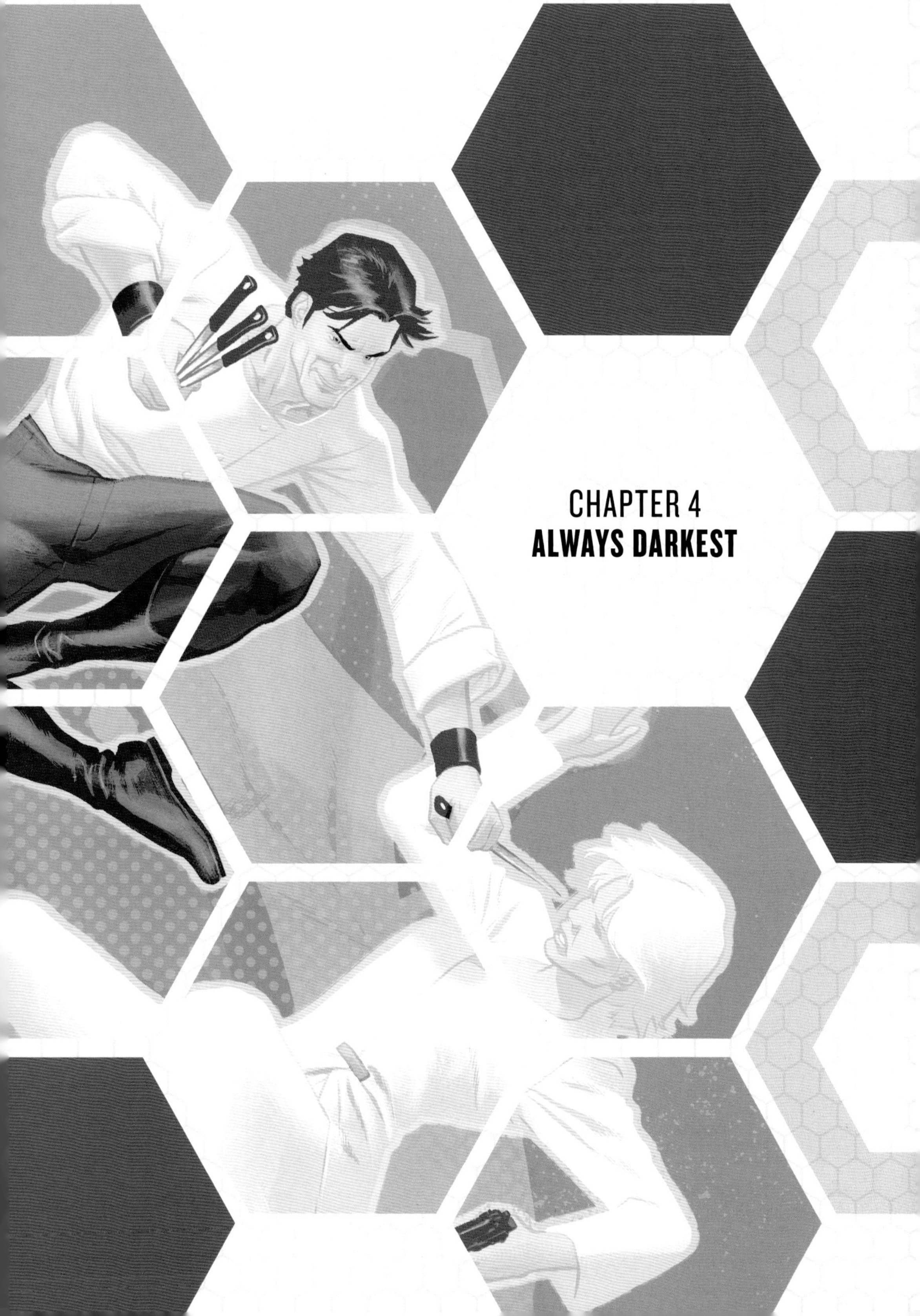

CHAPTER 4
ALWAYS DARKEST

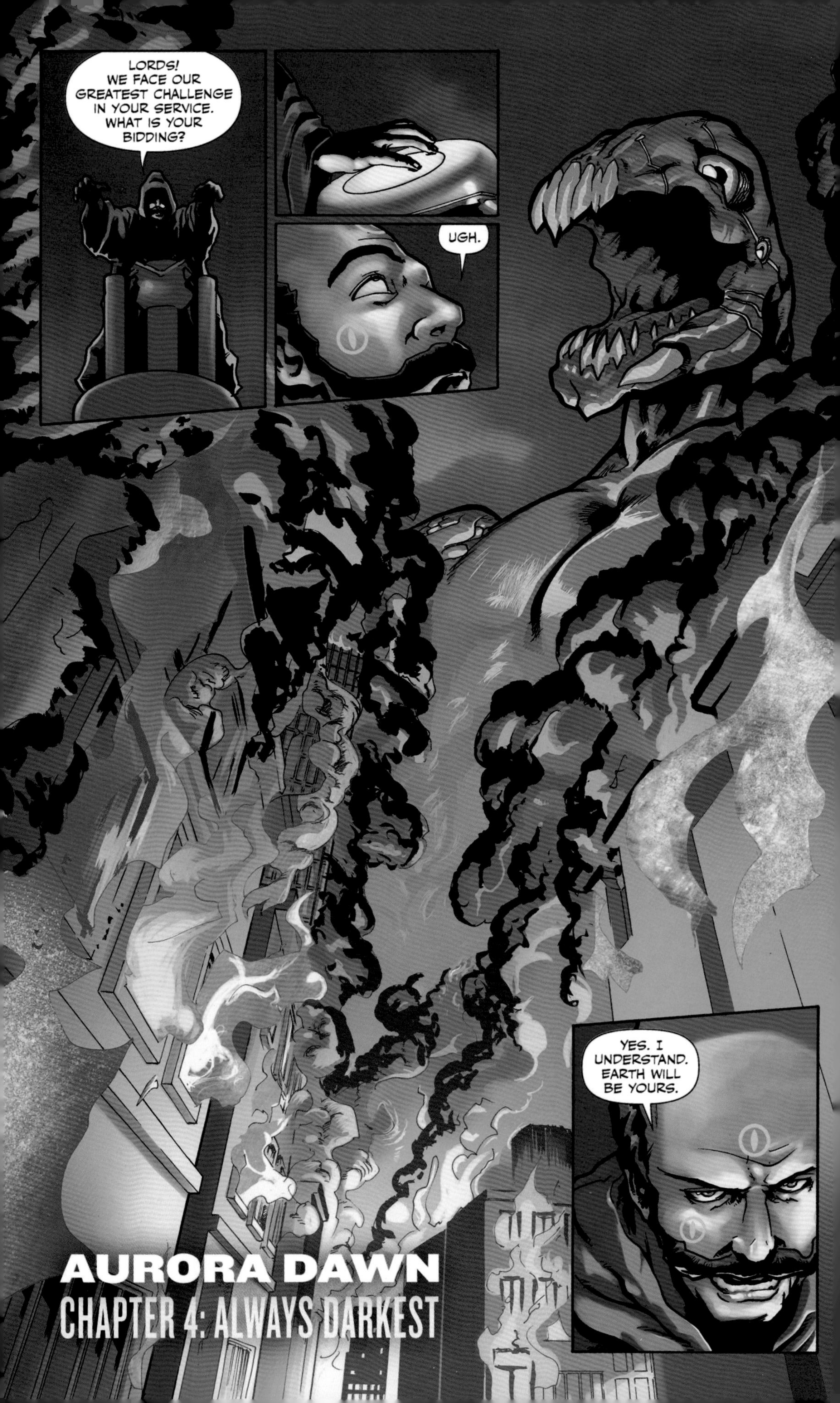

LORDS! WE FACE OUR GREATEST CHALLENGE IN YOUR SERVICE. WHAT IS YOUR BIDDING?
UGH.
YES. I UNDERSTAND. EARTH WILL BE YOURS.
AURORA DAWN
CHAPTER 4: ALWAYS DARKEST

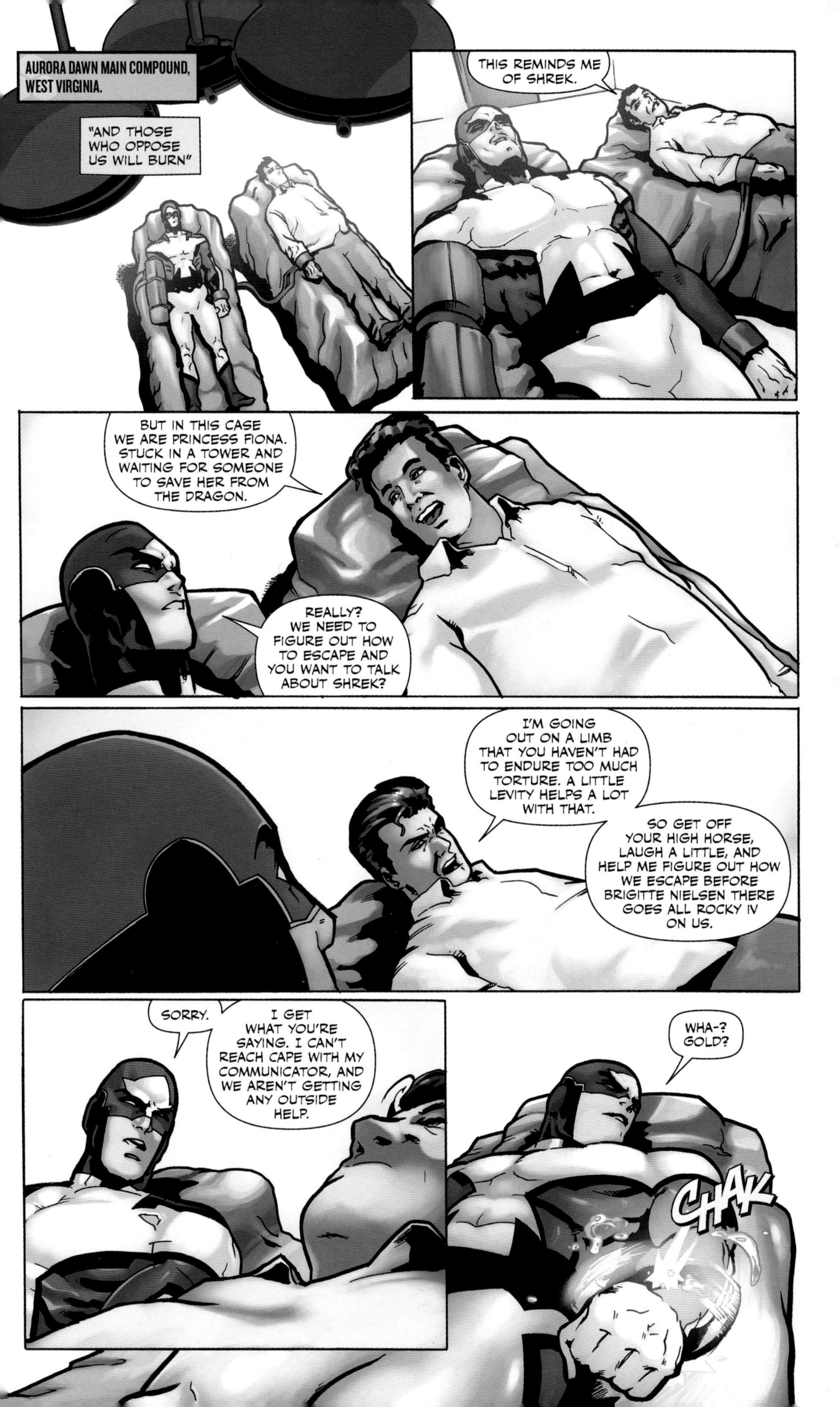
AURORA DAWN MAIN COMPOUND, WEST VIRGINIA.
"AND THOSE WHO OPPOSE US WILL BURN"
THIS REMINDS ME OF SHREK.
BUT IN THIS CASE WE ARE PRINCESS FIONA. STUCK IN A TOWER AND WAITING FOR SOMEONE TO SAVE HER FROM THE DRAGON.
REALLY? WE NEED TO FIGURE OUT HOW TO ESCAPE AND YOU WANT TO TALK ABOUT SHREK?
I'M GOING OUT ON A LIMB THAT YOU HAVEN'T HAD TO ENDURE TOO MUCH TORTURE. A LITTLE LEVITY HELPS A LOT WITH THAT.
SO GET OFF YOUR HIGH HORSE, LAUGH A LITTLE, AND HELP ME FIGURE OUT HOW WE ESCAPE BEFORE BRIGITTE NIELSEN THERE GOES ALL ROCKY IV ON US.
SORRY.
I GET WHAT YOU'RE SAYING. I CAN'T REACH CAPE WITH MY COMMUNICATOR, AND WE AREN'T GETTING ANY OUTSIDE HELP.
WHA-? GOLD?
CHAK

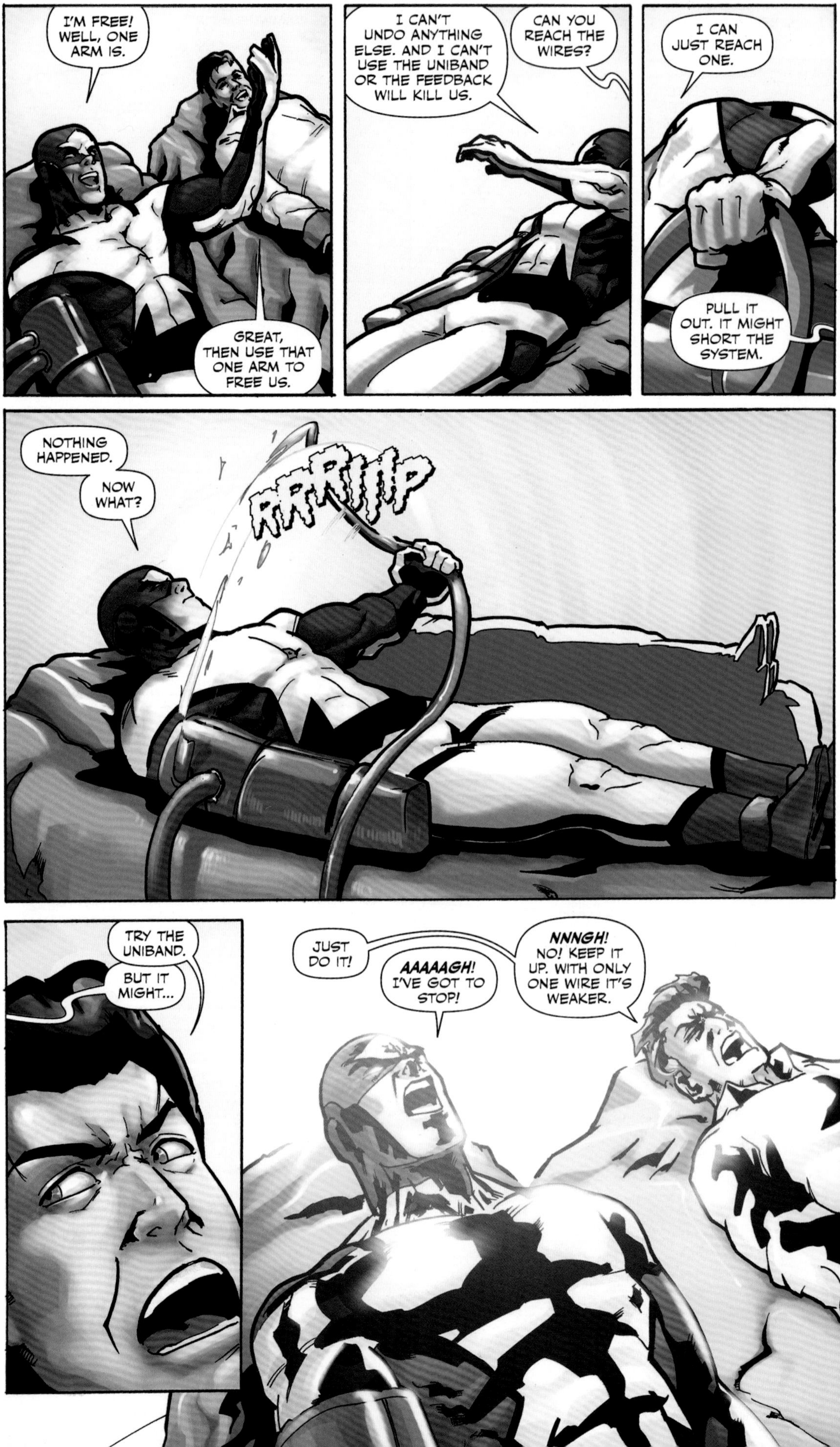
I'M FREE! WELL, ONE ARM IS.
GREAT, THEN USE THAT ONE ARM TO FREE US.
I CAN'T UNDO ANYTHING ELSE. AND I CAN'T USE THE UNIBAND OR THE FEEDBACK WILL KILL US.
CAN YOU REACH THE WIRES?
I CAN JUST REACH ONE.
PULL IT OUT. IT MIGHT SHORT THE SYSTEM.
NOTHING HAPPENED.
NOW WHAT?
RRRIIIP
TRY THE UNIBAND.
BUT IT MIGHT...
JUST DO IT!
AAAAAGH! I'VE GOT TO STOP!
NNNGH! NO! KEEP IT UP. WITH ONLY ONE WIRE IT'S WEAKER.

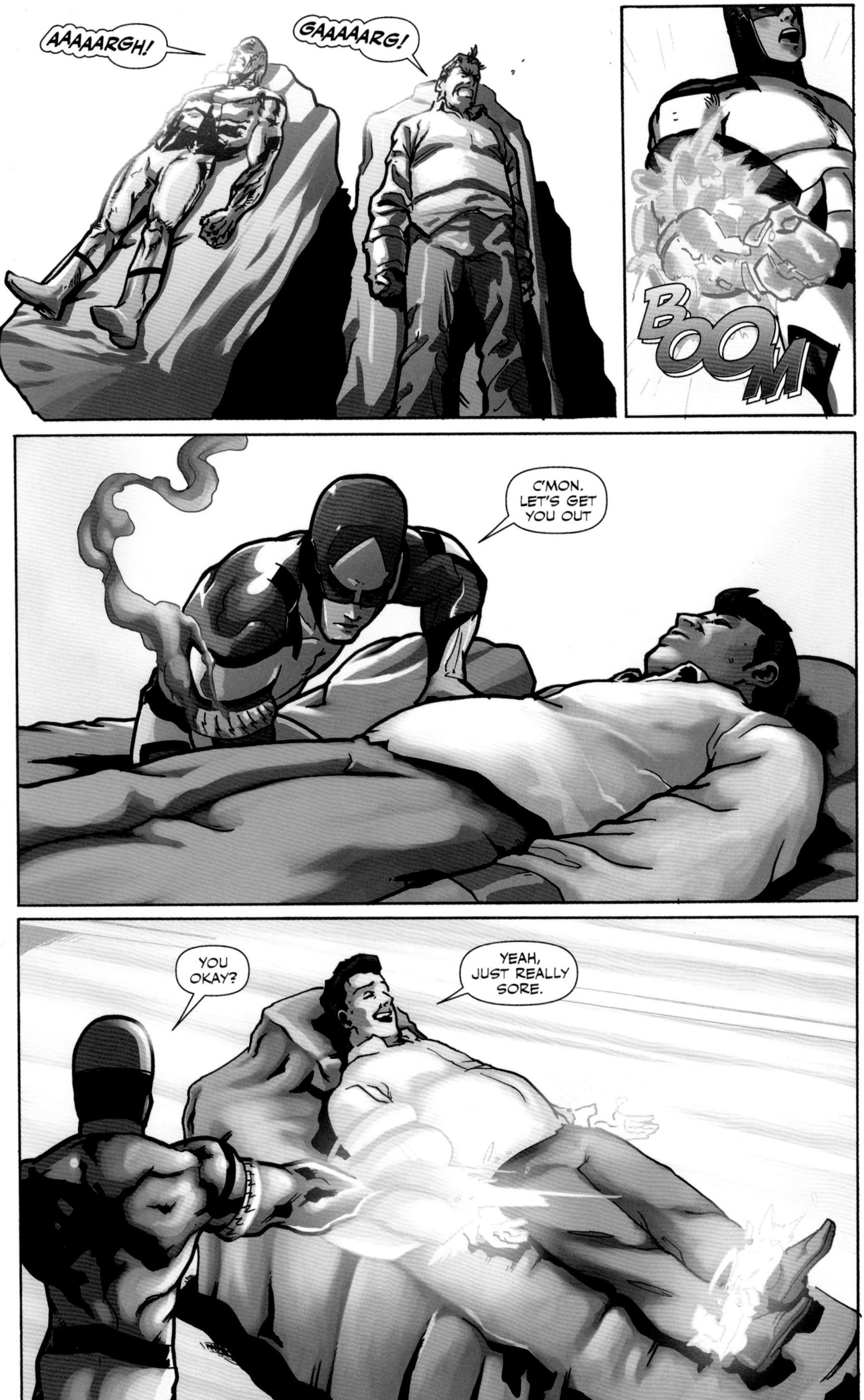
AAAAARGH!
GAAAAARG!
BOOM!
C'MON. LET'S GET YOU OUT
YOU OKAY?
YEAH, JUST REALLY SORE.

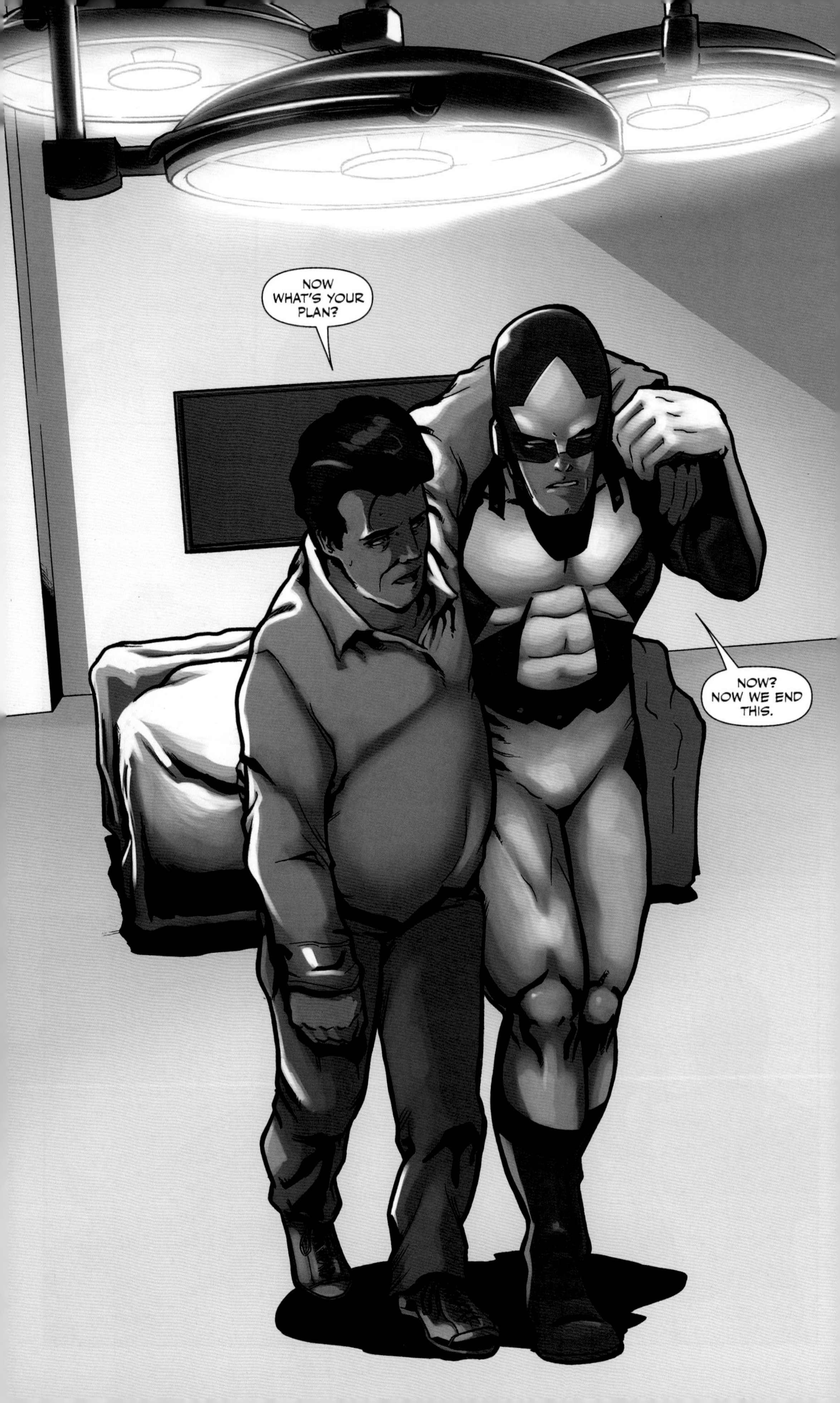
NOW WHAT'S YOUR PLAN?
NOW? NOW WE END THIS.

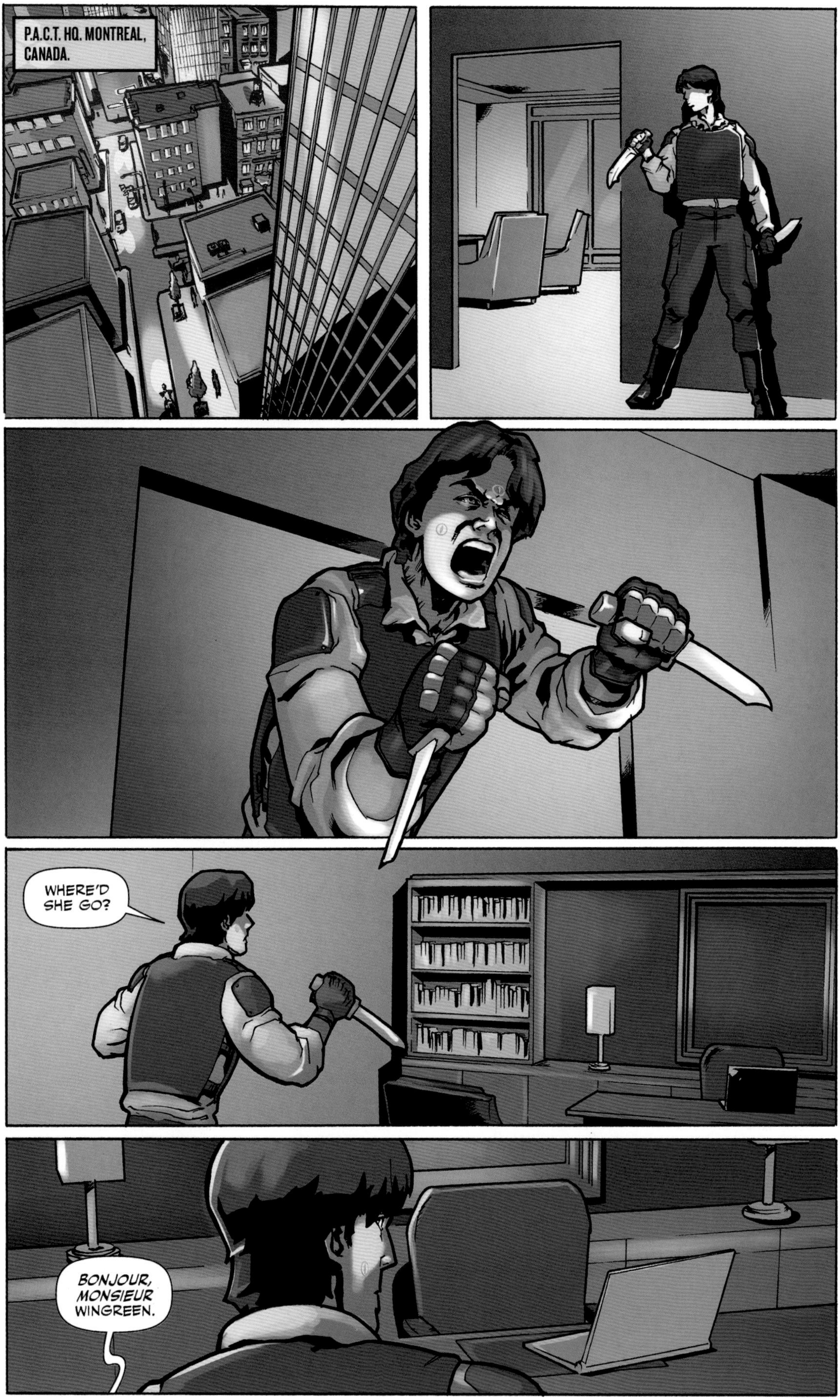
P.A.C.T. HQ. MONTREAL, CANADA.
WHERE'D SHE GO?
BONJOUR, MONSIEUR WINGREEN.

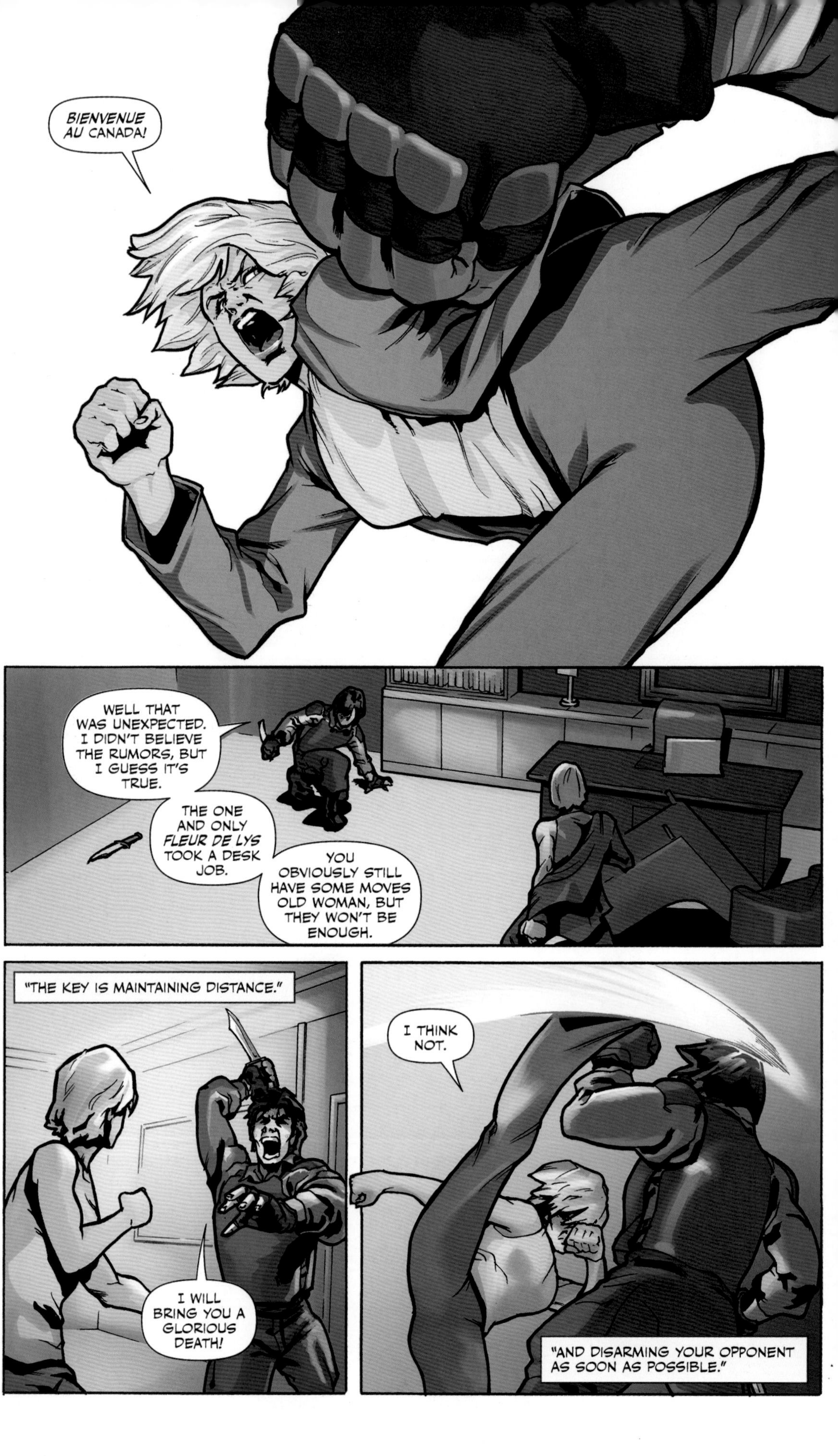

BIENVENUE AU CANADA!
WELL THAT WAS UNEXPECTED. I DIDN'T BELIEVE THE RUMORS, BUT I GUESS IT'S TRUE.
THE ONE AND ONLY FLEUR DE LYS TOOK A DESK JOB.
YOU OBVIOUSLY STILL HAVE SOME MOVES OLD WOMAN, BUT THEY WON'T BE ENOUGH.
"THE KEY IS MAINTAINING DISTANCE."
I WILL BRING YOU A GLORIOUS DEATH!
I THINK NOT.
"AND DISARMING YOUR OPPONENT AS SOON AS POSSIBLE."

WE SHALL SEE.

"FACING AN OPPONENT WITH A KNIFE IS ALWAYS DIFFICULT."

ARGH!

SLASSH

"TOO FAST TO DODGE."

OOOOF!

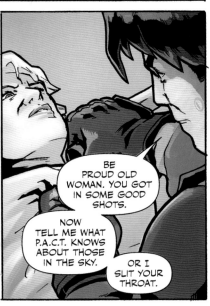

BE PROUD OLD WOMAN. YOU GOT IN SOME GOOD SHOTS.

NOW TELL ME WHAT P.A.C.T. KNOWS ABOUT THOSE IN THE SKY.

OR I SLIT YOUR THROAT.

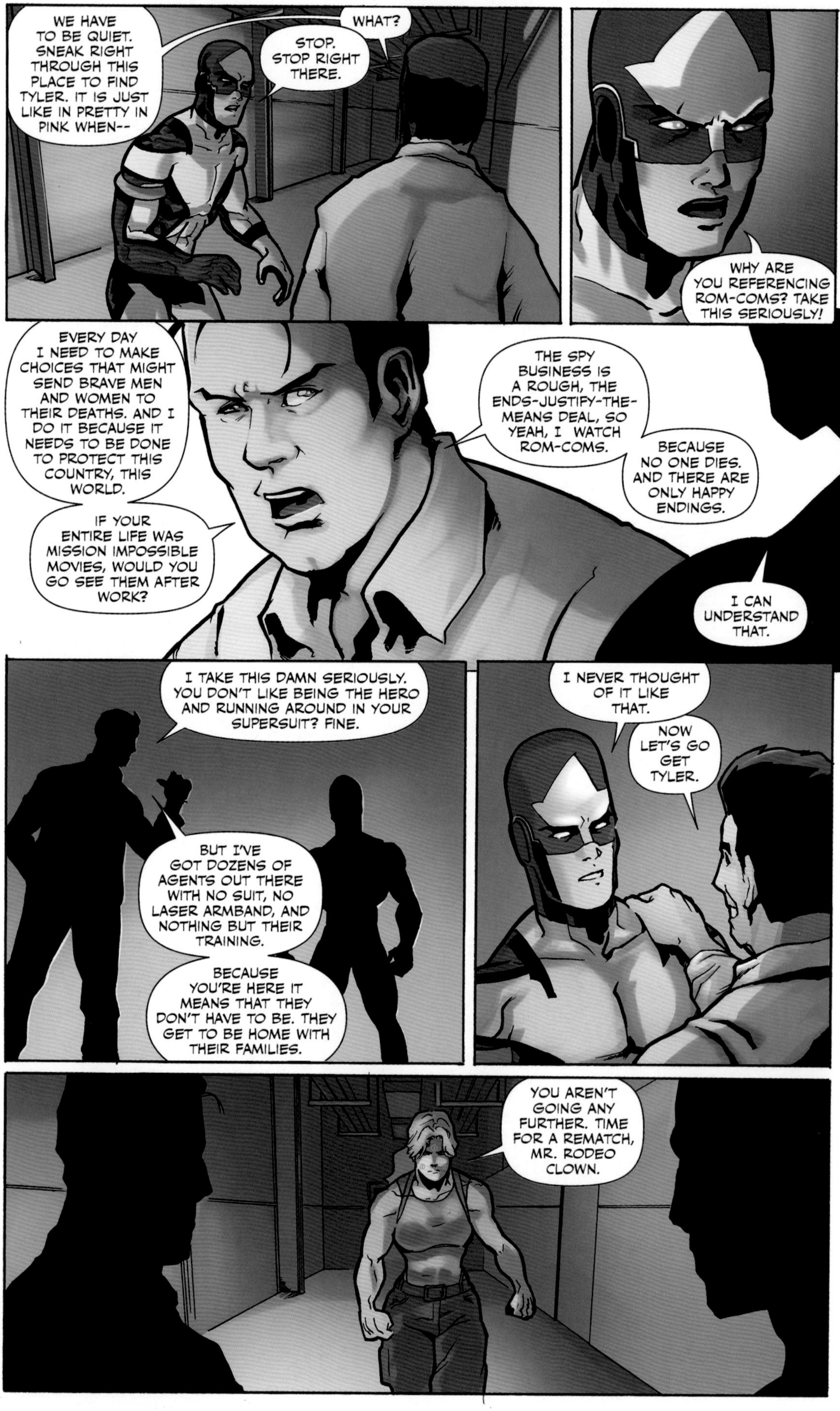
WE HAVE TO BE QUIET. SNEAK RIGHT THROUGH THIS PLACE TO FIND TYLER. IT IS JUST LIKE IN PRETTY IN PINK WHEN--
WHAT?
STOP. STOP RIGHT THERE.
WHY ARE YOU REFERENCING ROM-COMS? TAKE THIS SERIOUSLY!
EVERY DAY I NEED TO MAKE CHOICES THAT MIGHT SEND BRAVE MEN AND WOMEN TO THEIR DEATHS. AND I DO IT BECAUSE IT NEEDS TO BE DONE TO PROTECT THIS COUNTRY, THIS WORLD.
IF YOUR ENTIRE LIFE WAS MISSION IMPOSSIBLE MOVIES, WOULD YOU GO SEE THEM AFTER WORK?
THE SPY BUSINESS IS A ROUGH, THE ENDS-JUSTIFY-THE-MEANS DEAL, SO YEAH, I WATCH ROM-COMS.
BECAUSE NO ONE DIES. AND THERE ARE ONLY HAPPY ENDINGS.
I CAN UNDERSTAND THAT.
I TAKE THIS DAMN SERIOUSLY. YOU DON'T LIKE BEING THE HERO AND RUNNING AROUND IN YOUR SUPERSUIT? FINE.
BUT I'VE GOT DOZENS OF AGENTS OUT THERE WITH NO SUIT, NO LASER ARMBAND, AND NOTHING BUT THEIR TRAINING.
BECAUSE YOU'RE HERE IT MEANS THAT THEY DON'T HAVE TO BE. THEY GET TO BE HOME WITH THEIR FAMILIES.
I NEVER THOUGHT OF IT LIKE THAT.
NOW LET'S GO GET TYLER.
YOU AREN'T GOING ANY FURTHER. TIME FOR A REMATCH, MR. RODEO CLOWN.

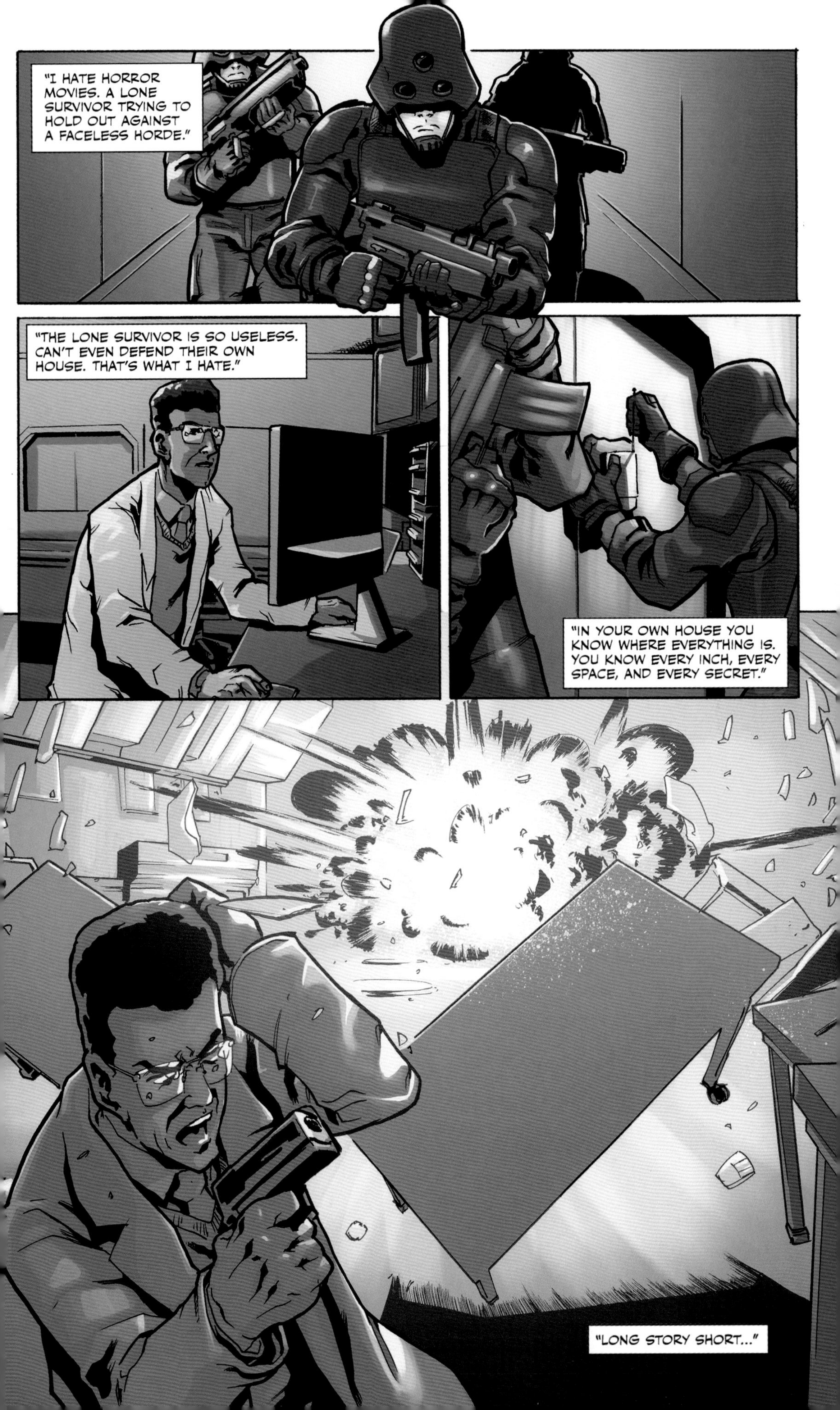
"I HATE HORROR MOVIES. A LONE SURVIVOR TRYING TO HOLD OUT AGAINST A FACELESS HORDE."
"THE LONE SURVIVOR IS SO USELESS. CAN'T EVEN DEFEND THEIR OWN HOUSE. THAT'S WHAT I HATE."
"IN YOUR OWN HOUSE YOU KNOW WHERE EVERYTHING IS. YOU KNOW EVERY INCH, EVERY SPACE, AND EVERY SECRET."
"LONG STORY SHORT..."

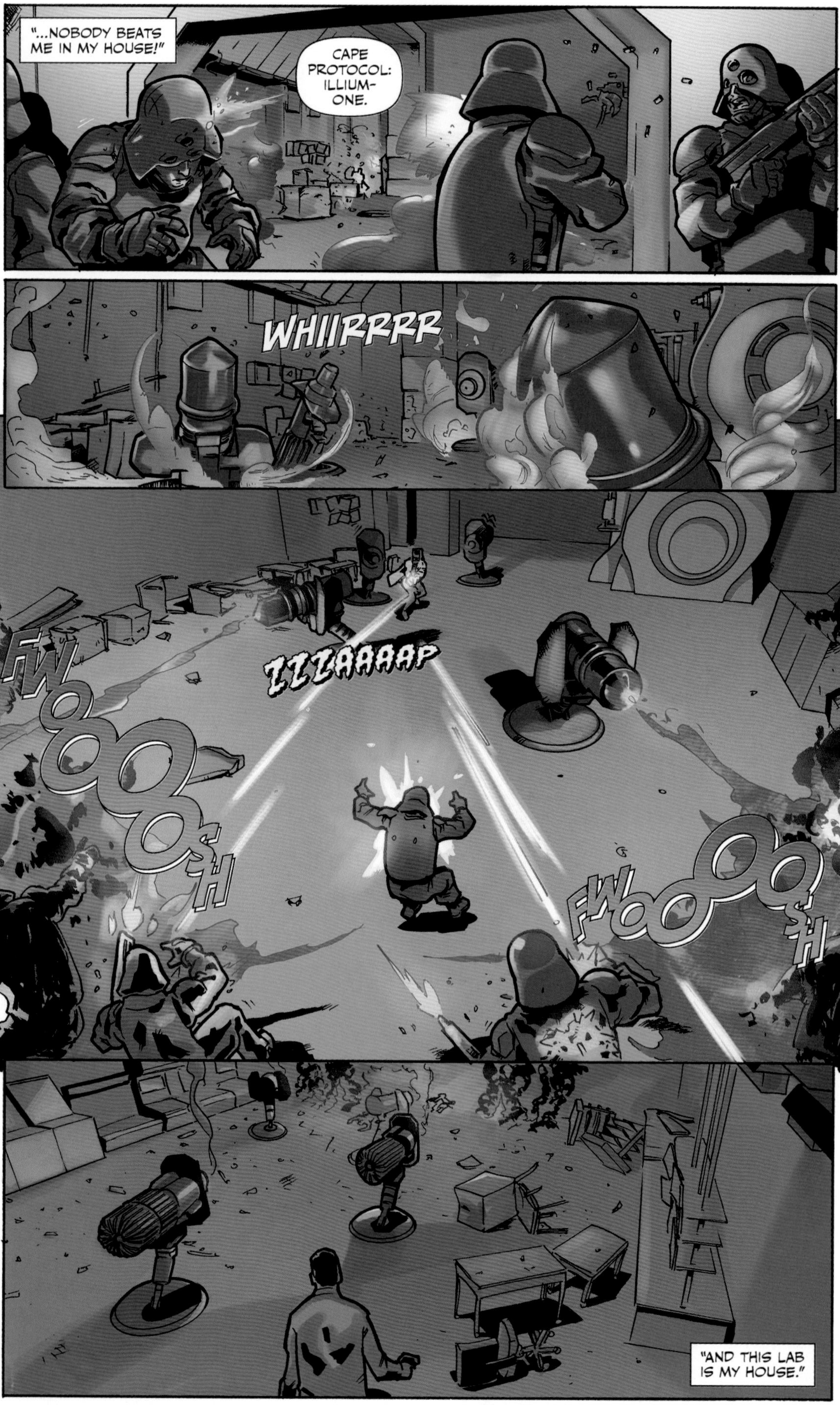
"...NOBODY BEATS ME IN MY HOUSE!"
CAPE PROTOCOL: ILLIUM-ONE.
WHIIRRRR
ZZZAAAAP
FWOOOOSH
FWOOOOSH
"AND THIS LAB IS MY HOUSE."

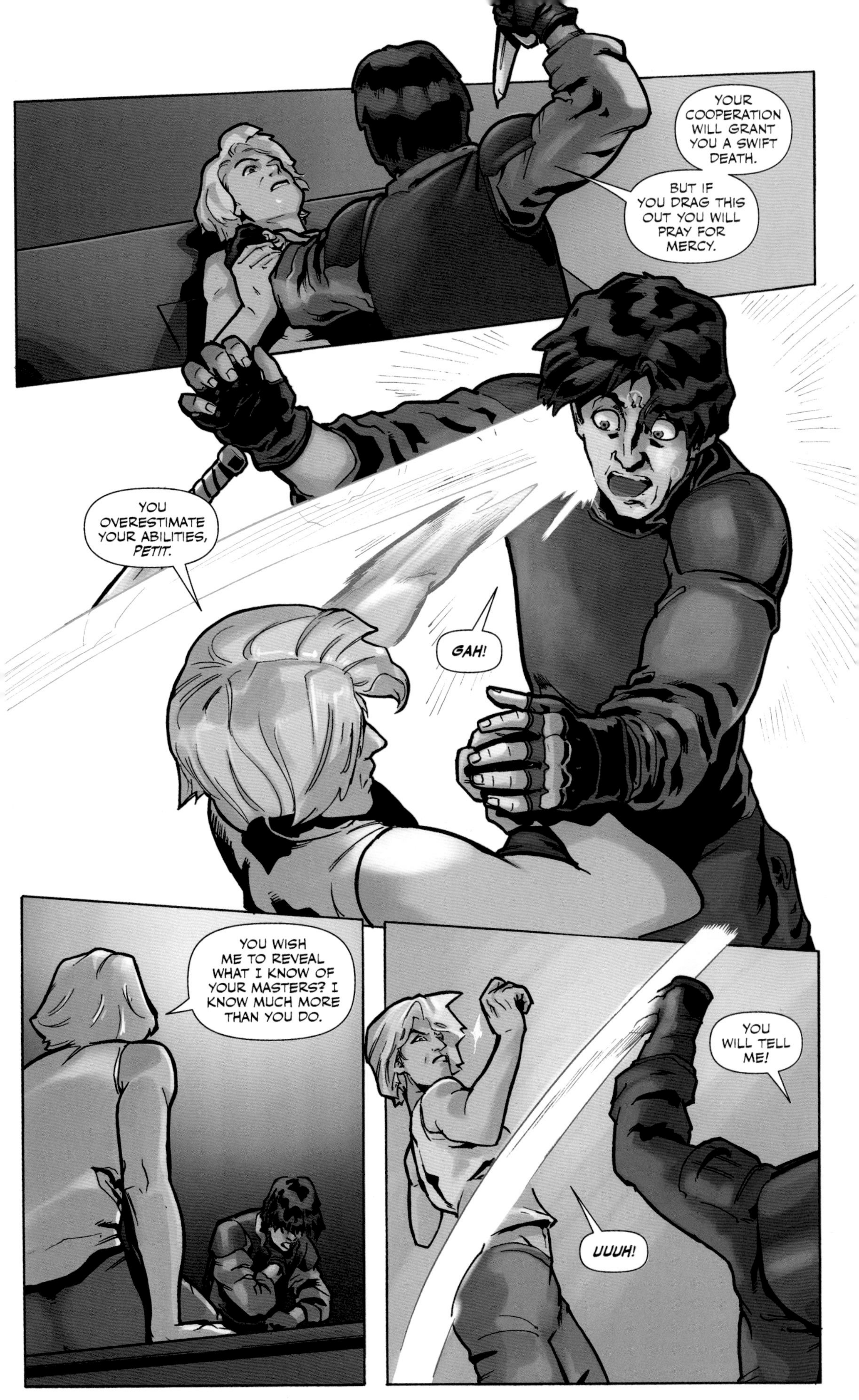
YOUR COOPERATION WILL GRANT YOU A SWIFT DEATH.
BUT IF YOU DRAG THIS OUT YOU WILL PRAY FOR MERCY.
YOU OVERESTIMATE YOUR ABILITIES, *PETIT.*
GAH!
YOU WISH ME TO REVEAL WHAT I KNOW OF YOUR MASTERS? I KNOW MUCH MORE THAN YOU DO.
YOU WILL TELL ME!
UUUH!

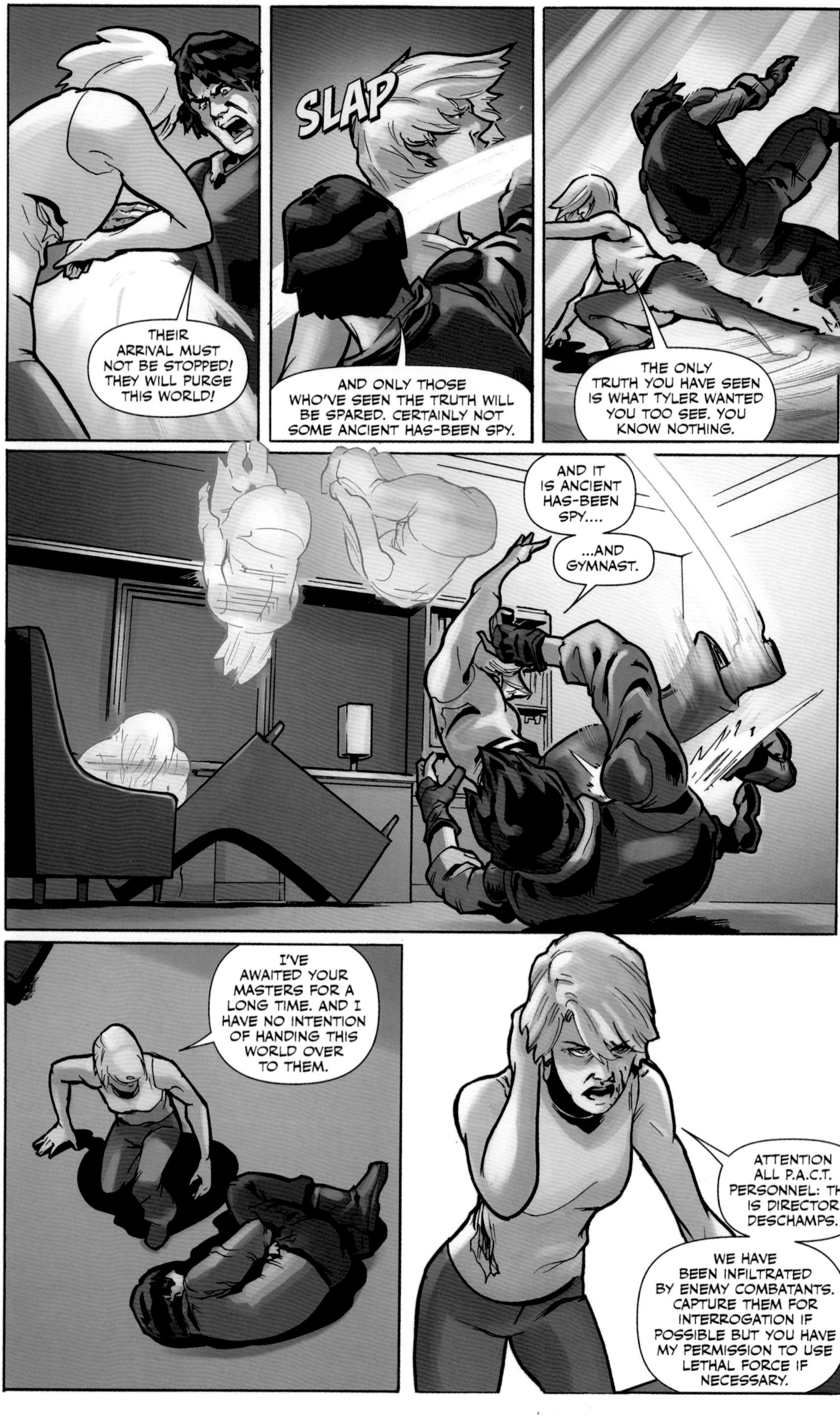
THEIR ARRIVAL MUST NOT BE STOPPED! THEY WILL PURGE THIS WORLD!
SLAP
AND ONLY THOSE WHO'VE SEEN THE TRUTH WILL BE SPARED. CERTAINLY NOT SOME ANCIENT HAS-BEEN SPY.
THE ONLY TRUTH YOU HAVE SEEN IS WHAT TYLER WANTED YOU TOO SEE. YOU KNOW NOTHING.
AND IT IS ANCIENT HAS-BEEN SPY....
...AND GYMNAST.
I'VE AWAITED YOUR MASTERS FOR A LONG TIME. AND I HAVE NO INTENTION OF HANDING THIS WORLD OVER TO THEM.
ATTENTION ALL P.A.C.T. PERSONNEL: THIS IS DIRECTOR DESCHAMPS.
WE HAVE BEEN INFILTRATED BY ENEMY COMBATANTS. CAPTURE THEM FOR INTERROGATION IF POSSIBLE BUT YOU HAVE MY PERMISSION TO USE LETHAL FORCE IF NECESSARY.

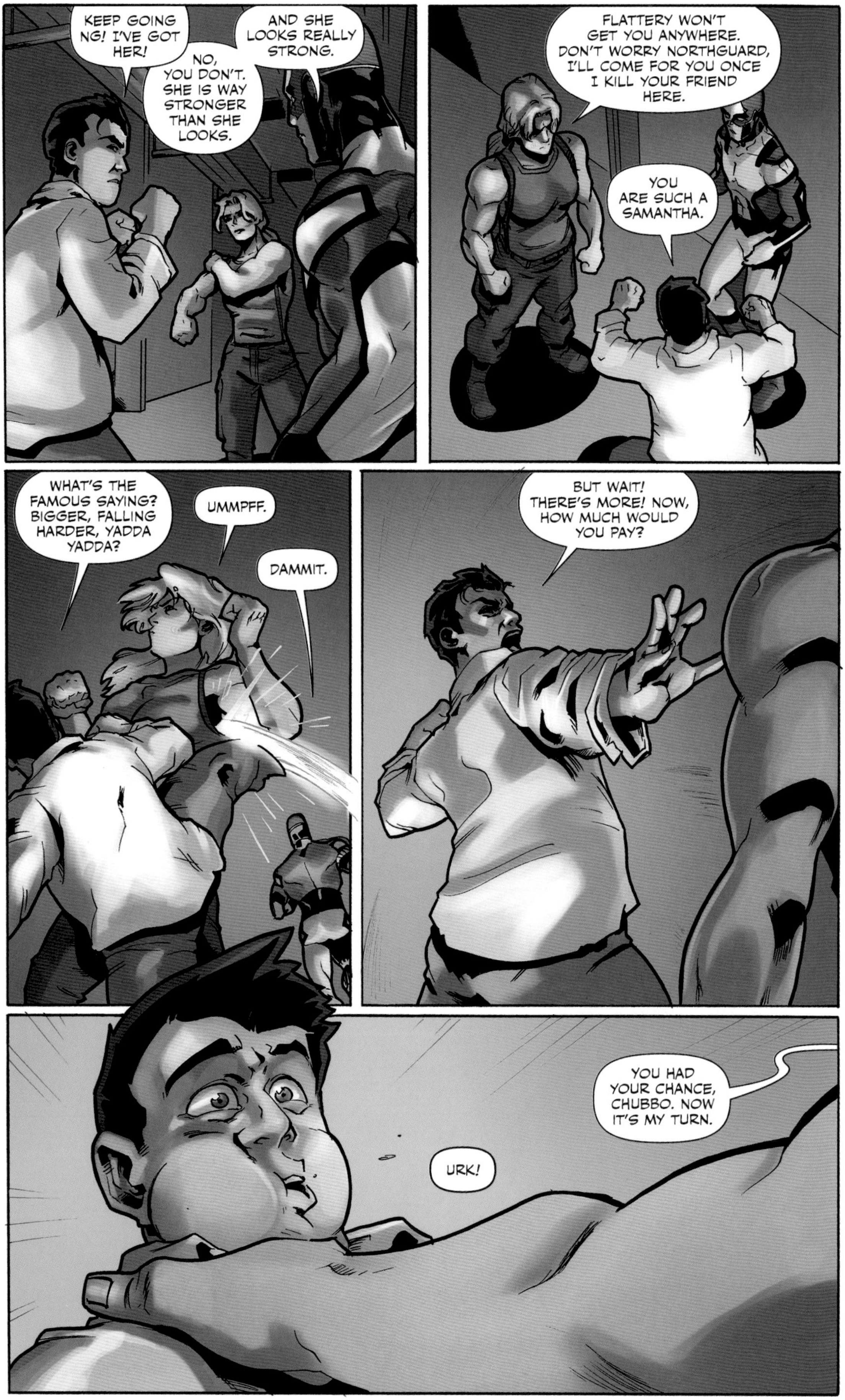
KEEP GOING NG! I'VE GOT HER!
NO, YOU DON'T. SHE IS WAY STRONGER THAN SHE LOOKS.
AND SHE LOOKS REALLY STRONG.
FLATTERY WON'T GET YOU ANYWHERE. DON'T WORRY NORTHGUARD, I'LL COME FOR YOU ONCE I KILL YOUR FRIEND HERE.
YOU ARE SUCH A SAMANTHA.
WHAT'S THE FAMOUS SAYING? BIGGER, FALLING HARDER, YADDA YADDA?
UMMPFF.
DAMMIT.
BUT WAIT! THERE'S MORE! NOW, HOW MUCH WOULD YOU PAY?
YOU HAD YOUR CHANCE, CHUBBO. NOW IT'S MY TURN.
URK!

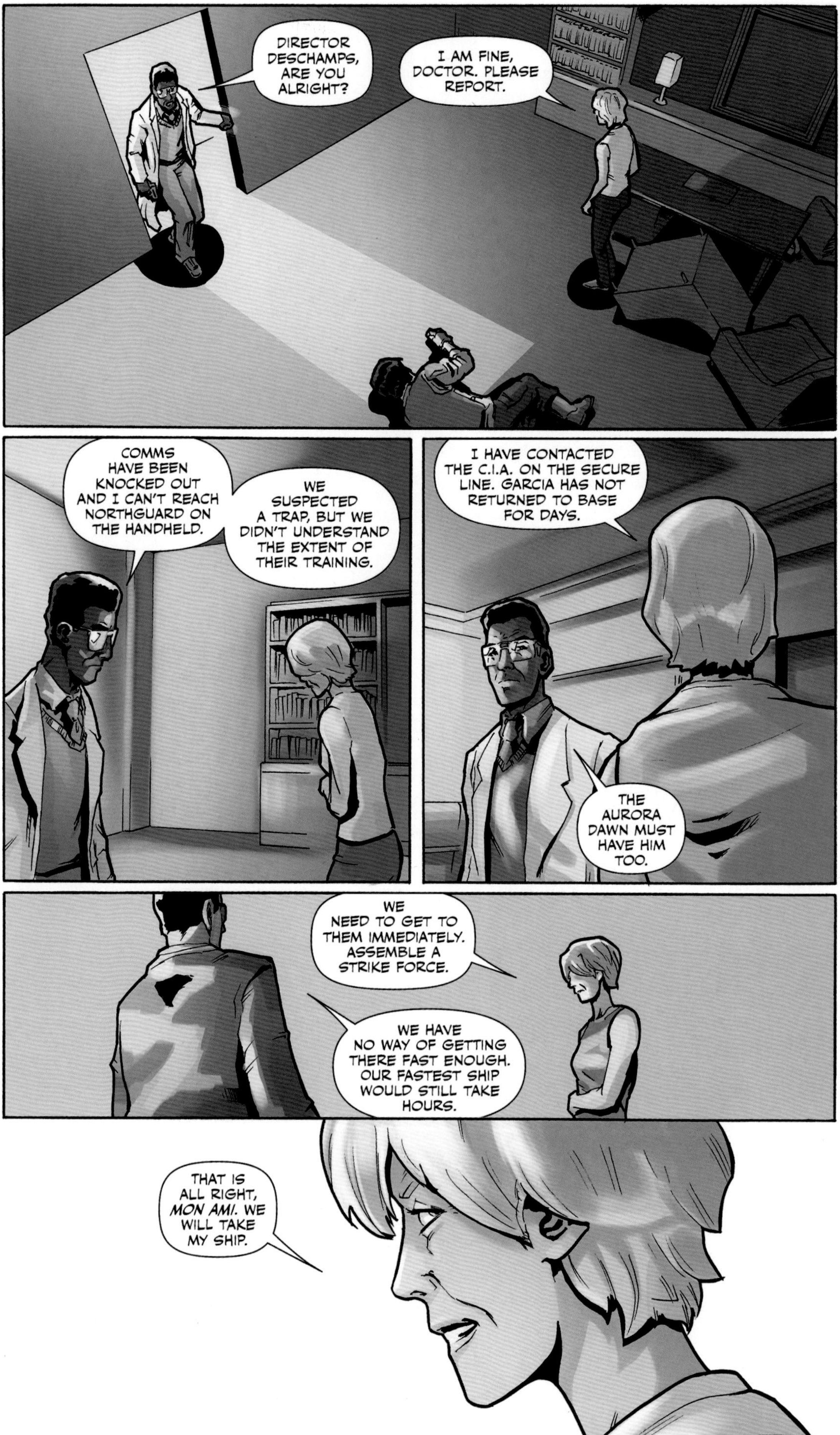
DIRECTOR DESCHAMPS, ARE YOU ALRIGHT?
I AM FINE, DOCTOR. PLEASE REPORT.
COMMS HAVE BEEN KNOCKED OUT AND I CAN'T REACH NORTHGUARD ON THE HANDHELD.
WE SUSPECTED A TRAP, BUT WE DIDN'T UNDERSTAND THE EXTENT OF THEIR TRAINING.
I HAVE CONTACTED THE C.I.A. ON THE SECURE LINE. GARCIA HAS NOT RETURNED TO BASE FOR DAYS.
THE AURORA DAWN MUST HAVE HIM TOO.
WE NEED TO GET TO THEM IMMEDIATELY. ASSEMBLE A STRIKE FORCE.
WE HAVE NO WAY OF GETTING THERE FAST ENOUGH. OUR FASTEST SHIP WOULD STILL TAKE HOURS.
THAT IS ALL RIGHT, *MON AMI*. WE WILL TAKE MY SHIP.

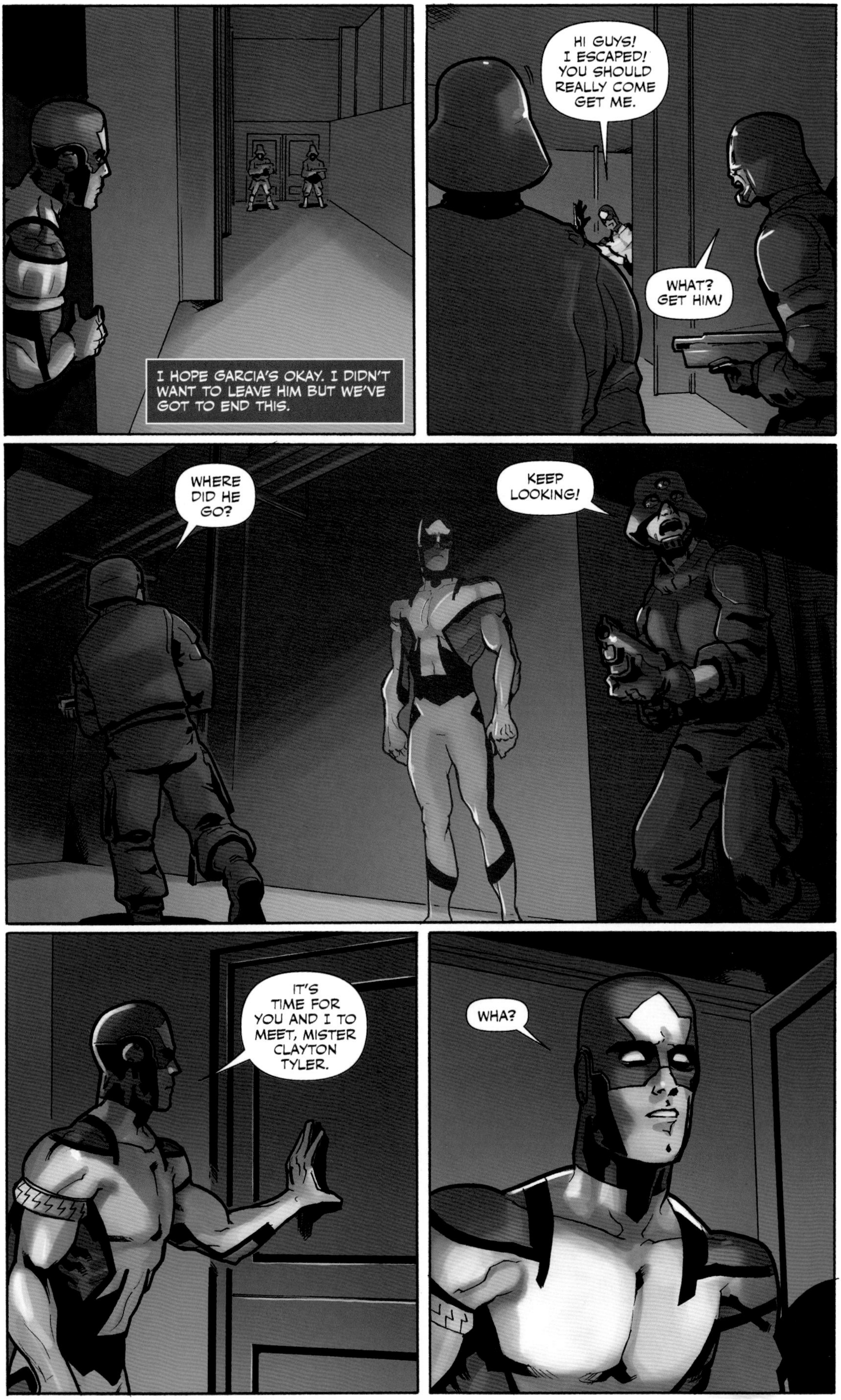
I HOPE GARCIA'S OKAY. I DIDN'T WANT TO LEAVE HIM BUT WE'VE GOT TO END THIS.
HI GUYS! I ESCAPED! YOU SHOULD REALLY COME GET ME.
WHAT? GET HIM!
WHERE DID HE GO?
KEEP LOOKING!
IT'S TIME FOR YOU AND I TO MEET, MISTER CLAYTON TYLER.
WHA?

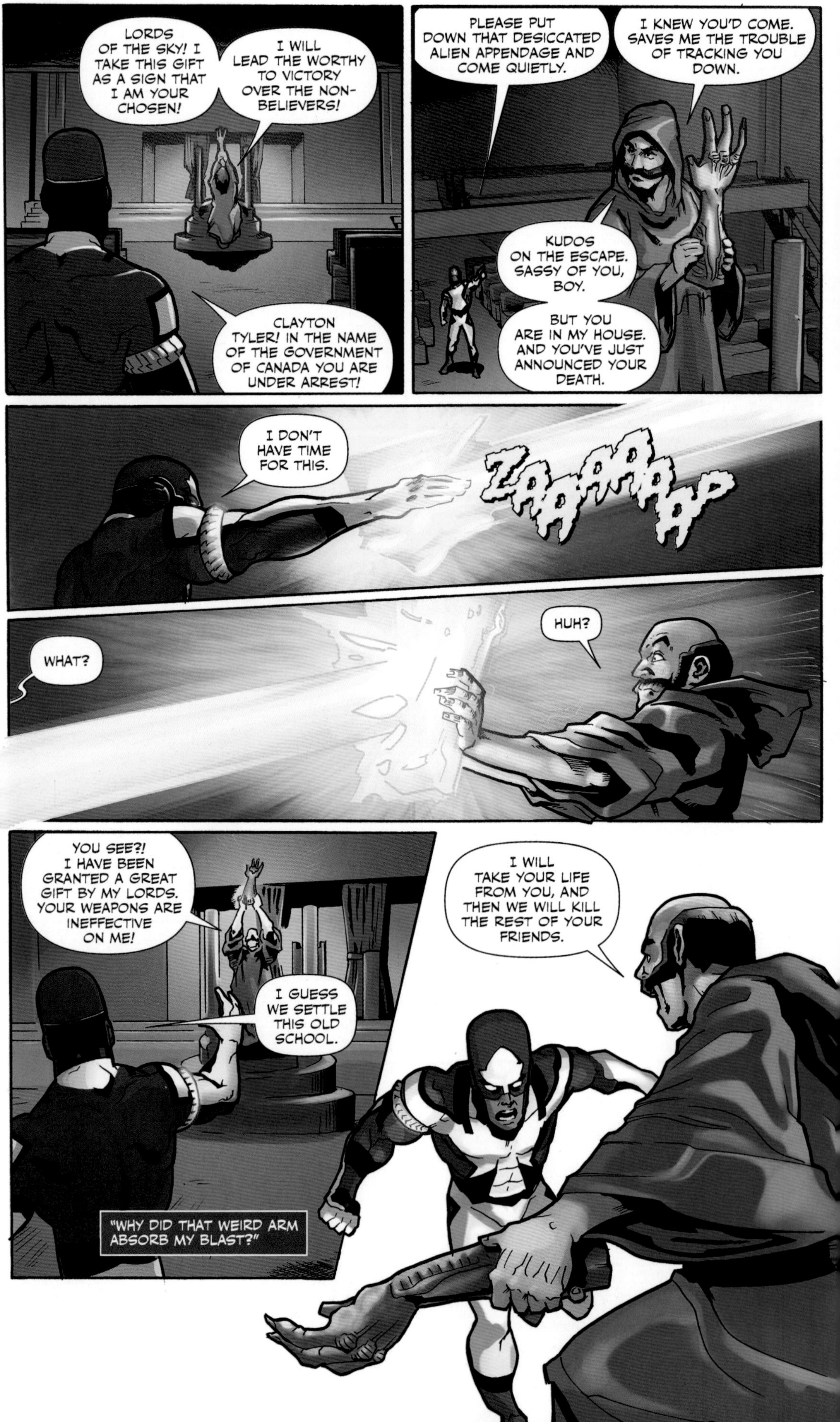
LORDS OF THE SKY! I TAKE THIS GIFT AS A SIGN THAT I AM YOUR CHOSEN!
I WILL LEAD THE WORTHY TO VICTORY OVER THE NON-BELIEVERS!
CLAYTON TYLER! IN THE NAME OF THE GOVERNMENT OF CANADA YOU ARE UNDER ARREST!
PLEASE PUT DOWN THAT DESICCATED ALIEN APPENDAGE AND COME QUIETLY.
I KNEW YOU'D COME. SAVES ME THE TROUBLE OF TRACKING YOU DOWN.
KUDOS ON THE ESCAPE. SASSY OF YOU, BOY.
BUT YOU ARE IN MY HOUSE. AND YOU'VE JUST ANNOUNCED YOUR DEATH.
I DON'T HAVE TIME FOR THIS.
ZAAAAAAP
WHAT?
HUH?
YOU SEE?! I HAVE BEEN GRANTED A GREAT GIFT BY MY LORDS. YOUR WEAPONS ARE INEFFECTIVE ON ME!
I GUESS WE SETTLE THIS OLD SCHOOL.
"WHY DID THAT WEIRD ARM ABSORB MY BLAST?"
I WILL TAKE YOUR LIFE FROM YOU, AND THEN WE WILL KILL THE REST OF YOUR FRIENDS.

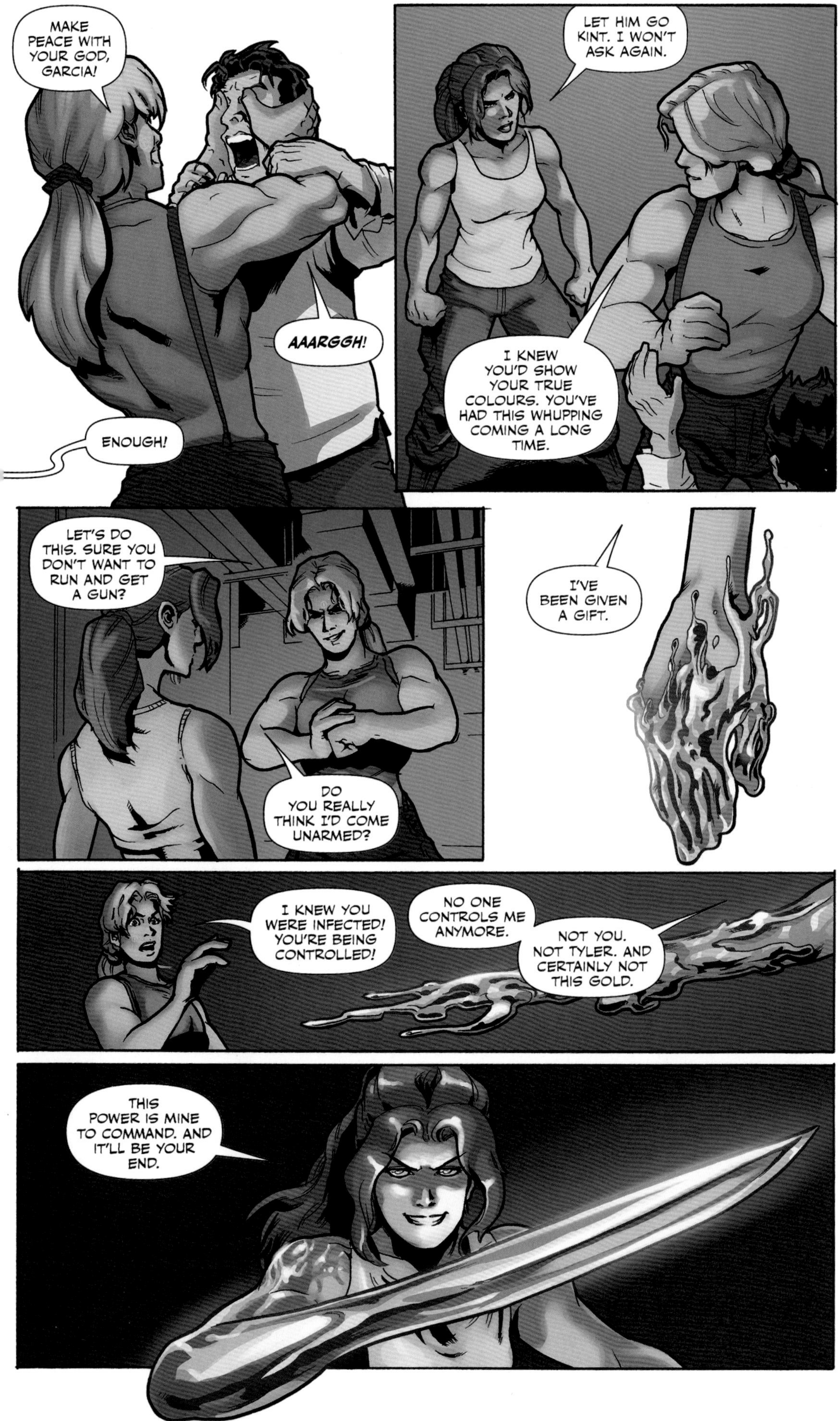
MAKE PEACE WITH YOUR GOD, GARCIA!
AAARGGH!
ENOUGH!
LET HIM GO KINT. I WON'T ASK AGAIN.
I KNEW YOU'D SHOW YOUR TRUE COLOURS. YOU'VE HAD THIS WHUPPING COMING A LONG TIME.
LET'S DO THIS. SURE YOU DON'T WANT TO RUN AND GET A GUN?
DO YOU REALLY THINK I'D COME UNARMED?
I'VE BEEN GIVEN A GIFT.
I KNEW YOU WERE INFECTED! YOU'RE BEING CONTROLLED!
NO ONE CONTROLS ME ANYMORE.
NOT YOU. NOT TYLER. AND CERTAINLY NOT THIS GOLD.
THIS POWER IS MINE TO COMMAND. AND IT'LL BE YOUR END.

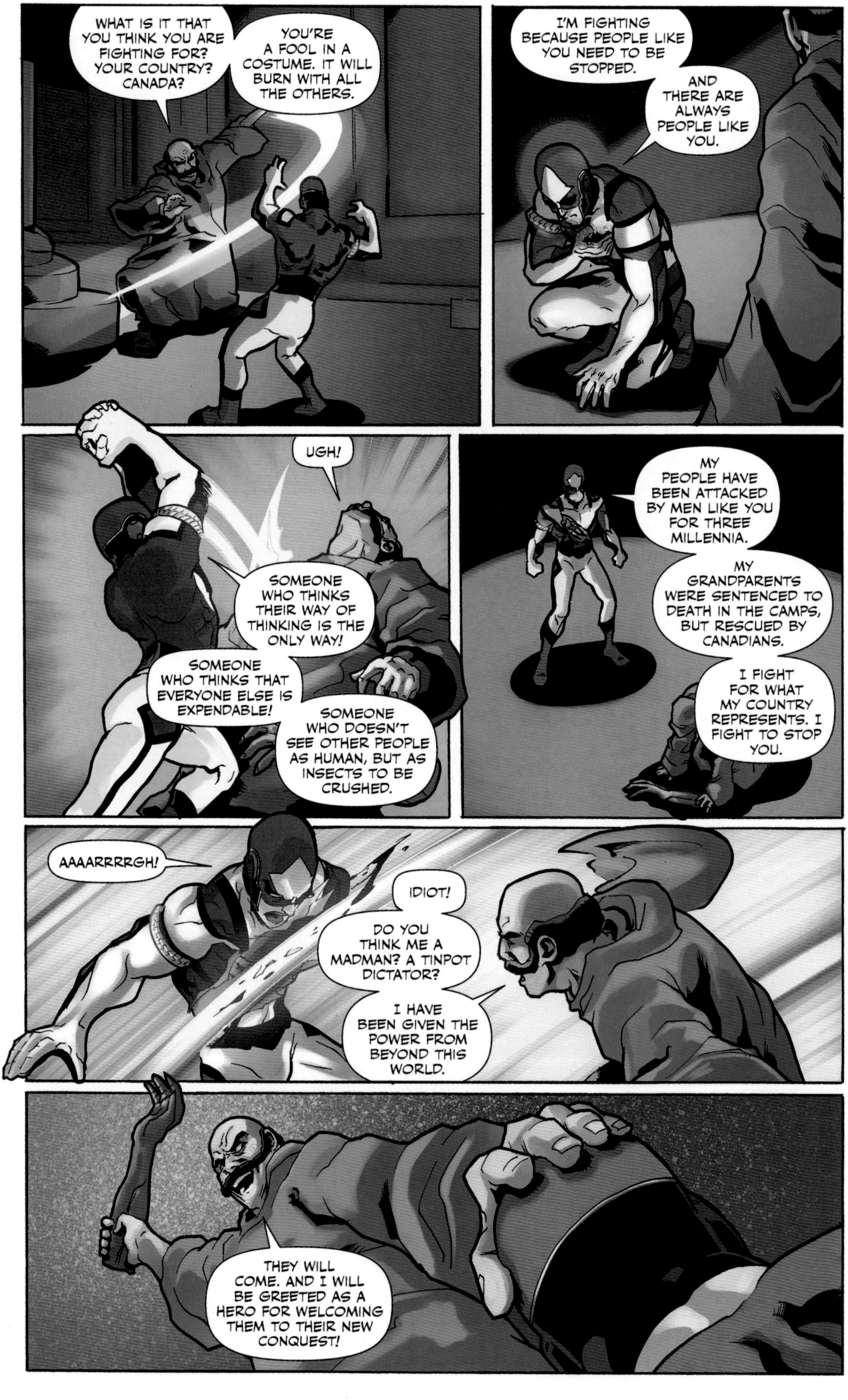
WHAT IS IT THAT YOU THINK YOU ARE FIGHTING FOR? YOUR COUNTRY? CANADA?
YOU'RE A FOOL IN A COSTUME. IT WILL BURN WITH ALL THE OTHERS.
I'M FIGHTING BECAUSE PEOPLE LIKE YOU NEED TO BE STOPPED.
AND THERE ARE ALWAYS PEOPLE LIKE YOU.
UGH!
SOMEONE WHO THINKS THEIR WAY OF THINKING IS THE ONLY WAY!
SOMEONE WHO THINKS THAT EVERYONE ELSE IS EXPENDABLE!
SOMEONE WHO DOESN'T SEE OTHER PEOPLE AS HUMAN, BUT AS INSECTS TO BE CRUSHED.
MY PEOPLE HAVE BEEN ATTACKED BY MEN LIKE YOU FOR THREE MILLENNIA.
MY GRANDPARENTS WERE SENTENCED TO DEATH IN THE CAMPS, BUT RESCUED BY CANADIANS.
I FIGHT FOR WHAT MY COUNTRY REPRESENTS. I FIGHT TO STOP YOU.
AAAARRRRGH!
IDIOT!
DO YOU THINK ME A MADMAN? A TINPOT DICTATOR?
I HAVE BEEN GIVEN THE POWER FROM BEYOND THIS WORLD.
THEY WILL COME. AND I WILL BE GREETED AS A HERO FOR WELCOMING THEM TO THEIR NEW CONQUEST!

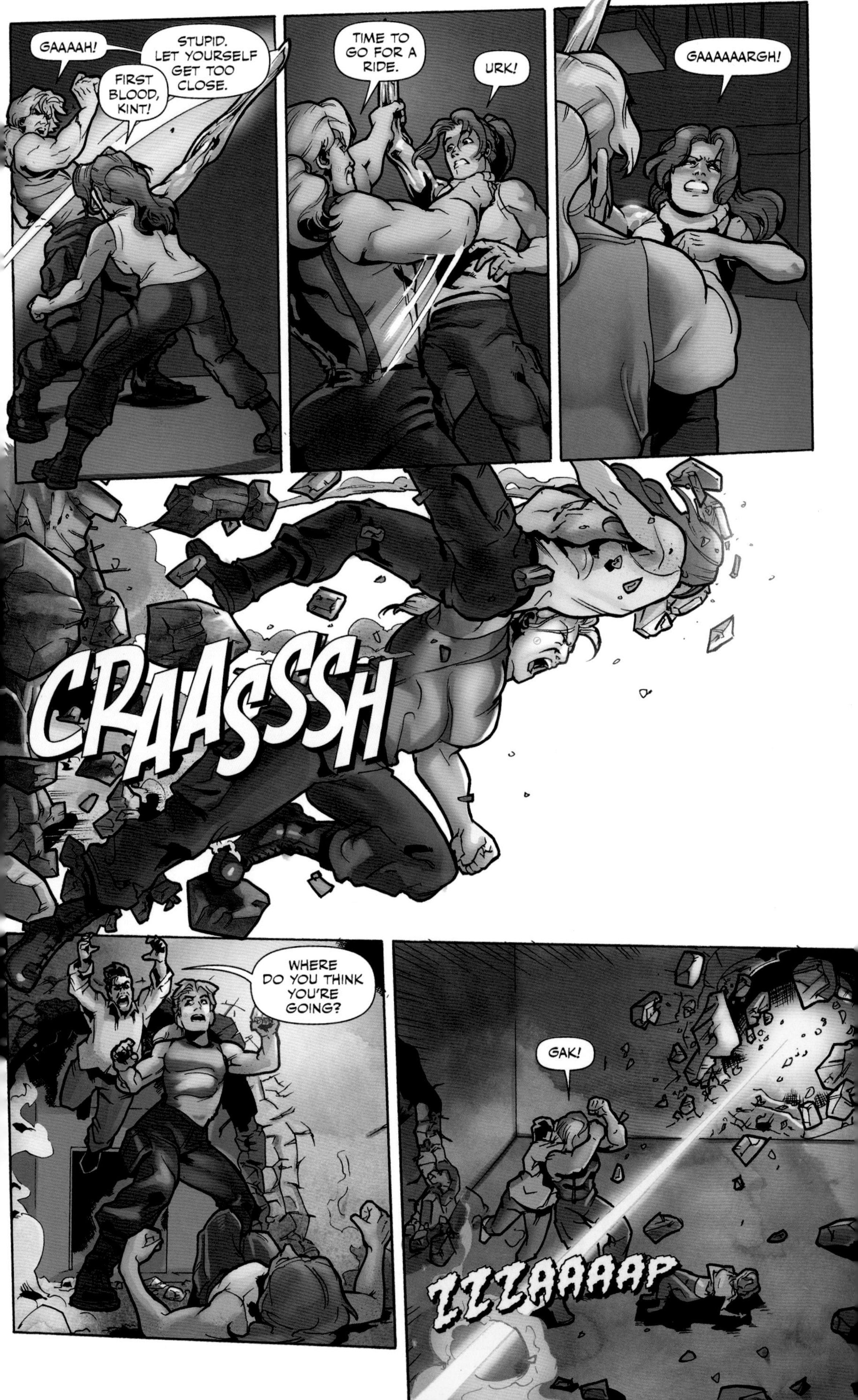
GAAAAH!
STUPID. LET YOURSELF GET TOO CLOSE.
FIRST BLOOD, KINT!
TIME TO GO FOR A RIDE.
URK!
GAAAAAARGH!
CRAASSSH
WHERE DO YOU THINK YOU'RE GOING?
GAK!
ZZZAAAAP

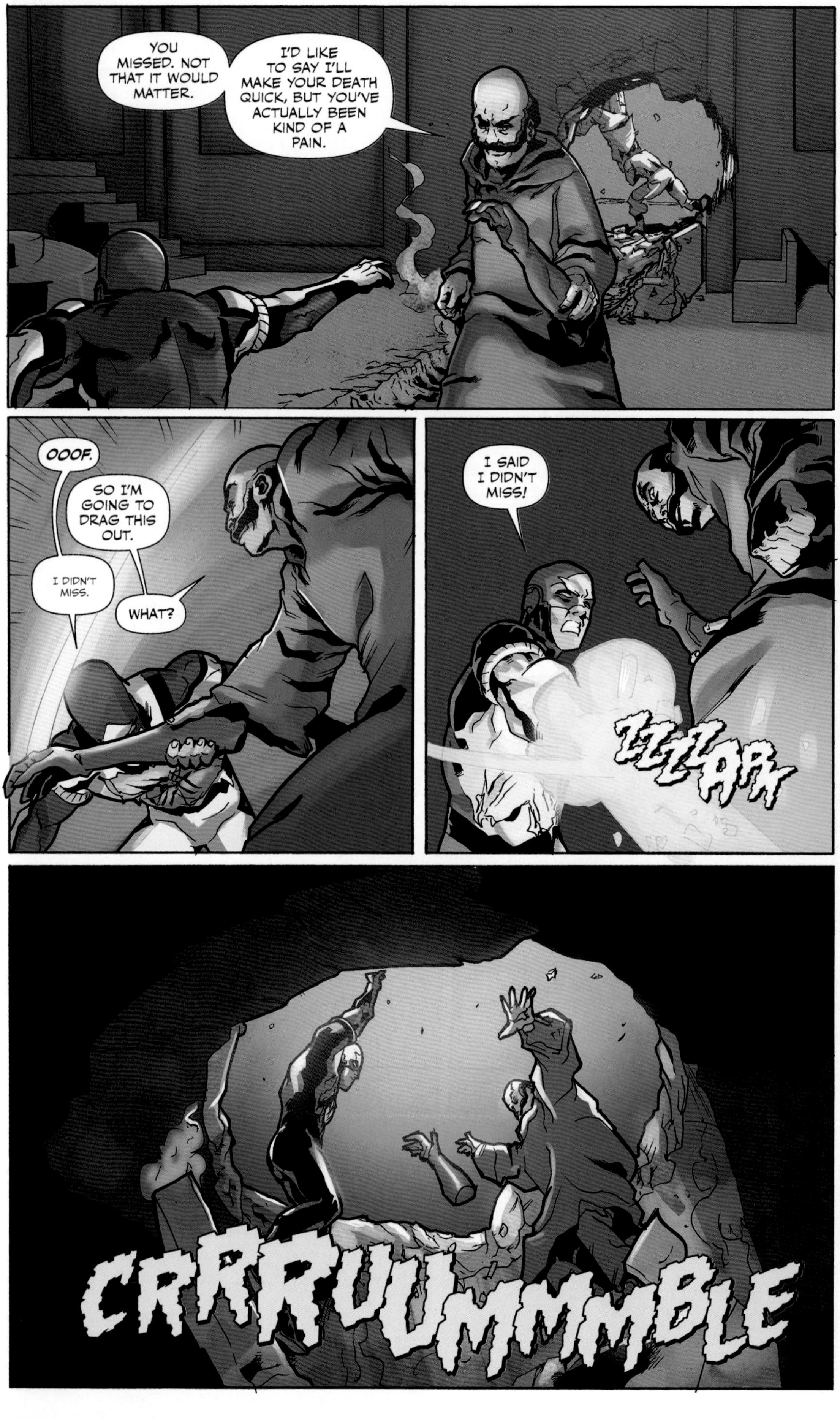
YOU MISSED. NOT THAT IT WOULD MATTER.
I'D LIKE TO SAY I'LL MAKE YOUR DEATH QUICK, BUT YOU'VE ACTUALLY BEEN KIND OF A PAIN.
OOOF.
SO I'M GOING TO DRAG THIS OUT.
I DIDN'T MISS.
WHAT?
I SAID I DIDN'T MISS!
ZZZZARK
CRRRUUMMMBLE

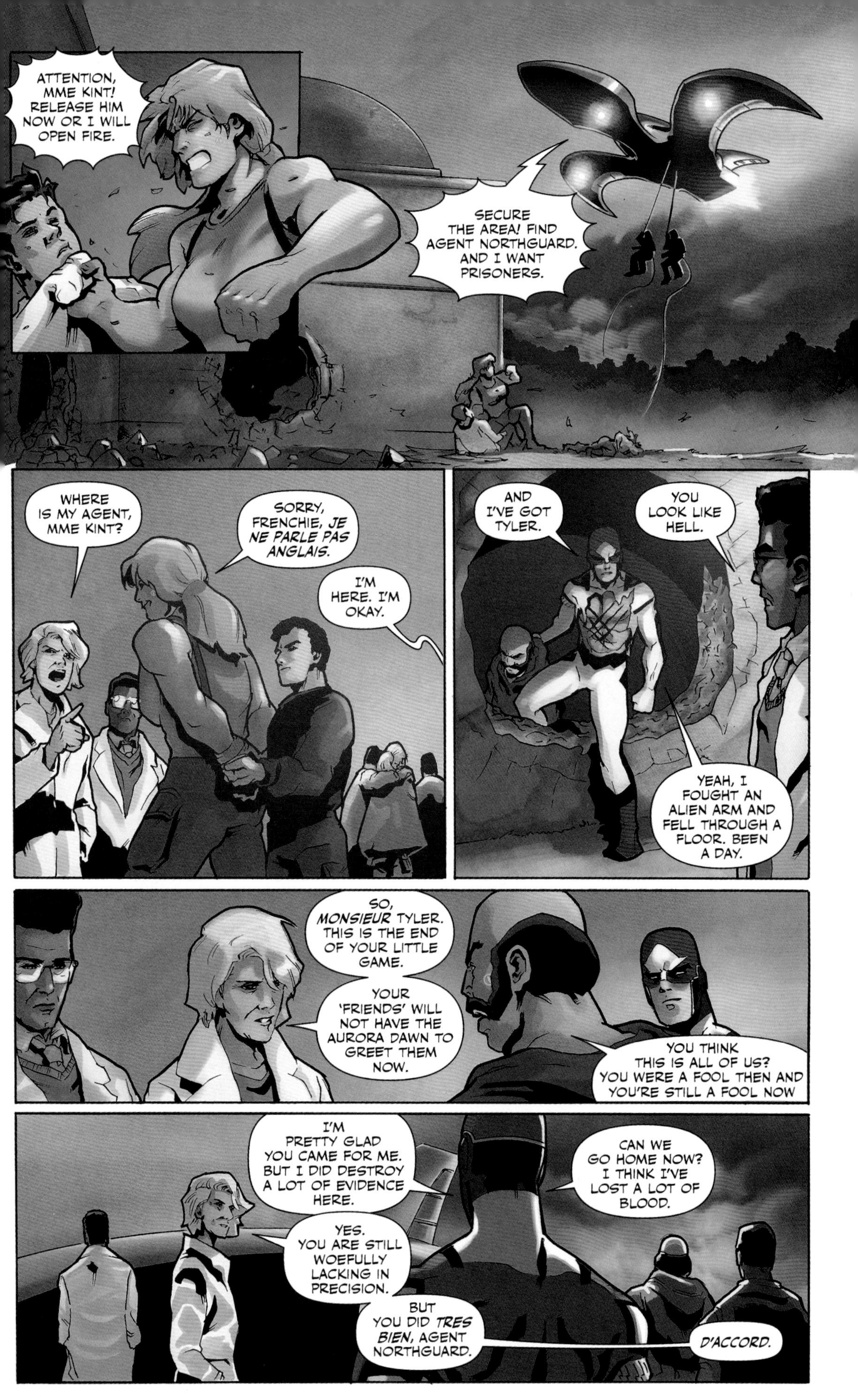

ATTENTION, MME KINT! RELEASE HIM NOW OR I WILL OPEN FIRE.
SECURE THE AREA! FIND AGENT NORTHGUARD. AND I WANT PRISONERS.
WHERE IS MY AGENT, MME KINT?
SORRY, FRENCHIE, *JE NE PARLE PAS ANGLAIS*.
I'M HERE. I'M OKAY.
AND I'VE GOT TYLER.
YOU LOOK LIKE HELL.
YEAH, I FOUGHT AN ALIEN ARM AND FELL THROUGH A FLOOR. BEEN A DAY.
SO, *MONSIEUR* TYLER. THIS IS THE END OF YOUR LITTLE GAME.
YOUR 'FRIENDS' WILL NOT HAVE THE AURORA DAWN TO GREET THEM NOW.
YOU THINK THIS IS ALL OF US? YOU WERE A FOOL THEN AND YOU'RE STILL A FOOL NOW
I'M PRETTY GLAD YOU CAME FOR ME. BUT I DID DESTROY A LOT OF EVIDENCE HERE.
CAN WE GO HOME NOW? I THINK I'VE LOST A LOT OF BLOOD.
YES. YOU ARE STILL WOEFULLY LACKING IN PRECISION.
BUT YOU DID *TRES BIEN*, AGENT NORTHGUARD.
D'ACCORD.

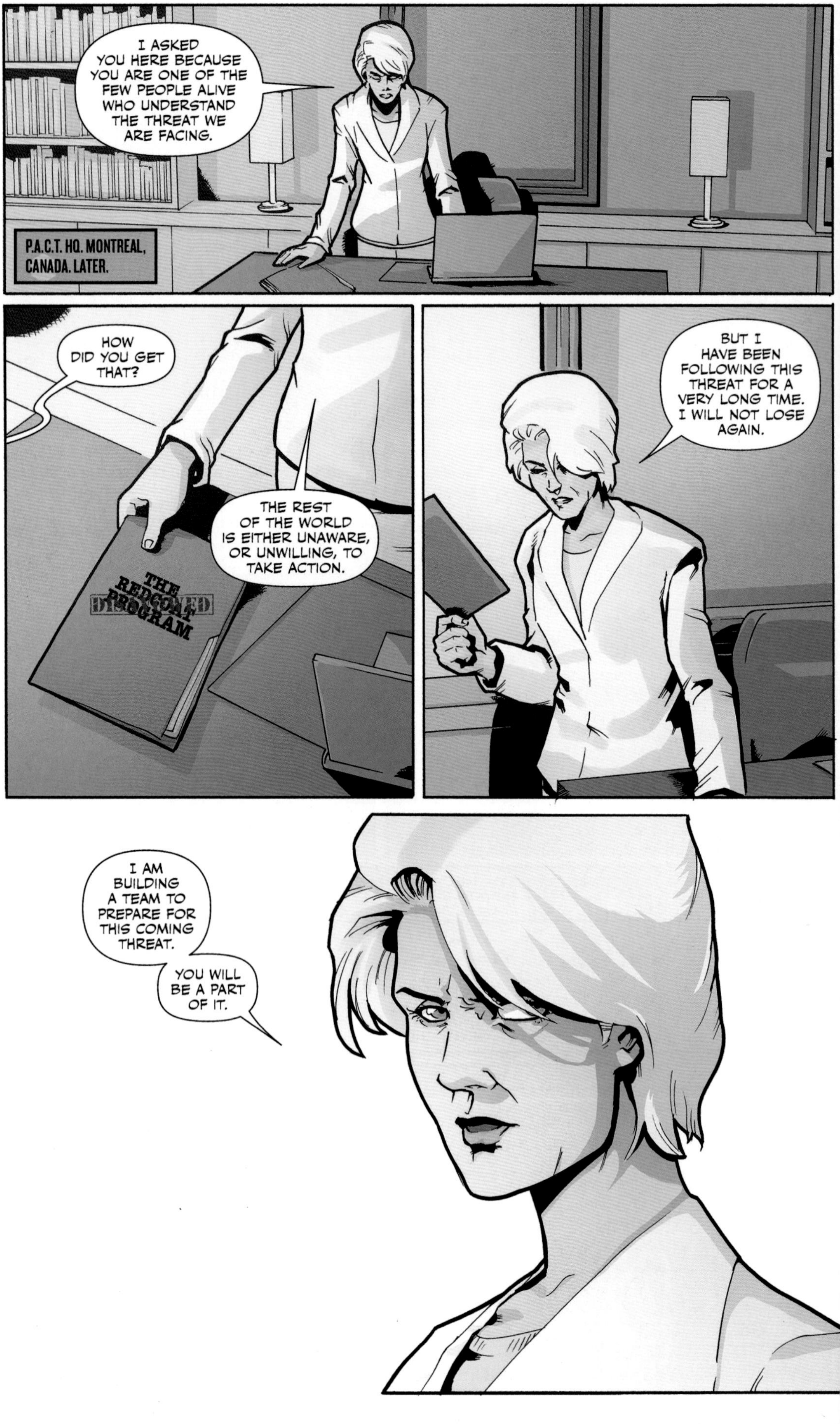
I ASKED YOU HERE BECAUSE YOU ARE ONE OF THE FEW PEOPLE ALIVE WHO UNDERSTAND THE THREAT WE ARE FACING.
P.A.C.T. HQ. MONTREAL, CANADA. LATER.
HOW DID YOU GET THAT?
THE REST OF THE WORLD IS EITHER UNAWARE, OR UNWILLING, TO TAKE ACTION.
BUT I HAVE BEEN FOLLOWING THIS THREAT FOR A VERY LONG TIME. I WILL NOT LOSE AGAIN.
I AM BUILDING A TEAM TO PREPARE FOR THIS COMING THREAT.
YOU WILL BE A PART OF IT.

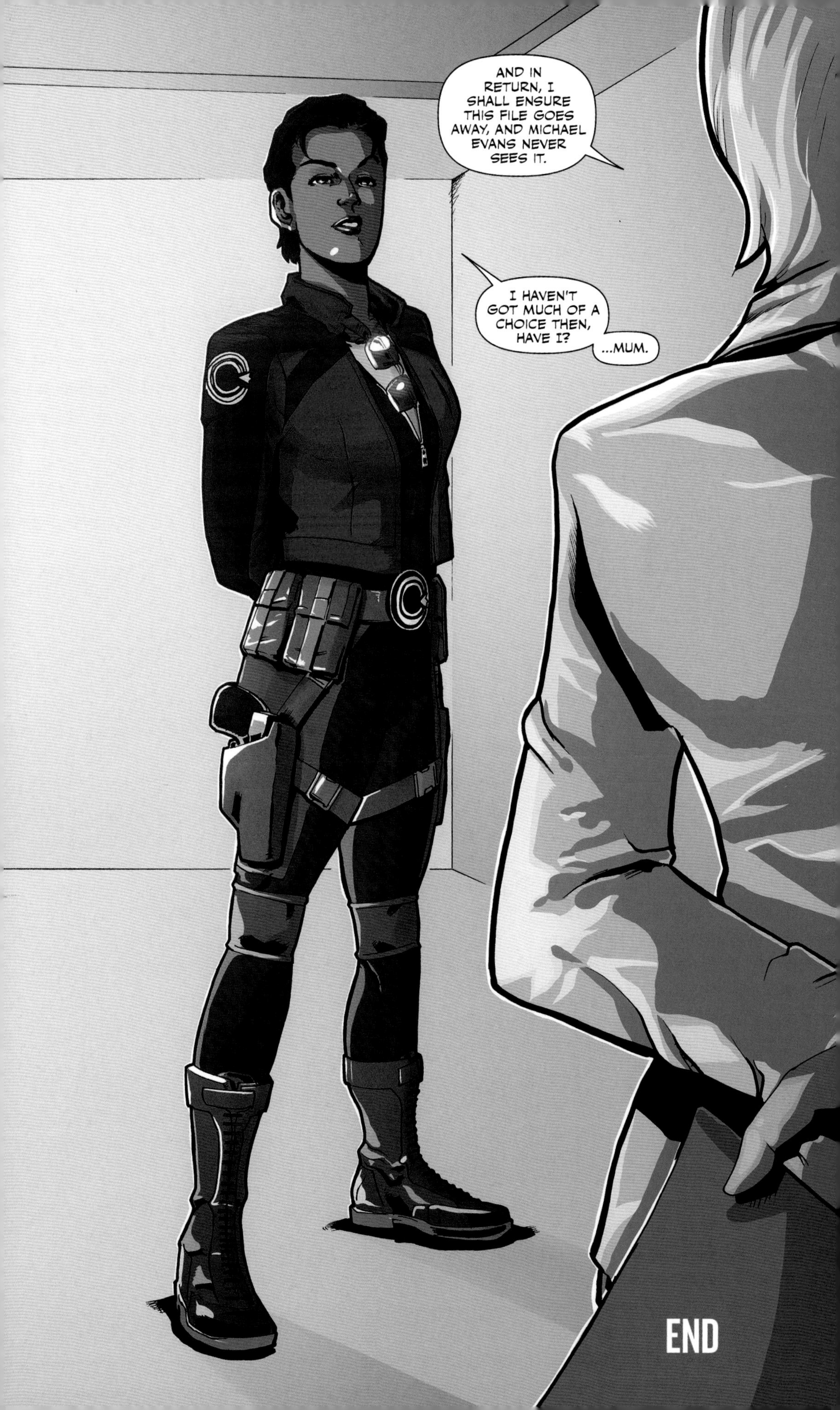
AND IN RETURN, I SHALL ENSURE THIS FILE GOES AWAY, AND MICHAEL EVANS NEVER SEES IT.
I HAVEN'T GOT MUCH OF A CHOICE THEN, HAVE I?
...MUM.
END

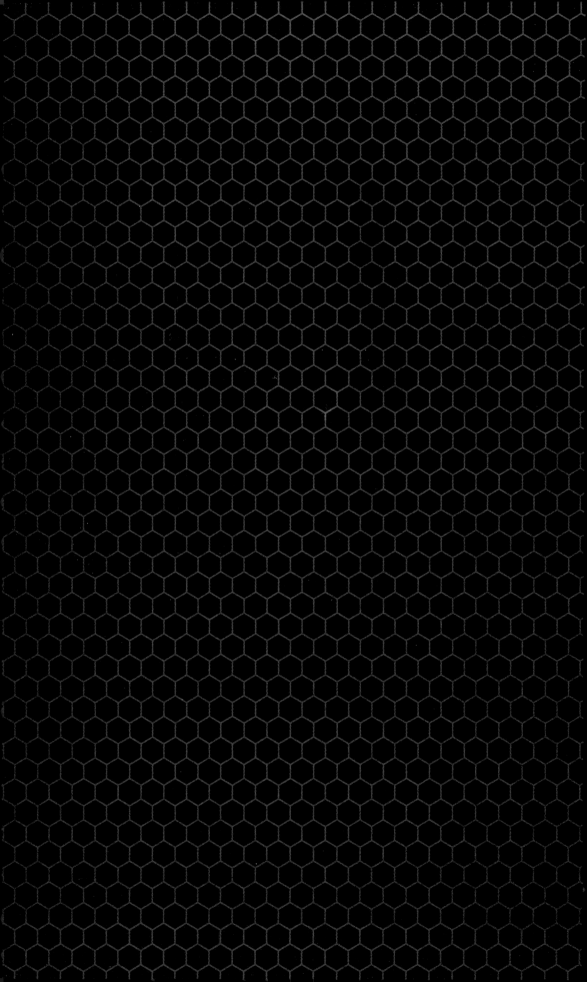

...EVERY PROBLEM
LOOKS LIKE A NAIL

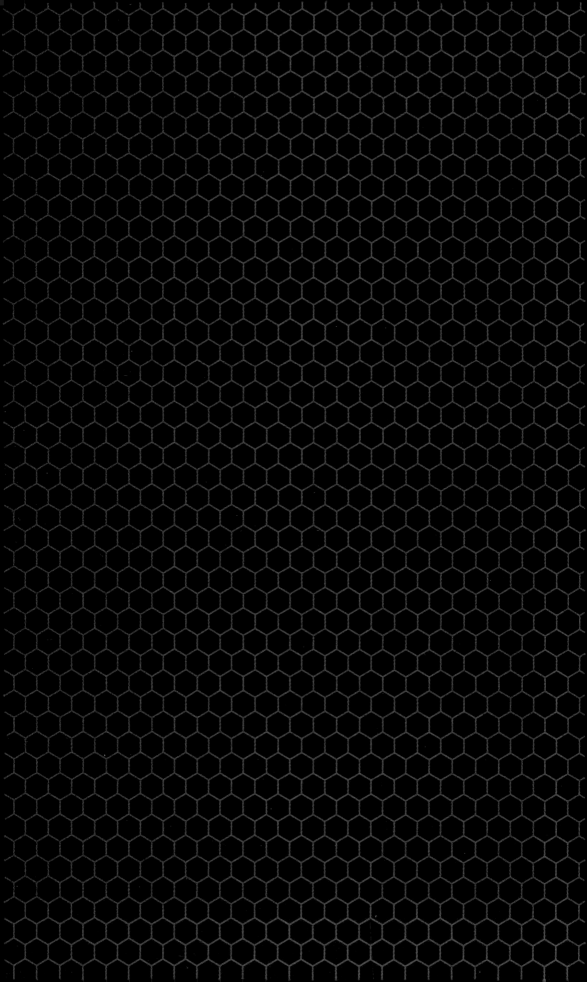

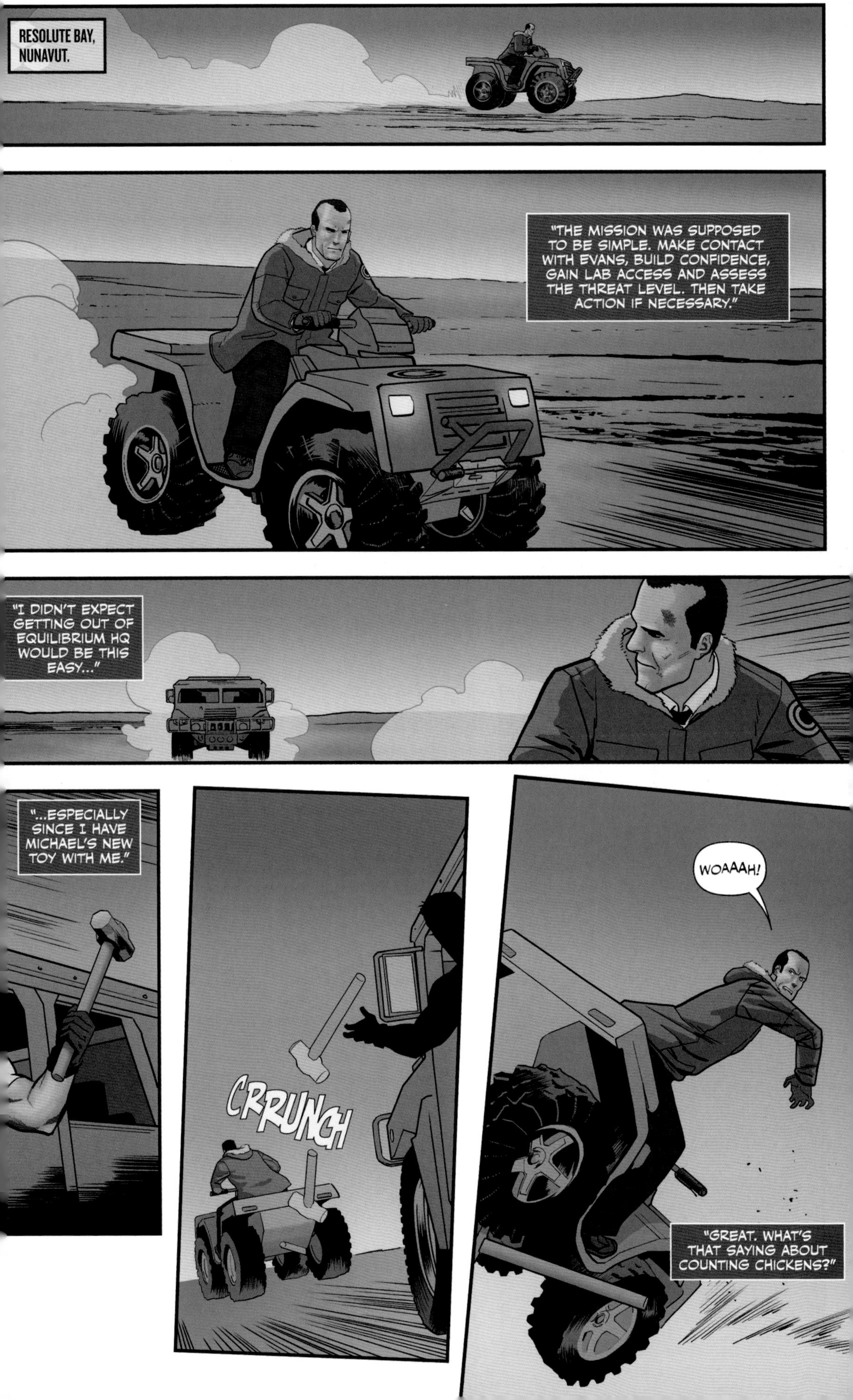
RESOLUTE BAY, NUNAVUT.
"THE MISSION WAS SUPPOSED TO BE SIMPLE. MAKE CONTACT WITH EVANS, BUILD CONFIDENCE, GAIN LAB ACCESS AND ASSESS THE THREAT LEVEL. THEN TAKE ACTION IF NECESSARY."
"I DIDN'T EXPECT GETTING OUT OF EQUILIBRIUM HQ WOULD BE THIS EASY..."
"...ESPECIALLY SINCE I HAVE MICHAEL'S NEW TOY WITH ME."
CRRUNCH
WOAAAH!
"GREAT. WHAT'S THAT SAYING ABOUT COUNTING CHICKENS?"

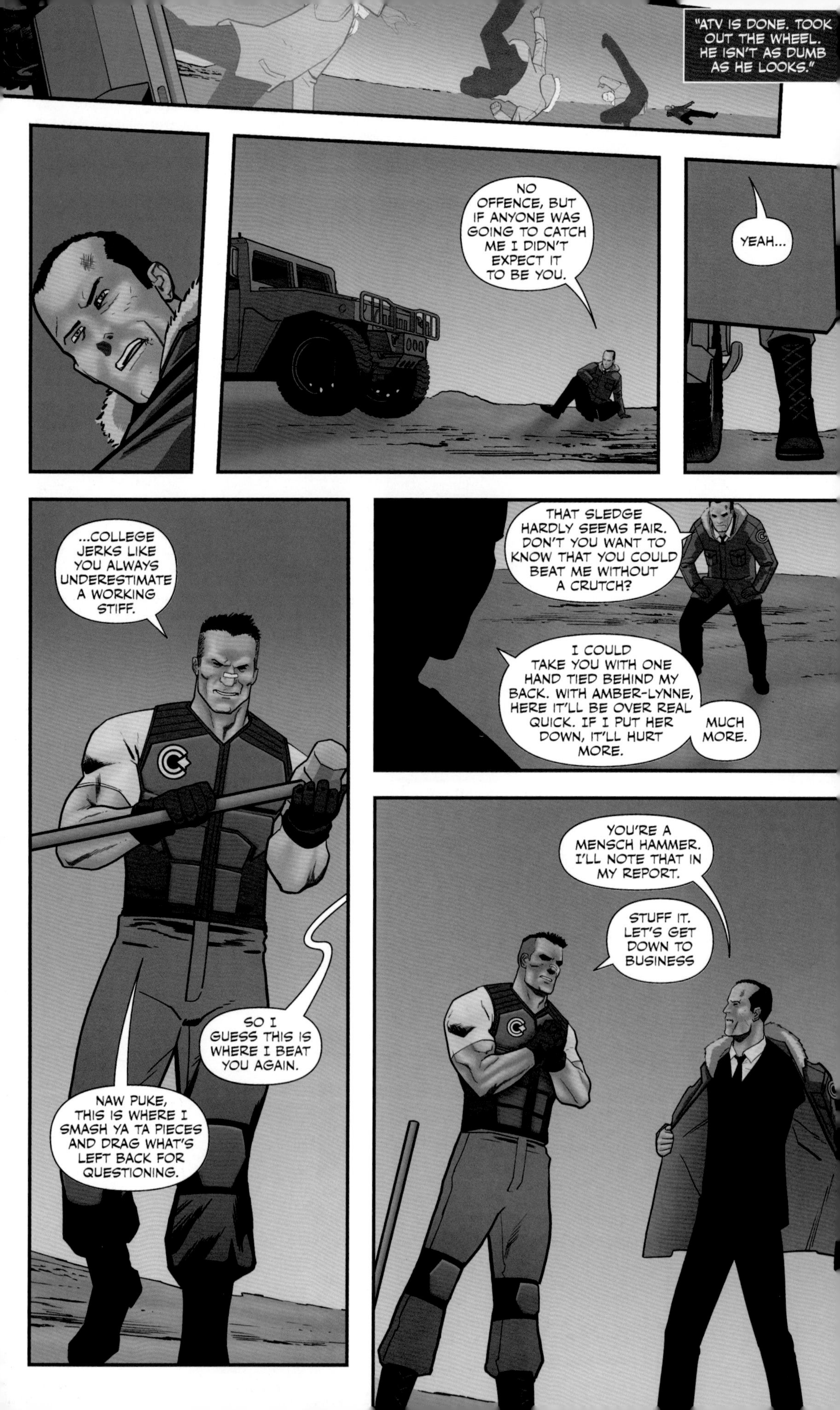
"ATV IS DONE. TOOK OUT THE WHEEL. HE ISN'T AS DUMB AS HE LOOKS."
NO OFFENCE, BUT IF ANYONE WAS GOING TO CATCH ME I DIDN'T EXPECT IT TO BE YOU.
YEAH...
...COLLEGE JERKS LIKE YOU ALWAYS UNDERESTIMATE A WORKING STIFF.
SO I GUESS THIS IS WHERE I BEAT YOU AGAIN.
NAW PUKE, THIS IS WHERE I SMASH YA TA PIECES AND DRAG WHAT'S LEFT BACK FOR QUESTIONING.
THAT SLEDGE HARDLY SEEMS FAIR. DON'T YOU WANT TO KNOW THAT YOU COULD BEAT ME WITHOUT A CRUTCH?
I COULD TAKE YOU WITH ONE HAND TIED BEHIND MY BACK. WITH AMBER-LYNNE, HERE IT'LL BE OVER REAL QUICK. IF I PUT HER DOWN, IT'LL HURT MORE.
MUCH MORE.
YOU'RE A MENSCH HAMMER. I'LL NOTE THAT IN MY REPORT.
STUFF IT. LET'S GET DOWN TO BUSINESS

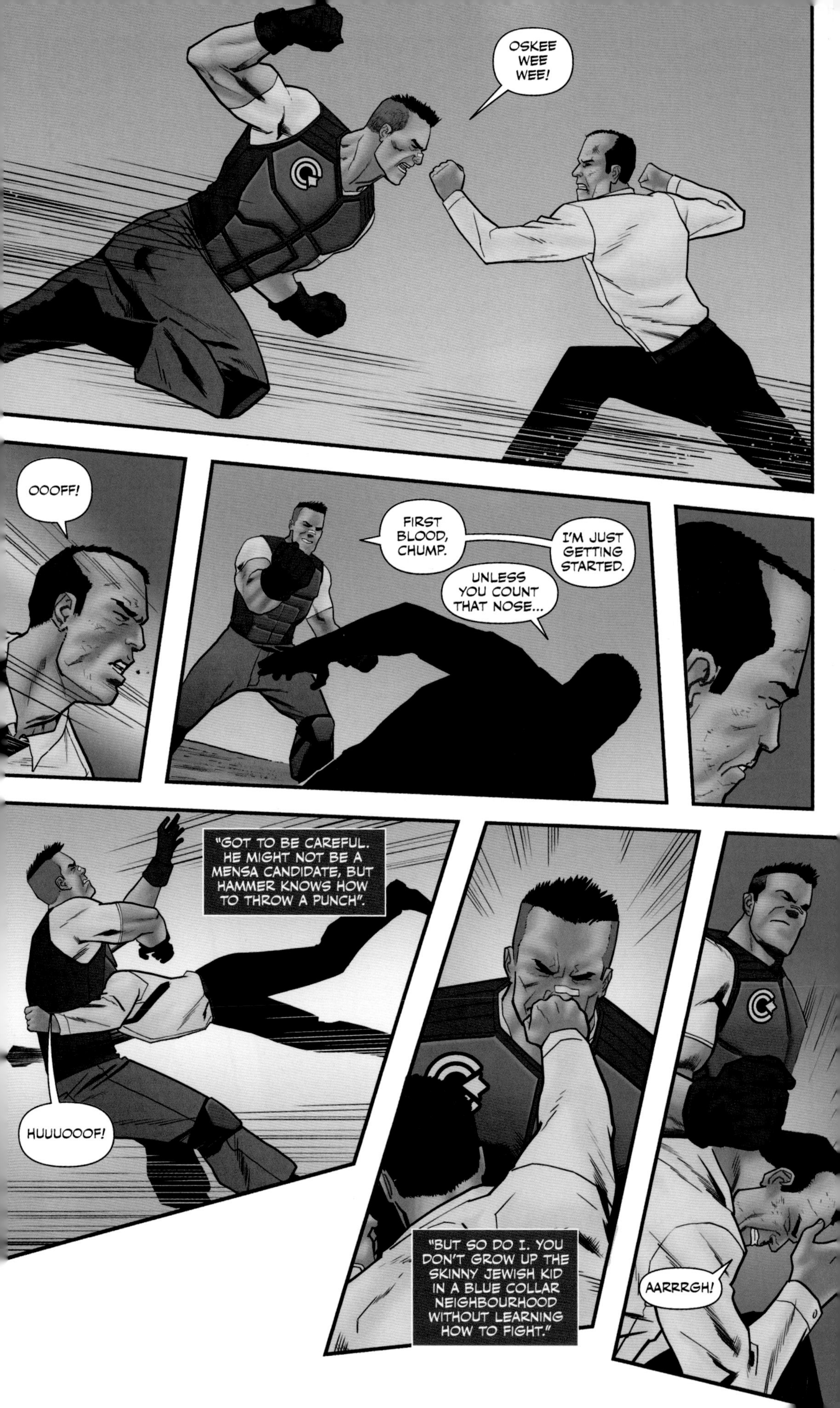
OSKEE WEE WEE!
OOOFF!
FIRST BLOOD, CHUMP.
I'M JUST GETTING STARTED.
UNLESS YOU COUNT THAT NOSE...
"GOT TO BE CAREFUL. HE MIGHT NOT BE A MENSA CANDIDATE, BUT HAMMER KNOWS HOW TO THROW A PUNCH".
HUUUOOOF!
"BUT SO DO I. YOU DON'T GROW UP THE SKINNY JEWISH KID IN A BLUE COLLAR NEIGHBOURHOOD WITHOUT LEARNING HOW TO FIGHT."
AARRRGH!

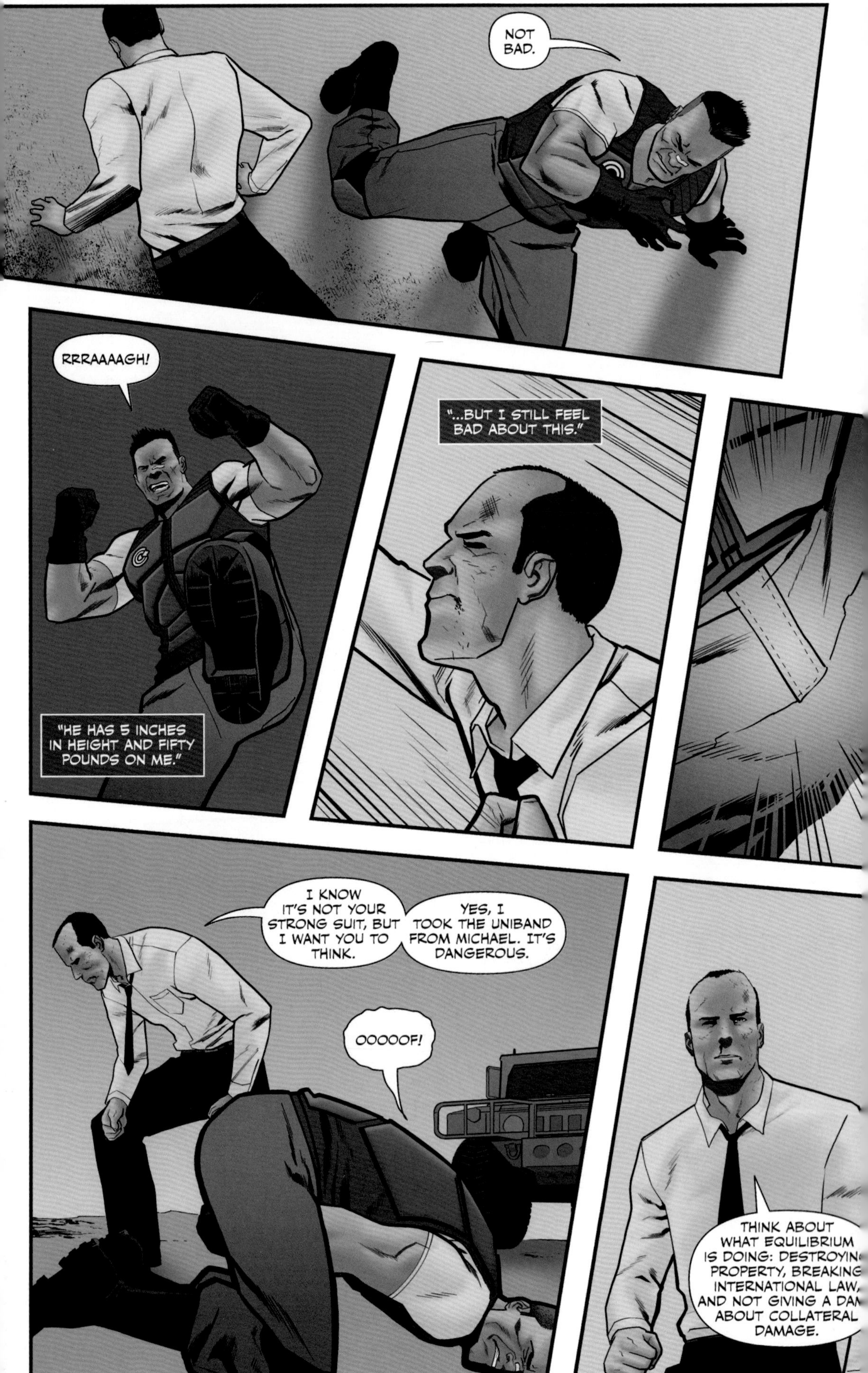
NOT BAD.
RRRAAAAGH!
"HE HAS 5 INCHES IN HEIGHT AND FIFTY POUNDS ON ME."
"...BUT I STILL FEEL BAD ABOUT THIS."
I KNOW IT'S NOT YOUR STRONG SUIT, BUT I WANT YOU TO THINK.
YES, I TOOK THE UNIBAND FROM MICHAEL. IT'S DANGEROUS.
OOOOOF!
THINK ABOUT WHAT EQUILIBRIUM IS DOING: DESTROYIN PROPERTY, BREAKIN INTERNATIONAL LAW, AND NOT GIVING A DAM ABOUT COLLATERAL DAMAGE.

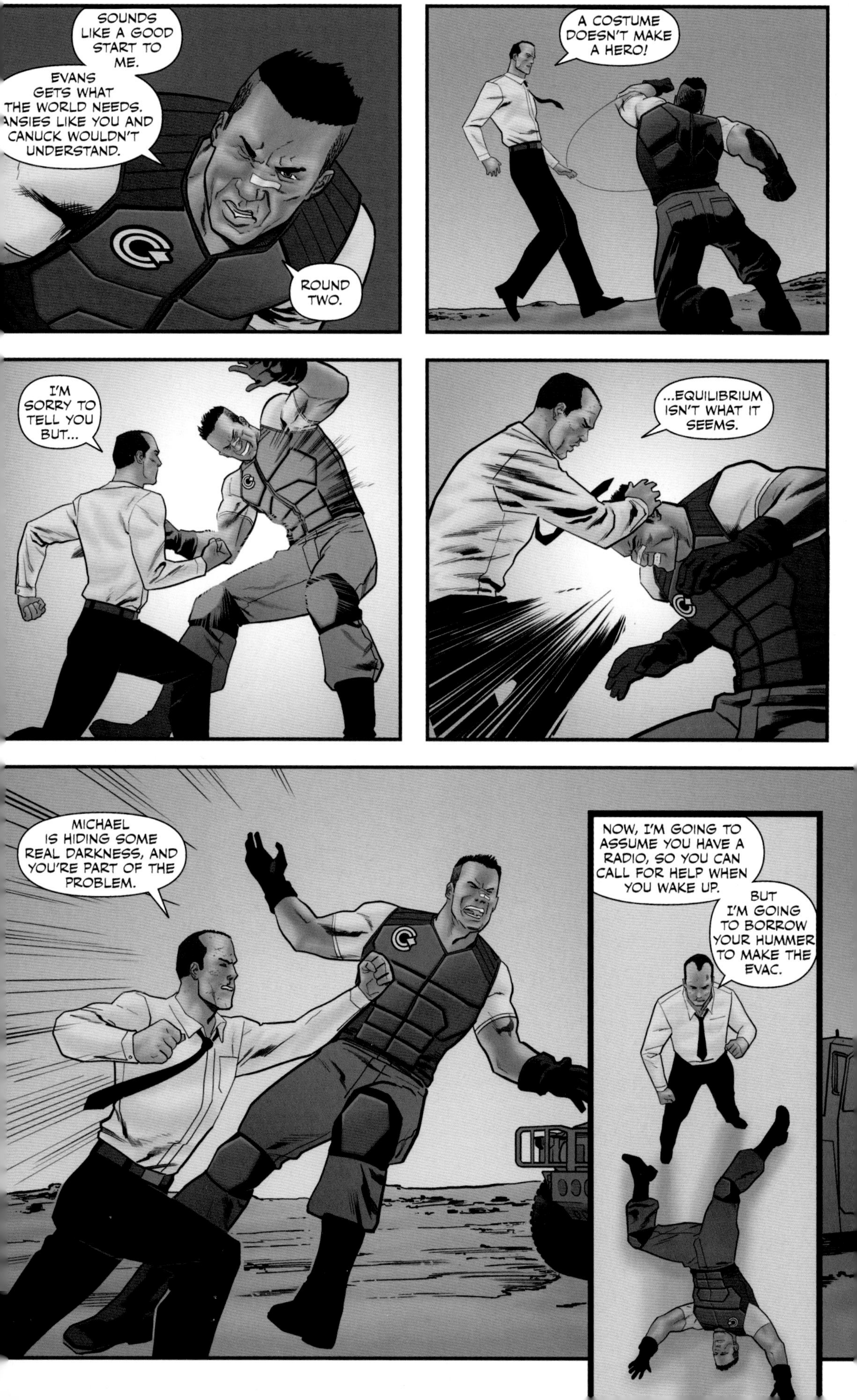
SOUNDS LIKE A GOOD START TO ME.
EVANS GETS WHAT THE WORLD NEEDS. ANSIES LIKE YOU AND CANUCK WOULDN'T UNDERSTAND.
ROUND TWO.
A COSTUME DOESN'T MAKE A HERO!
I'M SORRY TO TELL YOU BUT...
...EQUILIBRIUM ISN'T WHAT IT SEEMS.
MICHAEL IS HIDING SOME REAL DARKNESS, AND YOU'RE PART OF THE PROBLEM.
NOW, I'M GOING TO ASSUME YOU HAVE A RADIO, SO YOU CAN CALL FOR HELP WHEN YOU WAKE UP.
BUT I'M GOING TO BORROW YOUR HUMMER TO MAKE THE EVAC.

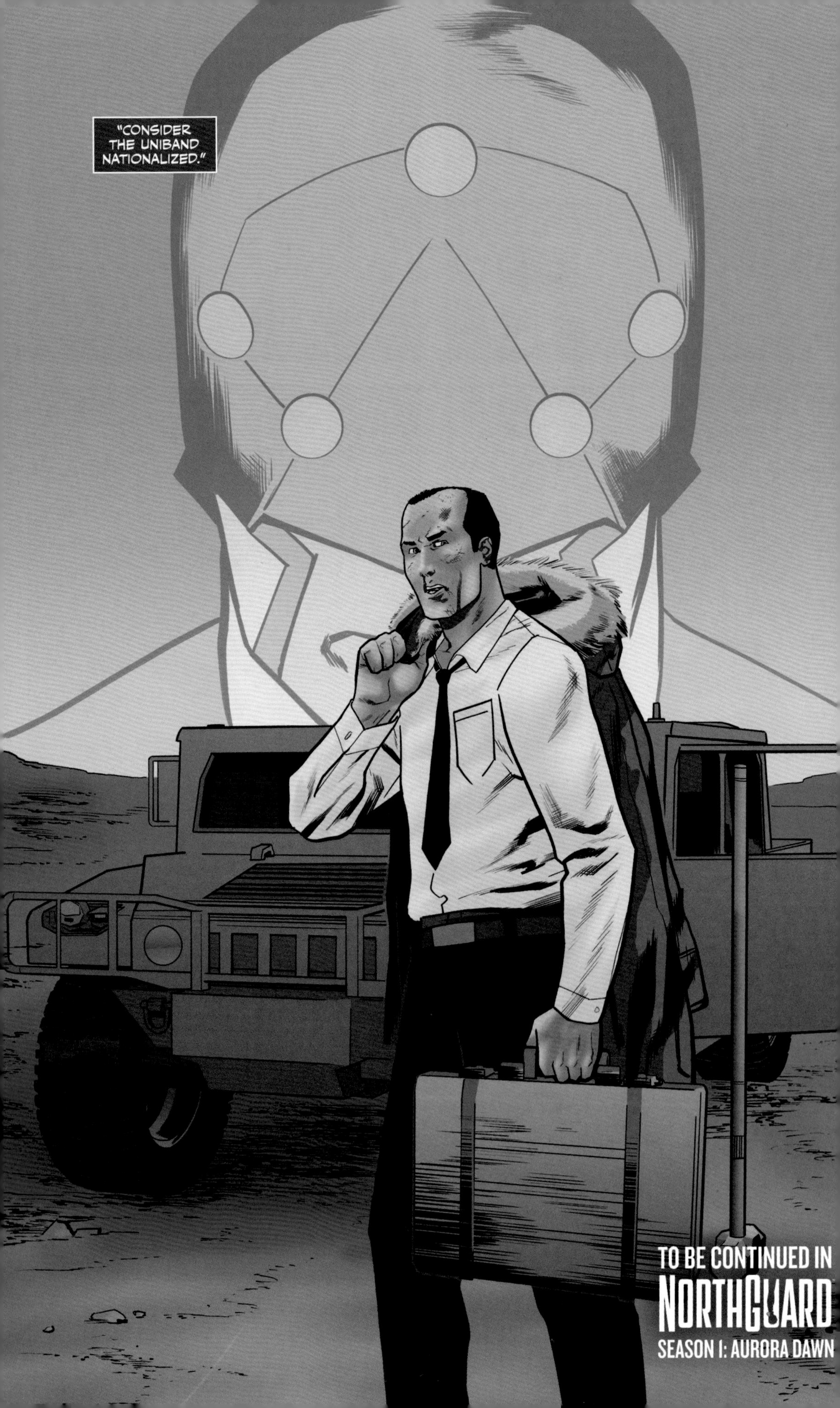

"CONSIDER THE UNIBAND NATIONALIZED."
TO BE CONTINUED IN
NORTHGUARD
SEASON 1: AURORA DAWN

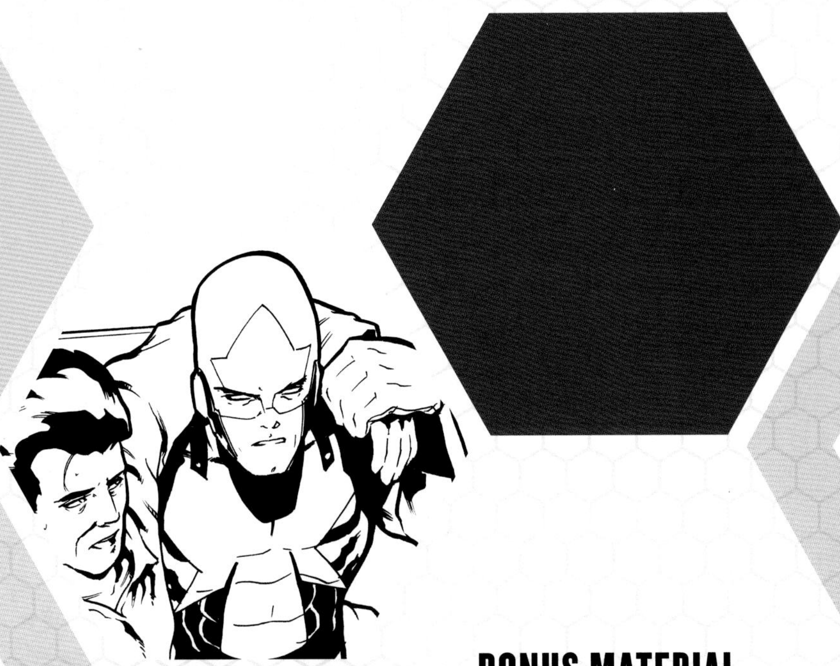

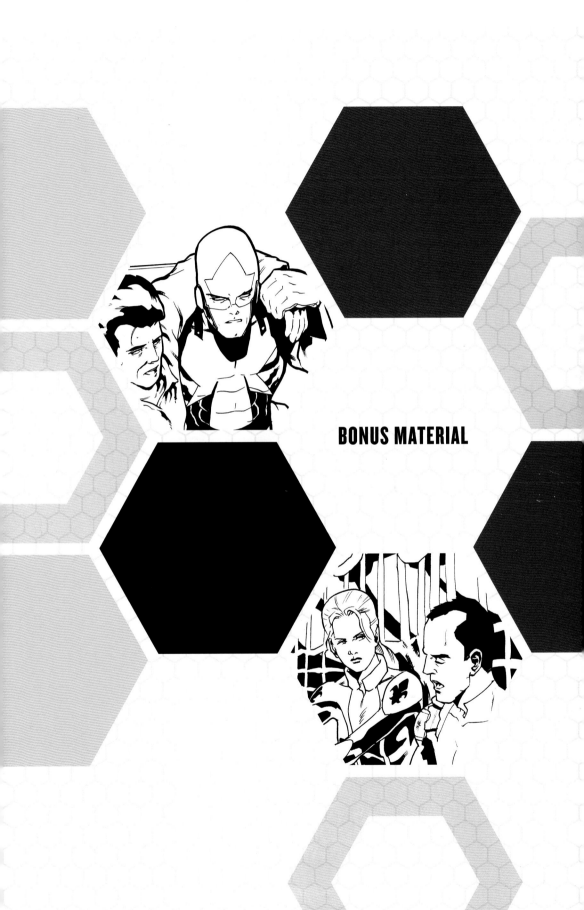

BONUS MATERIAL

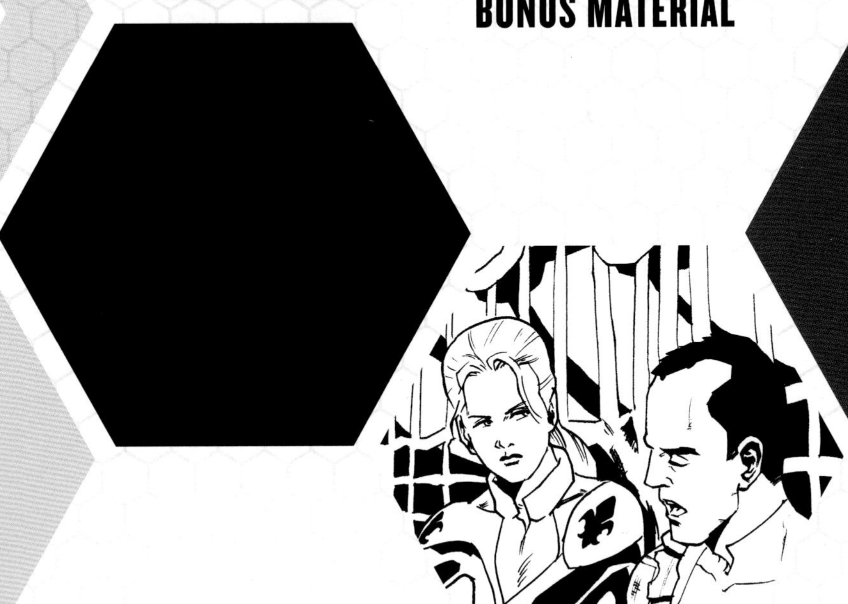

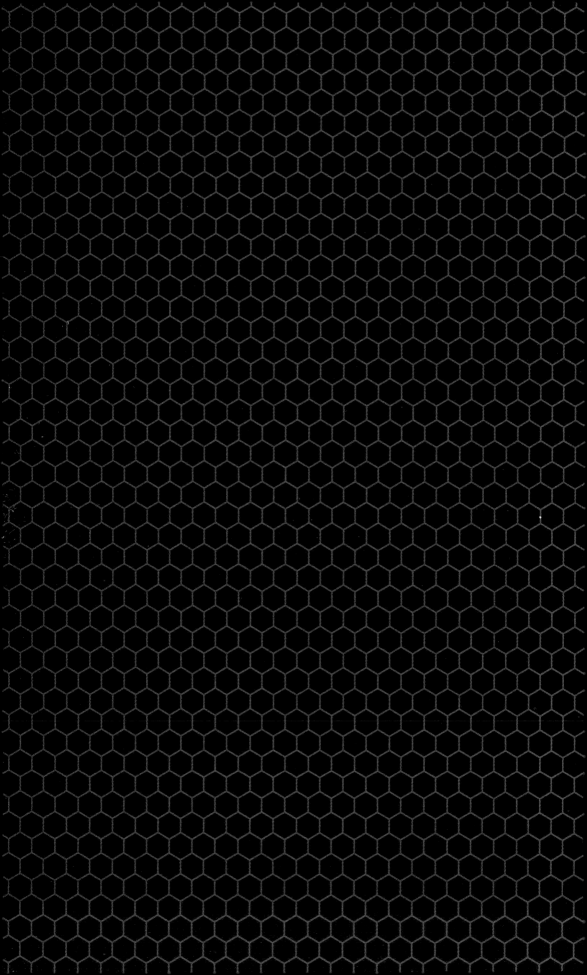

SEASON ONE COVER ART: ISSUE ONE

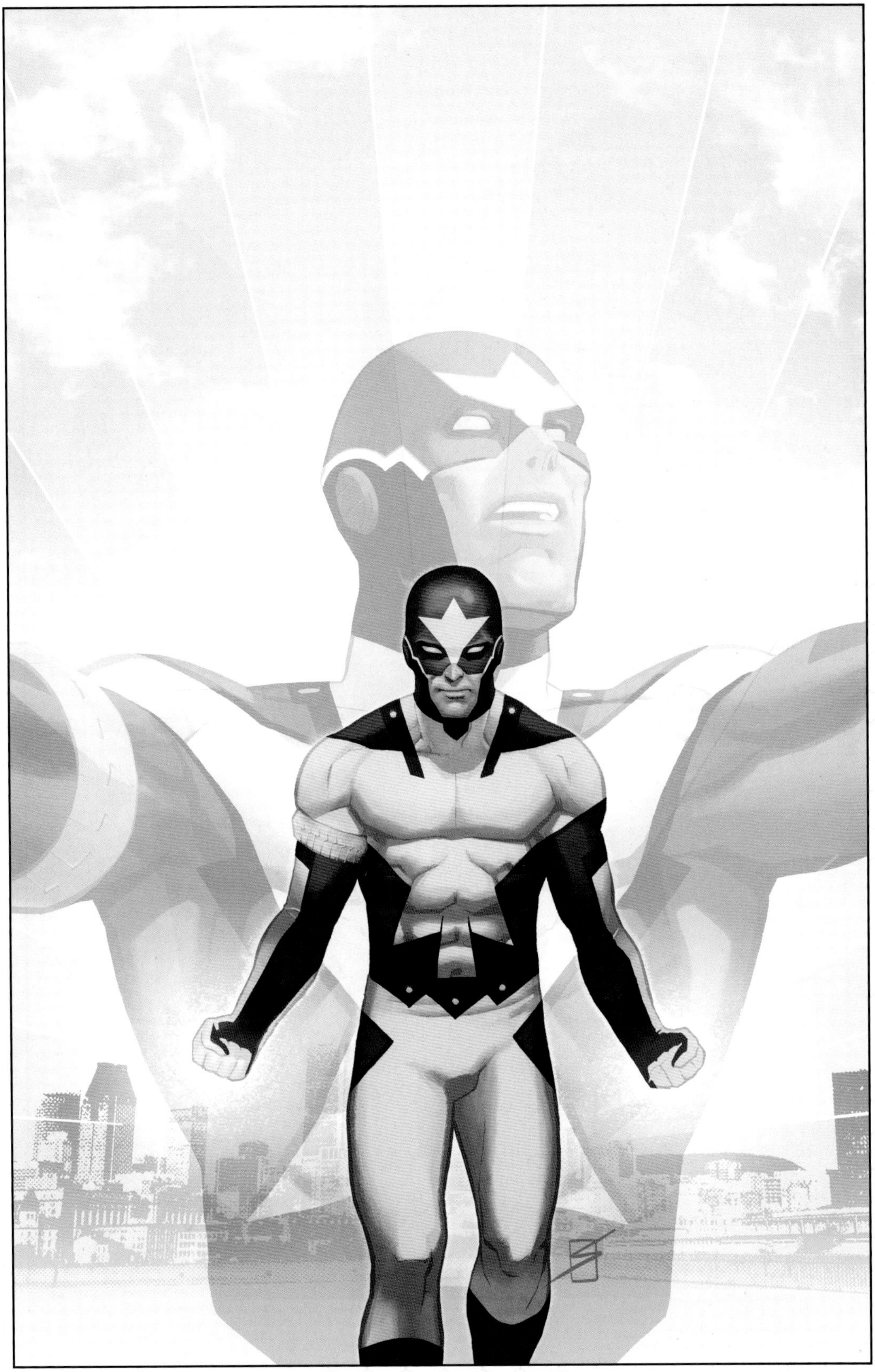

Northguard #1
Cover A
by Ron Salas

SEASON ONE COVER ART: ISSUE ONE VARIANT

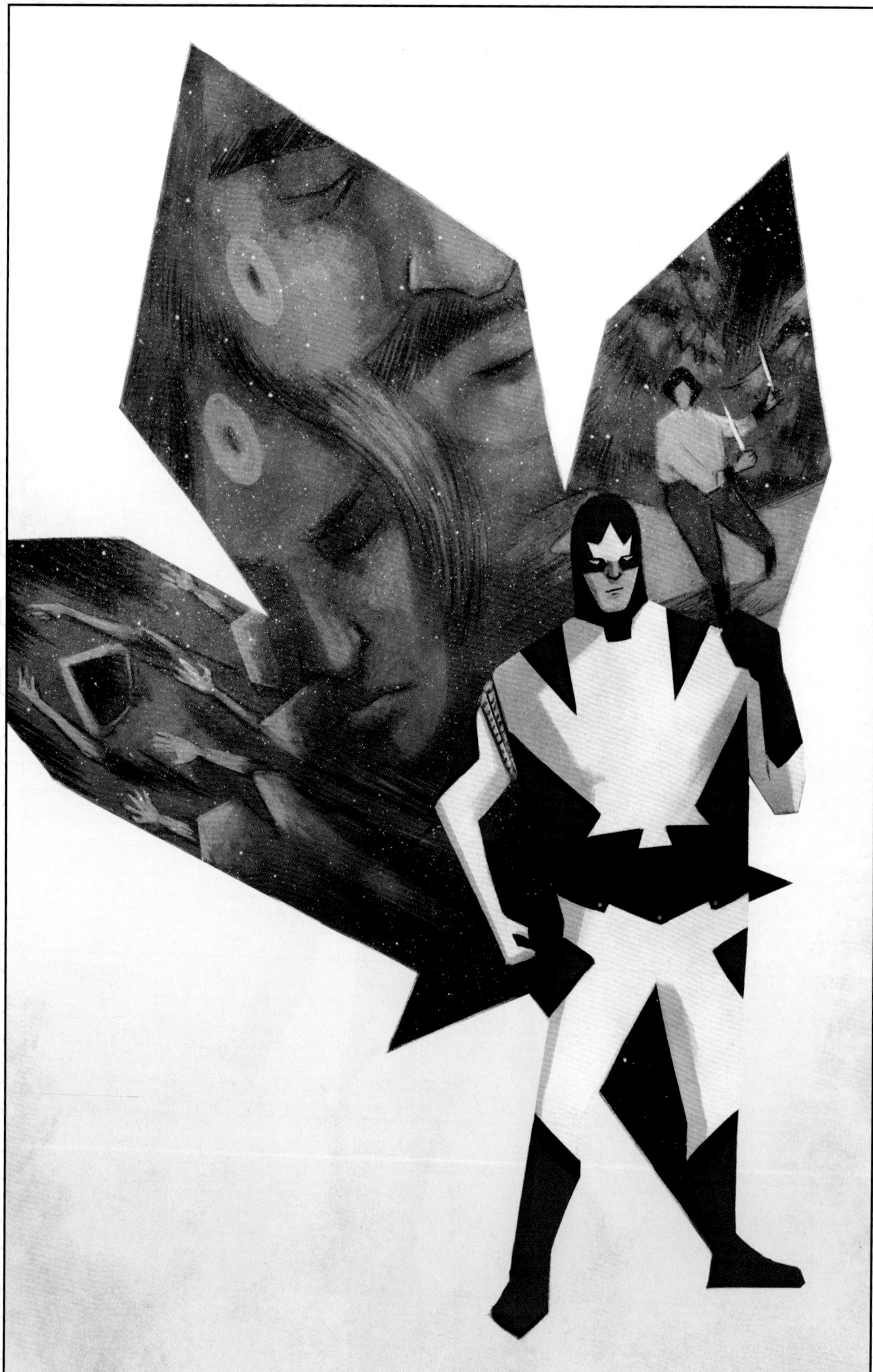

Northguard #1
Cover B
by Ian Herring

SEASON ONE COVER ART: ISSUE TWO

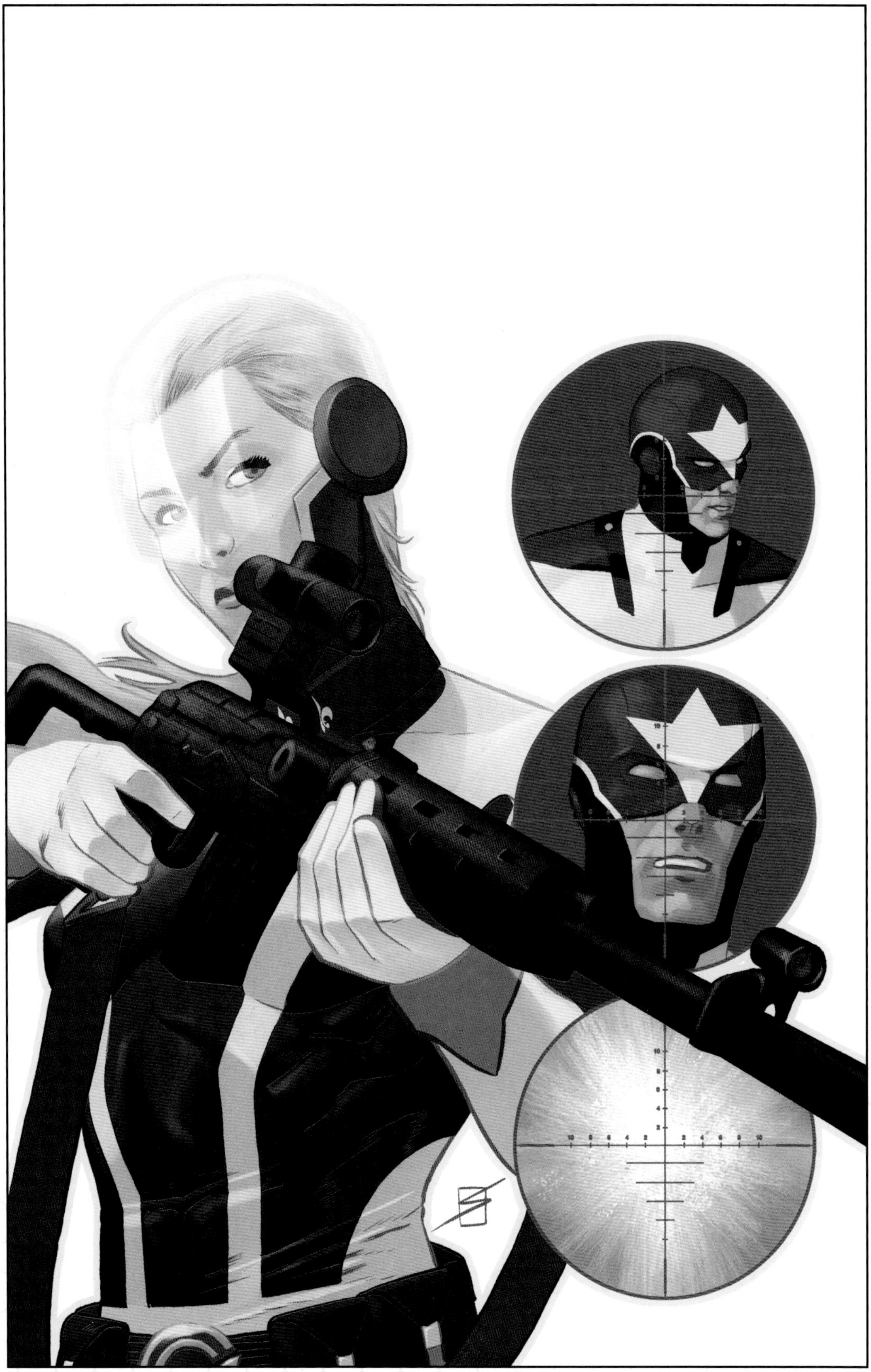

Northguard #2
Cover A
by Ron Salas

SEASON ONE COVER ART: ISSUE TWO VARIANT

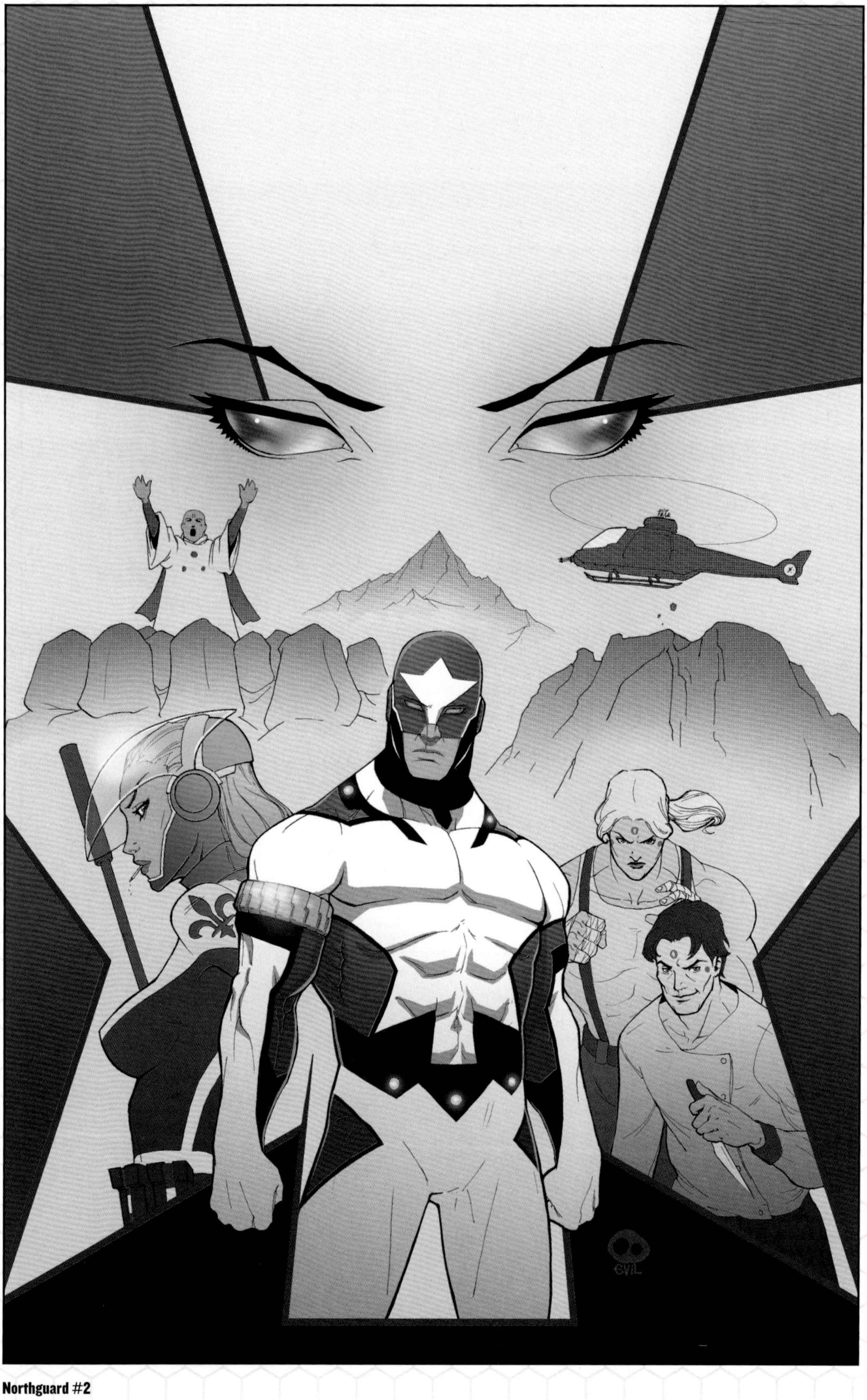
EVIL

Northguard #2
Cover B
by Eric Vedder

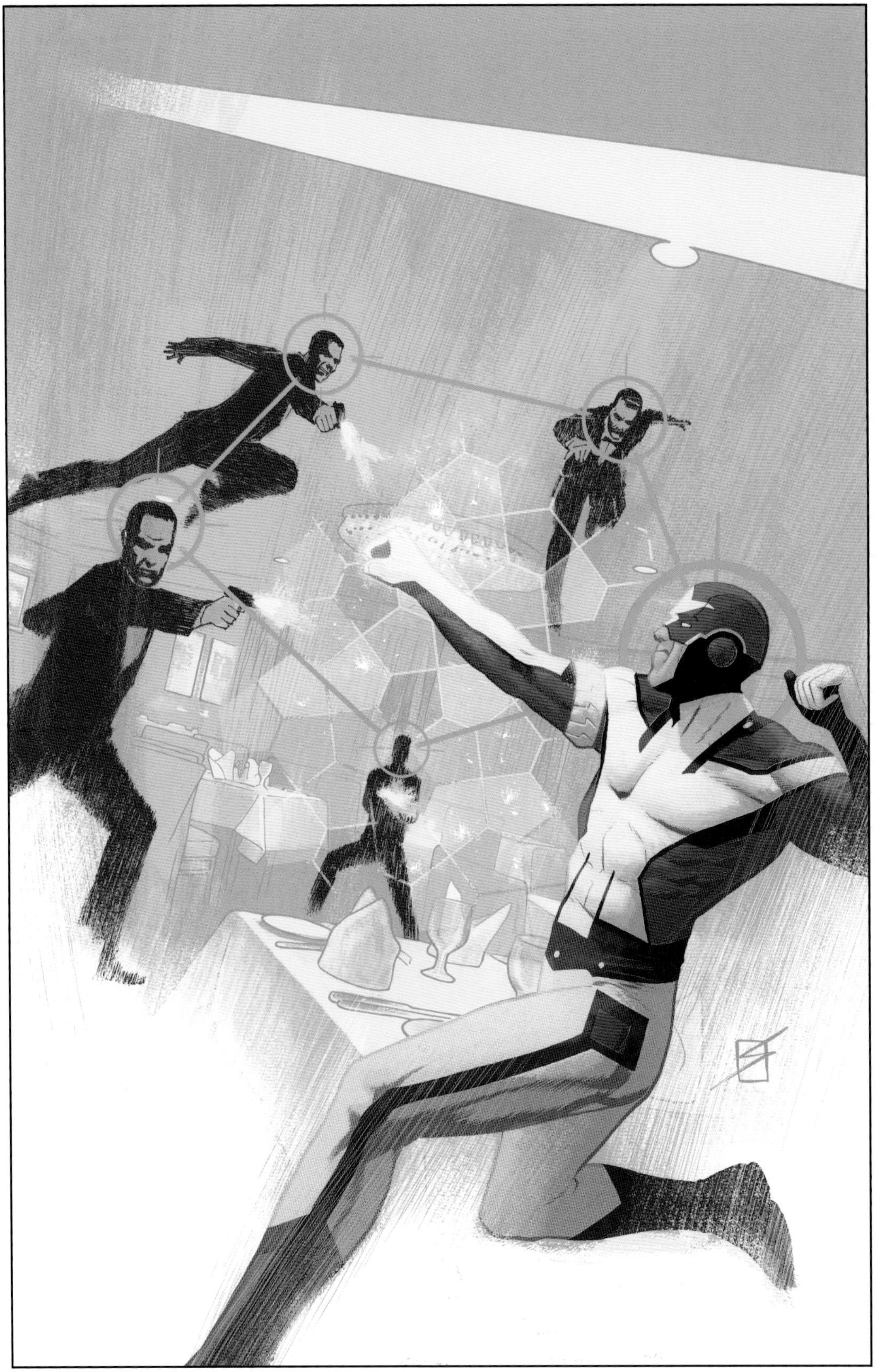

Northguard #3
Cover A
by Ron Salas

SEASON ONE COVER ART: ISSUE THREE VARIANT

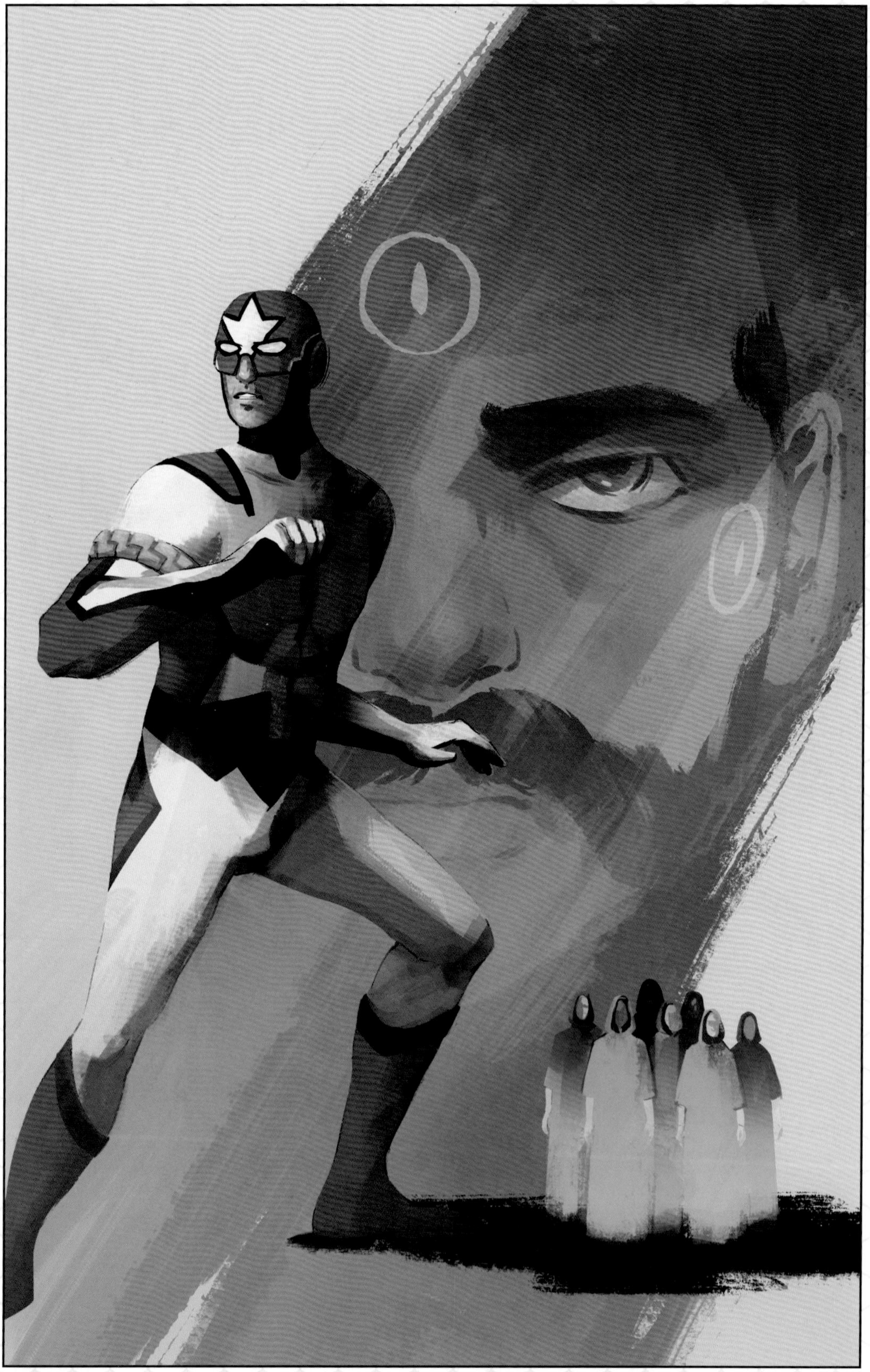

Northguard #3
Cover B
by Irma Kniivila

SEASON ONE COVER ART: ISSUE FOUR

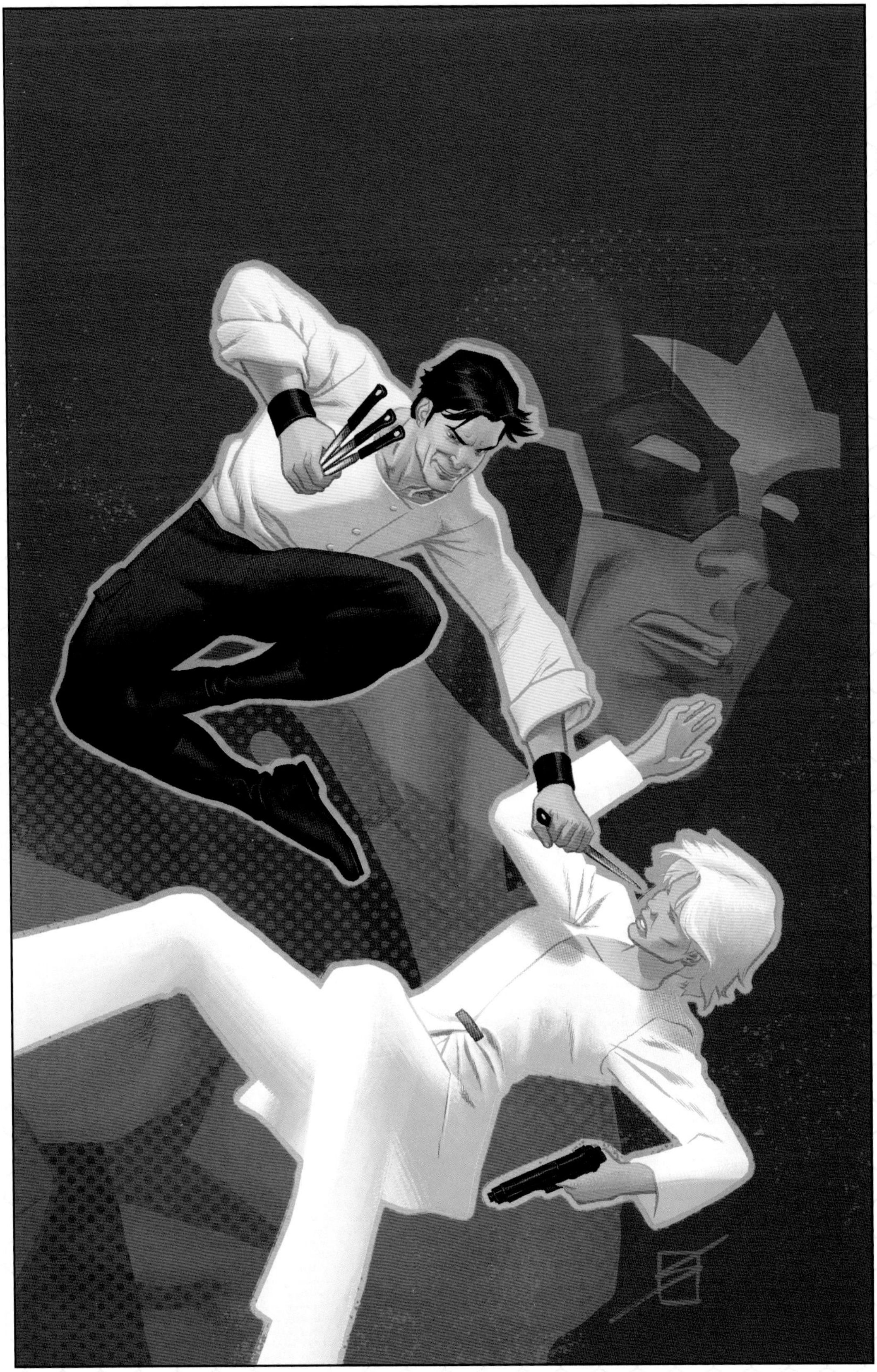

Northguard #4
Cover A
by Ron Salas

SEASON ONE COVER ART: ISSUE FOUR VARIANT

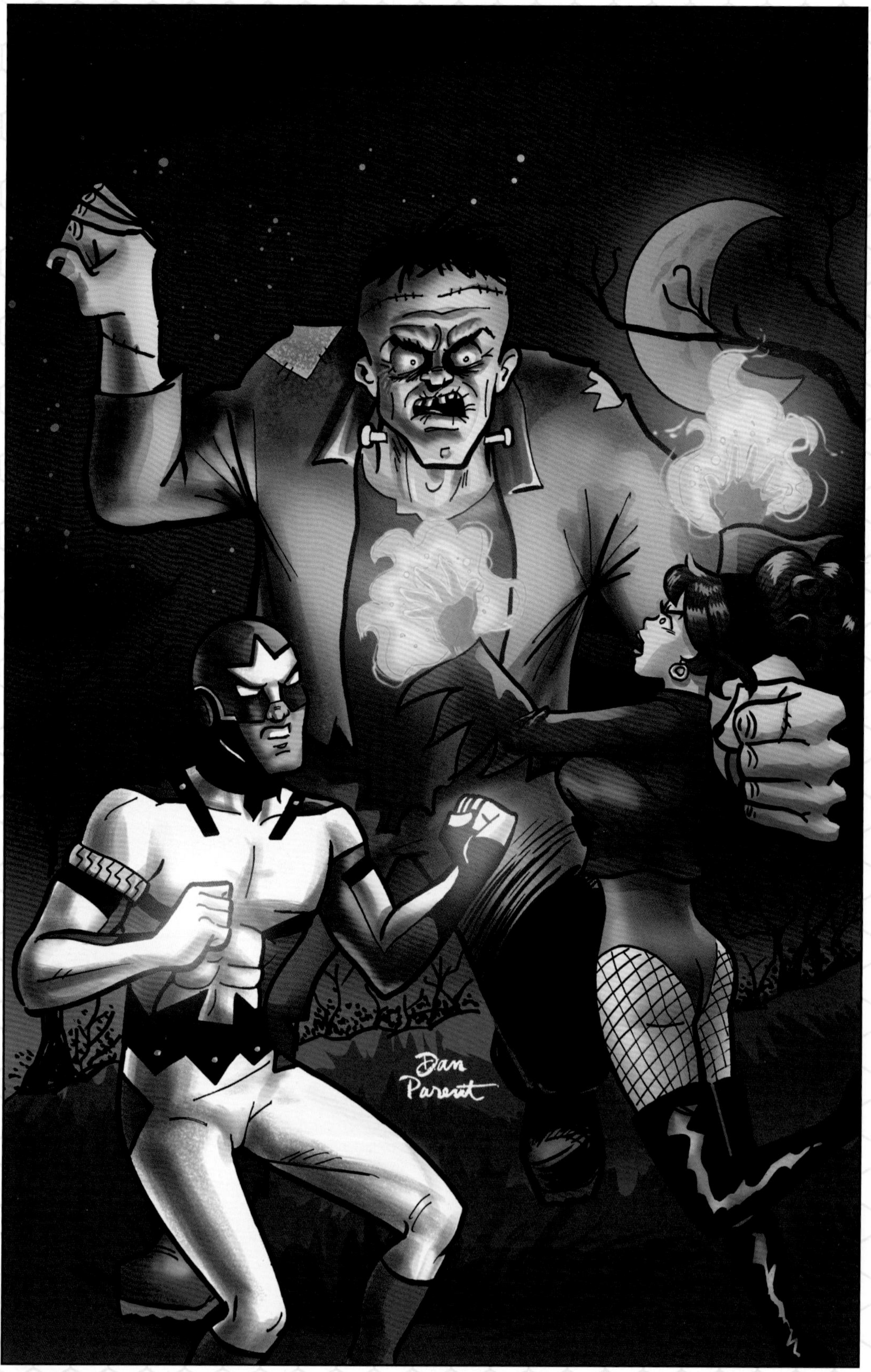
Dan Parent

Northguard #4
Cover B
by Dan Parent

PROCESS ART

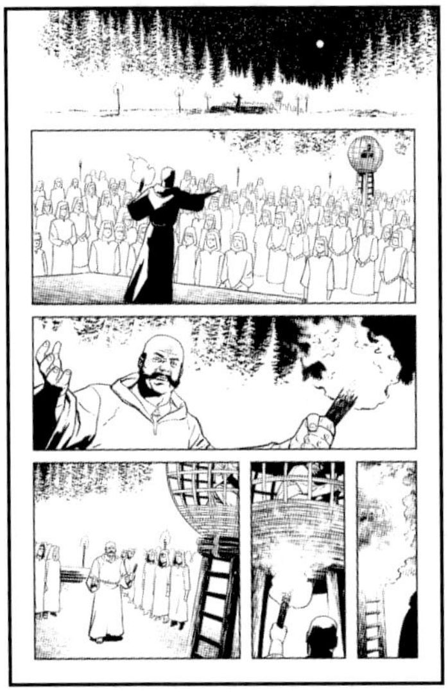

Issue 1: Page 1 inks
by Ron Salas

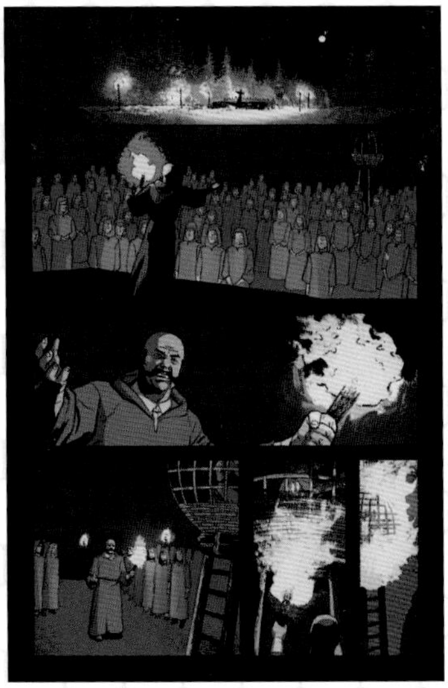

Issue 1: Page 1 colours
by Irma Kniivila

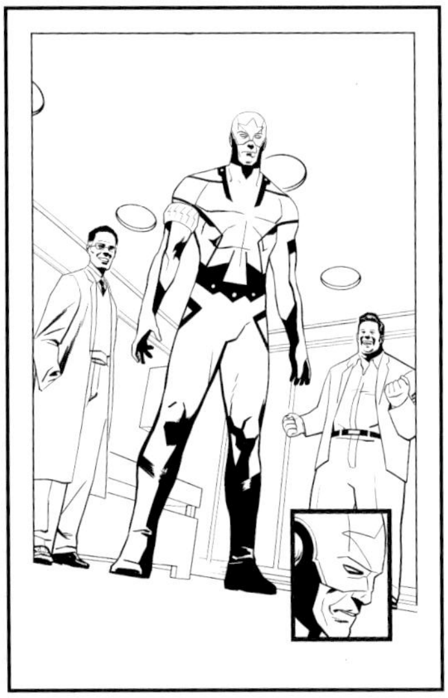

Issue 1: Page 7 inks
by Ron Salas

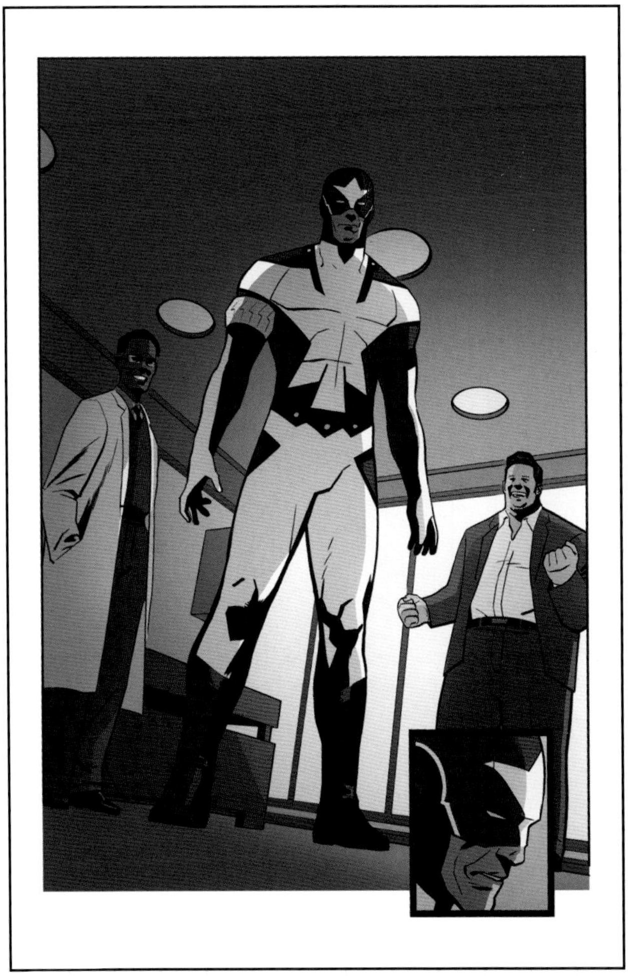

Issue 1: Page 7 colours
by Irma Kniivila

PROCESS ART

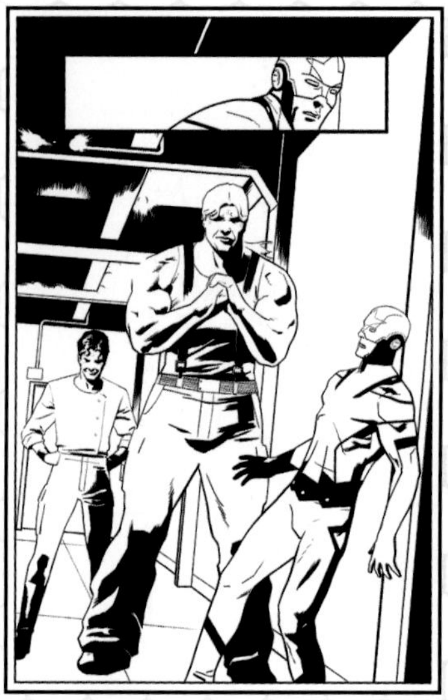

Issue 1: Page 12 inks
by Ron Salas

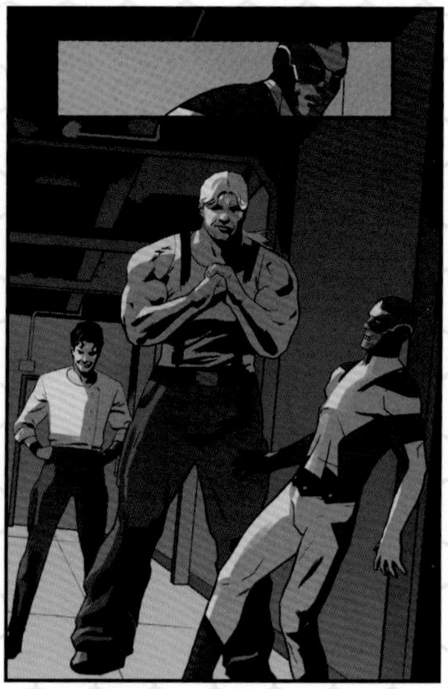

Issue 1: Page 12 colours
by Irma Kniivila

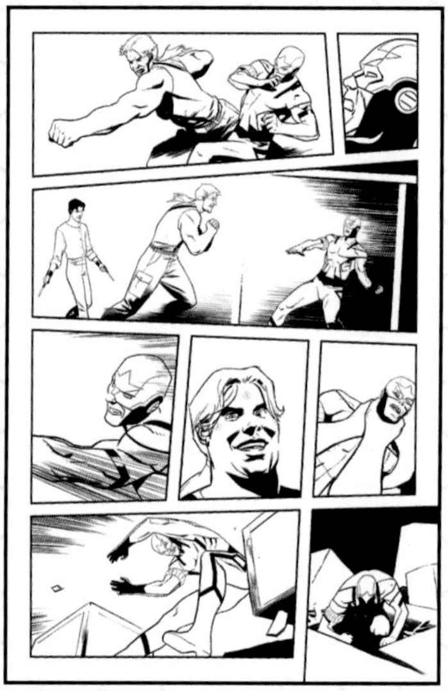

Issue 1: Page 13 inks
by Ron Salas

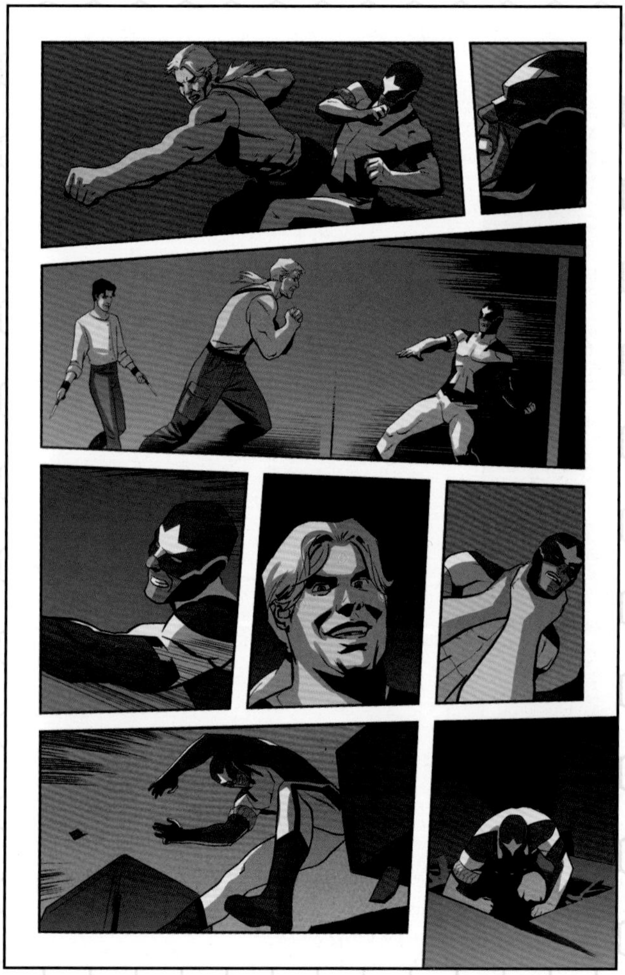

Issue 1: Page 13 colours
by Irma Kniivila

PROCESS ART

Issue 1: Page 17 inks
by Ron Salas

Issue 1: Page 17 colours
by Irma Kniivila

PROCESS ART

Issue 2: Page 9 colours
by Juancho

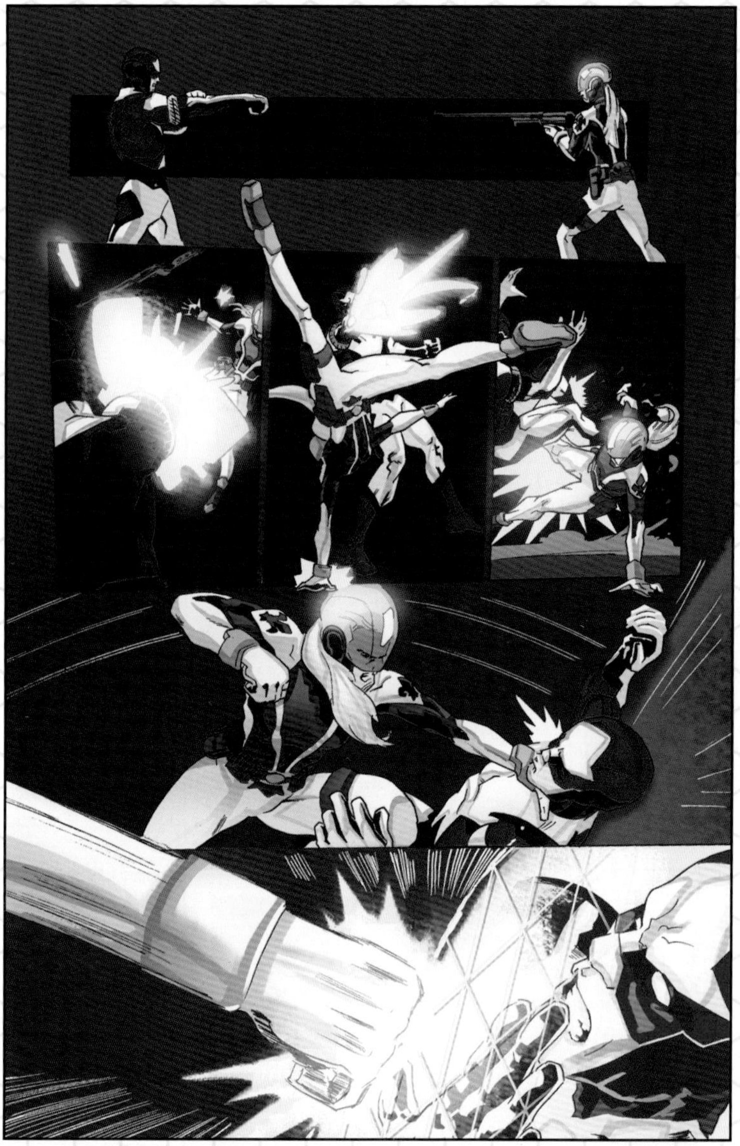

left:
Issue 2: Page 9 layout
by Eric Kim

right:
Issue 2: Page 9 inks
by Eric Kim

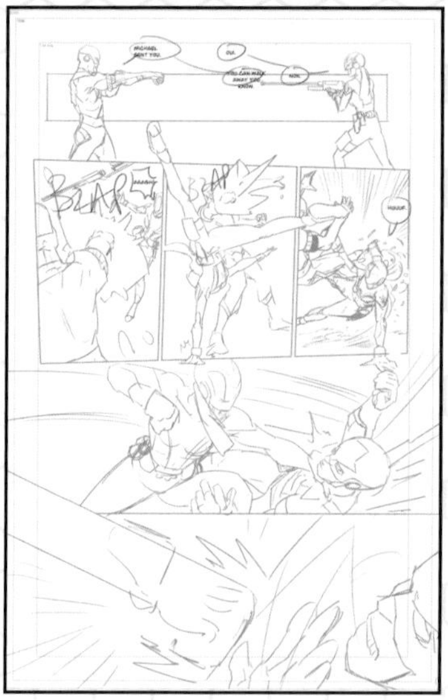

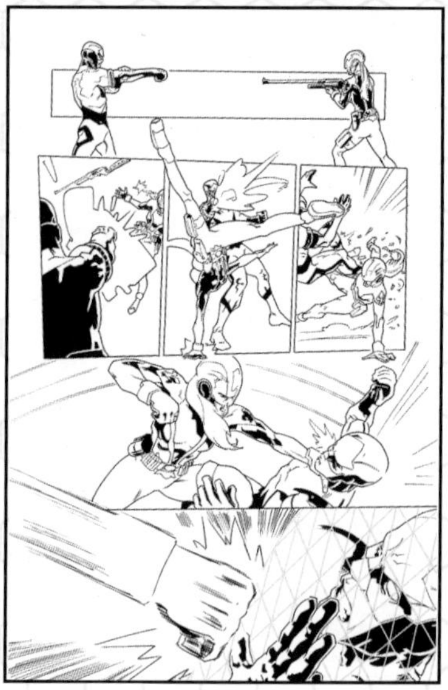

PROCESS ART

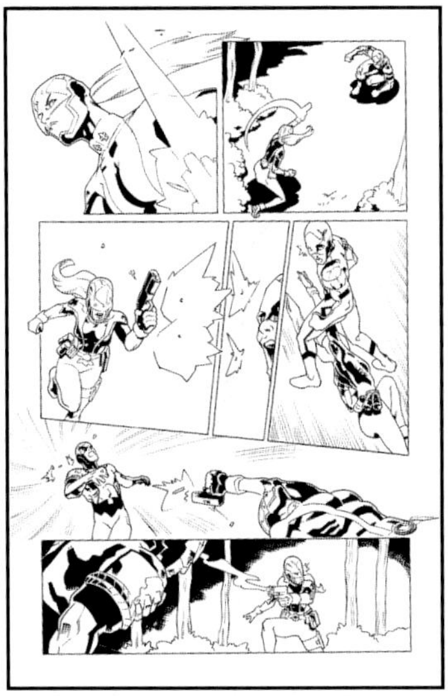

Issue 2: Page 10 inks
by Eric Kim

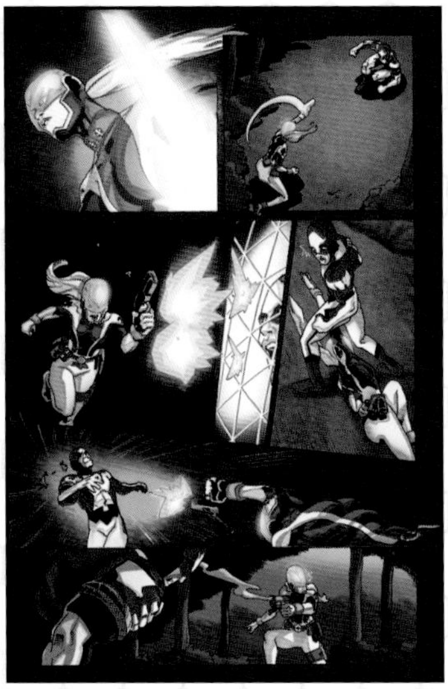

Issue 2: Page 10 colours
by Juancho

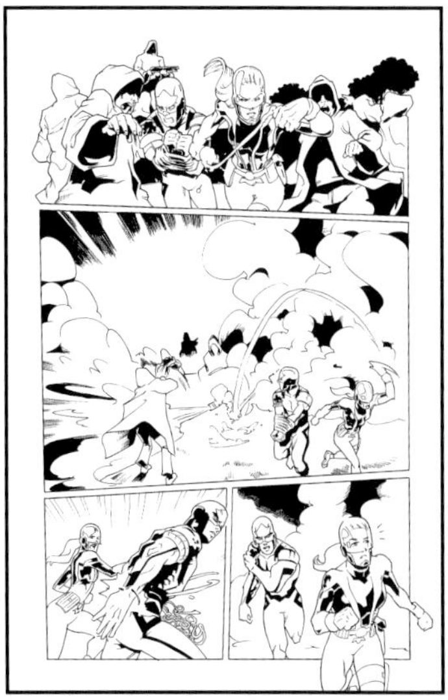

Issue 2: Page 14 inks
by Eric Kim

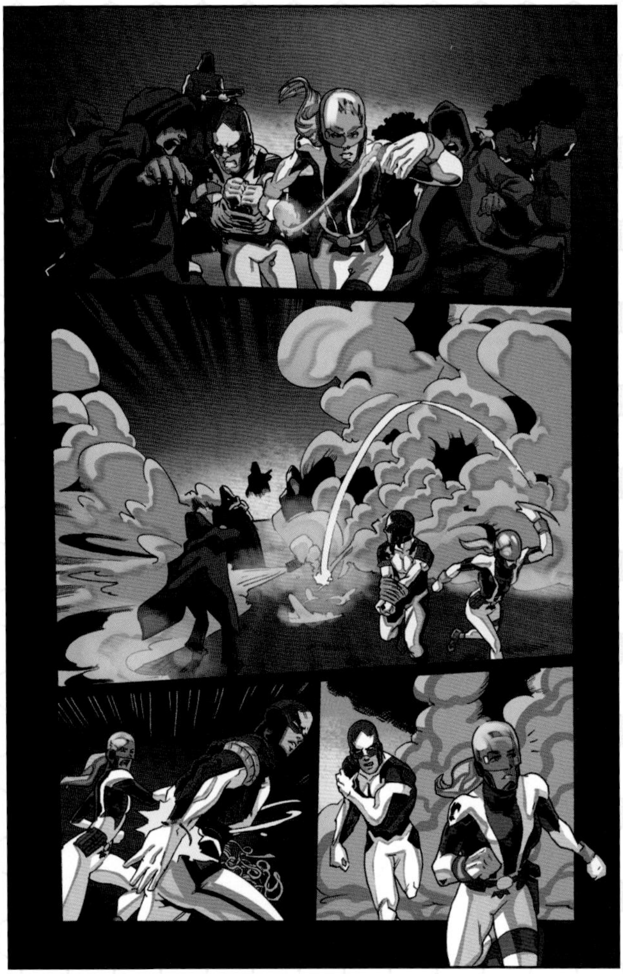

Issue 2: Page 14 colours
by Juancho

PROCESS ART

Issue 3: Page 7 inks
by Eric Kim

Issue 3: Page 7 colours
by Juancho

PROCESS ART

Issue 3: Page 14 colours
by Juancho

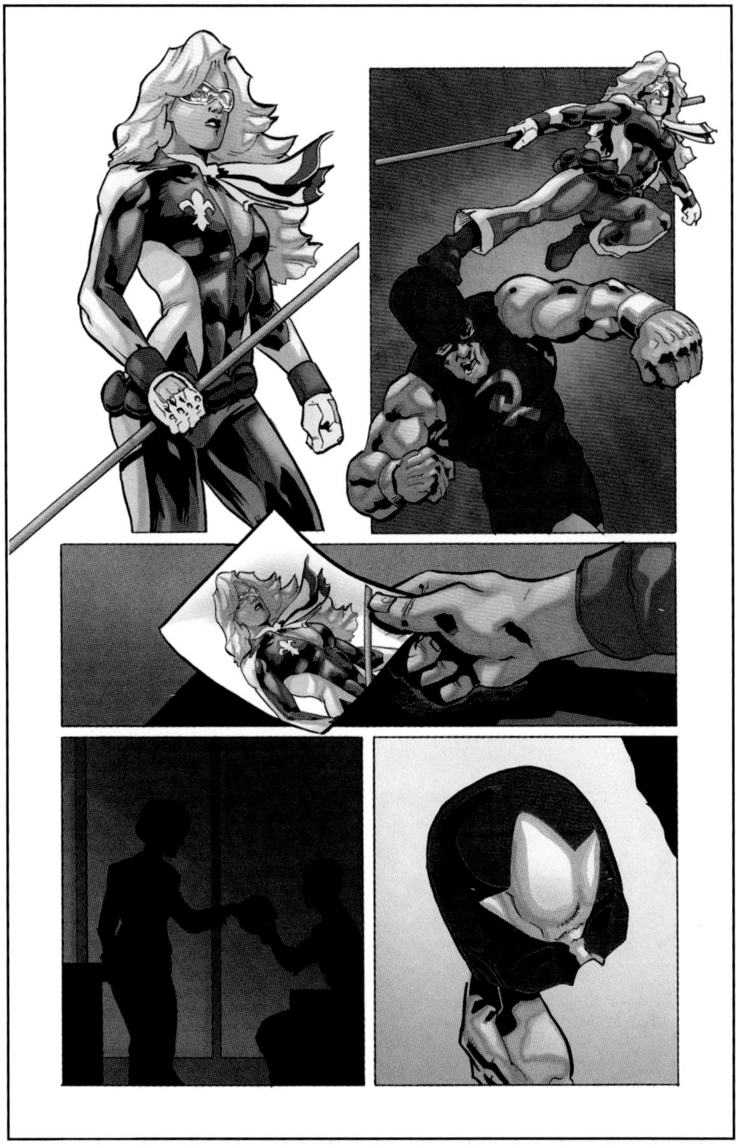

left:
Issue 3: Page 14 layout
by Eric Kim

right:
Issue 3: Page 14 inks
by Eric Kim

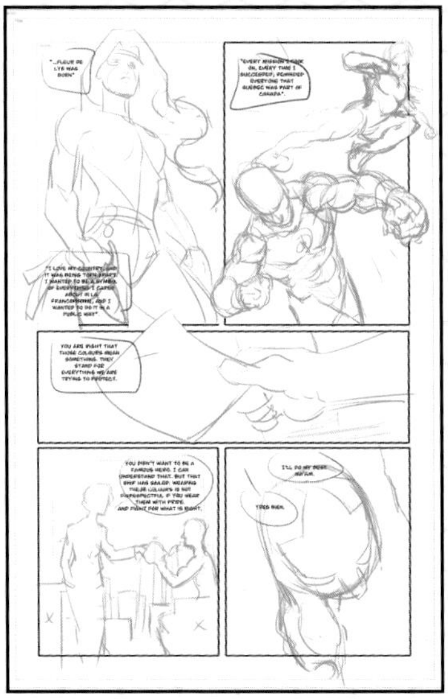

"...FLEUR DE LYS WAS BORN"
"EVERY MISSION I TOOK ON, EVERY TIME I SUCCEEDED, REMINDED EVERYONE THAT QUEBEC WAS PART OF CANADA".
"I LOVE MY COUNTRY, AND IT WAS BEING TORN APART. I WANTED TO BE A SYMBOL OF EVERYTHING I CARED ABOUT IN LA FRANCOPHONIE, AND I WANTED TO DO IT IN A PUBLIC WAY".
YOU ARE RIGHT THAT THOSE COLOURS MEAN SOMETHING. THEY STAND FOR EVERYTHING WE ARE TRYING TO PROTECT.
YOU DIDN'T WANT TO BE A FAMOUS HERO. I CAN UNDERSTAND THAT. BUT THAT SHIP HAS SAILED. WEARING THESE COLOURS IS NOT DISRESPECTFUL IF YOU WEAR THEM WITH PRIDE AND FIGHT FOR WHAT IS RIGHT.

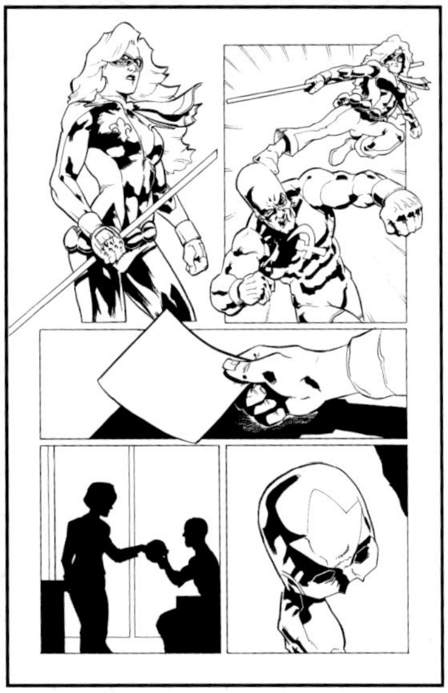

PROCESS ART: INKS

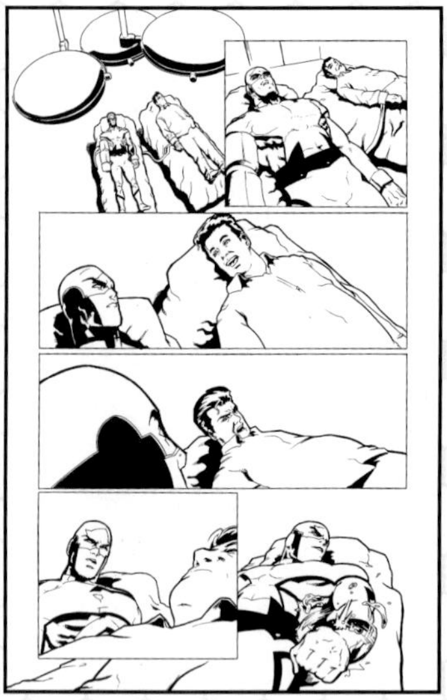

Issue 4: Page 2 inks
by Eric Kim

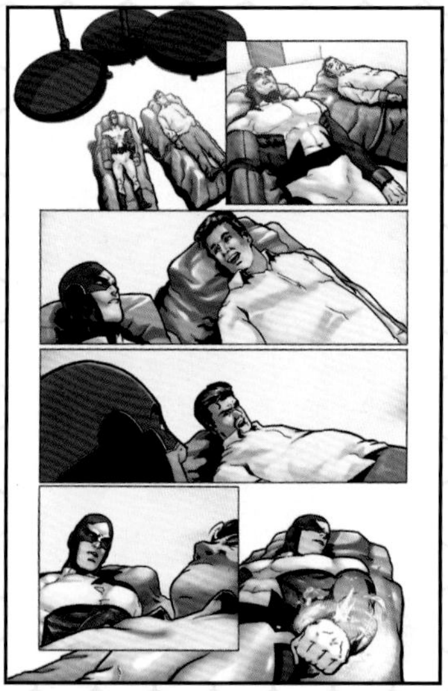

Issue 4: Page 2 colours
by Marco Pagnotta

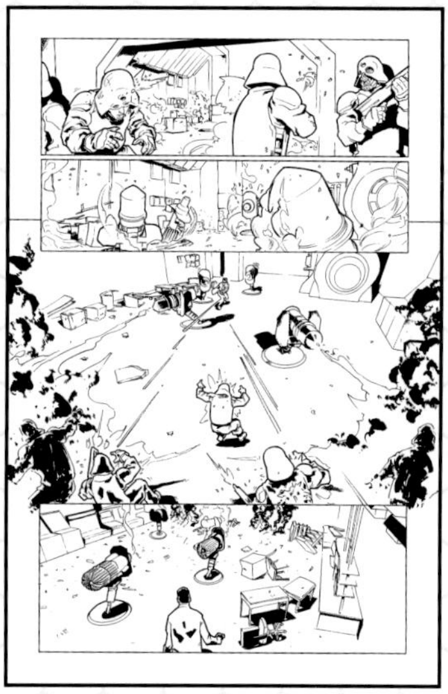

Issue 4: Page 11 inks
by Eric Kim

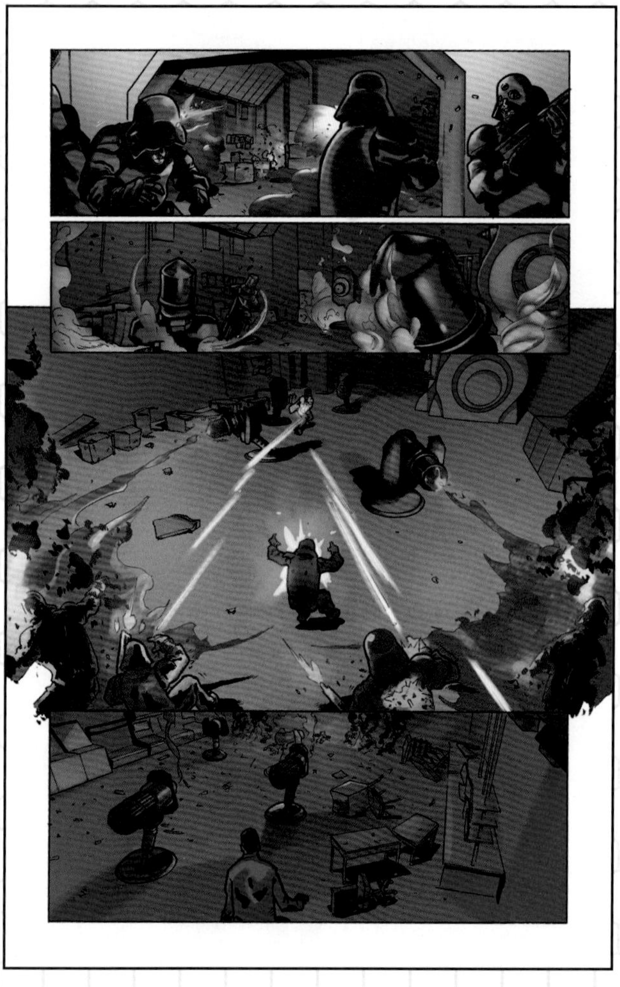

Issue 4: Page 11 colours
by Marco Pagnotta

CHAPTERVERSE RECOMMENDED READING ORDER

FOLLOW THE ADVENTURE!

CHAPTERHOUSE

CAPTAIN CANUCK
SUR SARAY

CAPTAIN CANUCK
SEASON ZERO:
SUR SARAY
BARUCHEL ANDRASOFSZKY
TO LEE VIREAK

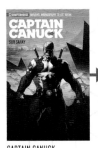

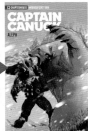

ALEPH

CAPTAIN CANUCK
SEASON ONE:
ALEPH
ANDRASOFSZKY KIRK

the Pitiful
HUMAN-LIZARD

THE PITIFUL HUMAN-LIZARD
SEASON ONE:
FAR FROM LEGENDARY
LOO

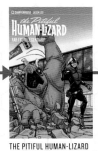

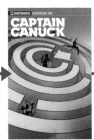

CAPTAIN
CANUCK

CAPTAIN CANUCK
SEASON TWO:
GAUNTLET
ANDRASOFSZKY KIRK

the Pitiful
HUMAN-LIZARD
STILL PRETTY PATHETIC

THE PITIFUL HUMAN-LIZARD
SEASON TWO:
STILL PRETTY PATHETIC
LOO RICHEY CARTER

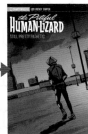

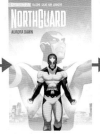

NORTHGUARD
AURORA DAWN

NORTHGUARD
SEASON ONE:
AURORA DAWN
FALCONE SALAS
KIM JUANCHO

AGENTS OF
PACT
FLEURS DE CONFLIT

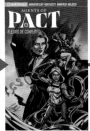

AGENTS OF P.A.C.T.
SEASON ONE:
FLEURS DE CONFLIT
ANDRASOFSZKY NORTHCOTT
MANFREDI NOLASCO

FREELANCE
ANGEL OF THE ABYSS

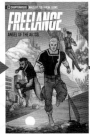

FREELANCE
SEASON ONE:
ANGEL OF THE ABYSS
WHEELER ZUB
VIREAK LEONG

Fantomah
UP FROM THE DEEP

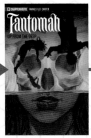

FANTOMAH
SEASON ONE:
UP FROM THE DEEP
FAWKES LEE
CARTER

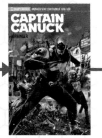

CAPTAIN
CANUCK

CAPTAIN CANUCK
SEASON THREE:
HARBINGER
ANDRASOFSZKY CHATEAUNEUF
KIRK LOO

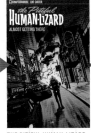

the Pitiful
HUMAN-LIZARD
ALMOST GETTING THERE

THE PITIFUL HUMAN-LIZARD
SEASON THREE:
ALMOST GETTING THERE
LOO CARTER

FALLEN SUNS

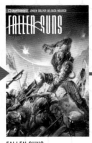

FALLEN SUNS
SEASON ONE:
THE ROOT
JENSEN COLLYER
DEL DUCA NOLASCO

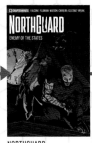

NORTHGUARD
ENEMY OF THE STATES

NORTHGUARD
SEASON TWO:
ENEMY OF THE STATES
FALCONE FELDMAN
WATSON CARRERA
IGLESIAS VIREAK

FREELANCE
LOST HISTORIES

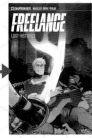

FREELANCE
SEASON TWO:
LOST HISTORIES
WHEELER SAMU
VIREAK

Fantomah
INTO THE FLAMES

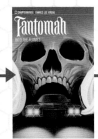

FANTOMAH
SEASON TWO:
INTO THE FLAMES
FAWKES LEE
VIREAK

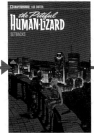

the Pitiful
HUMAN-LIZARD
SETBACKS

THE PITIFUL HUMAN-LIZARD
SEASON FOUR:
SETBACKS
LOO CARTER

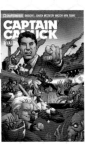

CAPTAIN

CAPTAIN CANUCK
SEASON FOUR:
INVASION
BARUCHEL JENSEN
MCCREERY MACCHI
KIRK ROANE

THE STORY CONTINUES
NEXT SEASON!

🔖 CHAPTERHOUSE

NORTHGUARD™

ENEMY OF THE STATES

Philip Wise, aka Northguard, lost his arm during the battle in Toronto with Pharos and is now working with PACT as a motivational speaker for amputee children.

When Wolf, one of the world's deadliest assassins, makes an attempt on Phil's life, Michael Evans shows up giving him an incredibly sophisticated cybernetic prosthesis complete with a brand new uniband. In exchange for his arm back, Phil has to acquire the weapon used by Wolf for Michael.

The search for these weapons will lead Phil and CIA Agent Terry Garcia straight into the clutches of a familiar foe, the newly evolved Aurora Dawn. Even more unexpected is the uneasy alliance Phil forms with Brian Dwyer, aka Steeltown Hammer.

"A darker, leaner, international hero with true Canadian spirit."
— *Rogues Portal*

"With solid writing, pacing and characterisation alongside some really nice interior artwork, you shouldn't be sleeping on this!"
— *Reading With A Flight Ring*

NORTHGUARD SEASON TWO: ENEMY OF THE STATES
Collects the complete Season Two of Northguard by **ANTHONY FALCONE, AARON FELDMAN, ALLEN WATSON, SERGIO CARRERA, FEDERICO IGLESIAS,** and **VANEDA VIREAK**